"There is no way I [would] make a decision on political grounds" — Hawke on the decision-making process for Sydney's airport

quoted in The Bulletin March 21 1989

(see p. 123)

" ~~ had developed a substantial public sector which supported private capital". (159)

"Control of the economy is an objective govts have rarely entertained"

(159) (162) (168)
(203)

PUBLIC POLICY

IN AUSTRALIA

G Davis   J Wanna   J Warhurst   P Weller

Sydney
ALLEN AND UNWIN
Wellington London Boston

First published in 1988

Allen & Unwin Australia Pty Ltd
An Unwin Hyman company
8 Napier Street, North Sydney, NSW 2060 Australia

Allen & Unwin New Zealand Limited
60 Cambridge Terrace, Wellington, New Zealand

Unwin Hyman Limited
37-39 Queen Elizabeth Street, London SE1 2QB England

Allen & Unwin Inc.
8 Winchester Place, Winchester, Mass 01890 USA

National Library of Australia
Cataloguing-in-Publication entry:

Public policy in Australia.

    Bibliography.
    ISBN 0 04 301285 X.

    1. Political planning − Australia. 2. Australia − Politics and government.
    I. Davis, Glyn.

354.9407'2

Library of Congress Catalog Card Number: 87−19451

Set in 10/11 Times by Setrite, Hong Kong
Produced by SRM Production Services Sdn Bhd, Malaysia

Contents

Acknowledgements

Public policy requires collective action, and we have shared the task of surveying this emerging field from an Australian perspective. Like the subject, our text reflects discussion, bargaining and cooperation. Computer discs have floated between authors and institutions, first drafts been held up to rigorous scrutiny over very long dinners, ideas and editorial roles exchanged, concepts debated and defended. The characteristic arguments which result can no longer be tied to an individual; this 'Brisbane line' has emerged, improbably and imperceptibly, from the enjoyable process of joint authorship.

Along the way David Corbett, Margaret Gardner, Brian Head, Jim Kitay and Ray McNamara commented on sections of the manuscript. Jeni Warburton, a hastily recruited research assistant, carried our contradictory requests, uncertain directions and ambiguous deadlines in her capable stride. The research committee of the School of Administration at Griffith University provided resources. David Gow offered an incisive critique of the project, and trialled chapters on sceptical students from the Masters of Public Administration course at the University of Queensland. Fragments were also inflicted on public policy undergraduates at Griffith University, and masters students from the University of New England. It is not their fault if stubborn academics fail to recognise good advice.

In Armidale, Cathy Cokeman and Yve Richards helped prepare draft chapters. Elsewhere, in the spirit of declining public funding for higher education, the authors typed their own pages. Any mistakes, then, belong only to us.

G.D. J.W.
J.W. P.W.
May 1987

1

Public Policy in Australia

The retrenched steelworkers, coalminers and their families arrived by chartered train and bus. Some came from the industrial cities of Wollongong and Port Kembla, others from Newcastle and the coal fields of the Hunter Valley. Fifteen hundred or more people had travelled to Canberra to protest against mass sackings by Australia's largest company, BHP, and its subsidiaries. On the afternoon of 26 October 1982 the workers held a rally on the parliament house lawns. They demanded that the government save their industry through protection against cheap steel imports.

'What do we want? Fraser out! What do we want? Jobs for dads!' The chants could be heard within the chamber of the House of Representatives, where the government was defending its economic record against an opposition censure motion. When the prime minister declined to come outside and address protesters, the crowd moved toward the building. Thirty police stationed behind yellow metal barriers erected across King's Avenue were unable to hold them back; people ran across the road, past the parked tourist buses, and up the front steps of parliament house. While startled attendants blocked the entrance with tables and desks, police hastily swung shut the main doors and stood shoulder to shoulder behind the glass panels.

For a brief moment it seemed the barricade might hold. Then the bullet-proof glass of the doors shattered over police. As defenders scrambled back over the pile of furniture, a hundred or so protesters pushed their way into King's Hall. While police lines reformed to guard the entrances to the House of Representatives and Senate, the workers sat amid the tourists, journalists and busts lining the hall, and demanded to see the prime minister.

Malcolm Fraser stayed in his office but the speaker, Sir Billy Snedden, arrived to appeal for an end to the protest. Storming the building, pleaded Snedden, had placed the institution in crisis; workers should realise that 'parliament is your protection'. He left to jeers. In his place a federal police inspector announced through a loudspeaker that

1

the prime minister would meet a delegation—provided the workers left the building. When the crowd remained seated, the inspector handed his loudspeaker to an official from the Miners' Federation who confirmed the promised meeting and suggested that the protesters had made their point. No parliamentarian could be left in any doubt about the anger and frustration of workers and their families at losing employment, security and prospects. As the steelworkers and coalminers filed out of King's Hall one commented 'we can always come back tomorrow. They can lock the doors but they can't lock the ballot boxes'. Workers' representatives later received a hearing—but few tangible promises— from the prime minister and senior cabinet ministers.

How can this event be understood? At one level as confirmation of the acceptance and stability of Australian political institutions; where else could the workers storm the parliament and then quietly leave after listening to speeches from politicians? At other levels it can be viewed as a corporation using the threat of retrenchments to obtain favourable treatment from government, or as an allegory of the usual exclusion of workers' interests from major decision making.

Most of all, the events of late October 1982 illustrate the pervasive Australian belief that politicians matter. There is no point charging the parliament building if you suspect that governments cannot override the decisions of the private sector. The workers wanted to put the future of their jobs, and their industry, on the agenda. They hoped to tell the prime minister of the damage mass retrenchments would cause coastal communities and of the cost to Australia of running down scarce industrial capacity. The symbolic capture of King's Hall was intended to dramatise their demand for action and to emphasise that employment was not just a private matter between BHP and its workers, but an issue of *public policy*.

What is Public Policy Analysis?

Much debate in Australia is about the legitimate boundaries of public policy. Those who oppose an extensive public sector seek to define issues in the narrow language of neo-classical economics, with its assumption that government intervention is inherently inefficient and usually ineffective. The fate of the steel industry should be decided by markets, not through measures prompted by the social cost of job losses. Public policy should be a question of management, with politicians behaving like accountants and being judged by the criteria of accountancy. Debate becomes the agreement of technicians, a discourse which excludes the overtly political and makes policy appear a logical process concerned only with limited issues. What is not expert cannot be rational.

Those committed to maintaining or extending the activities of government promote a different notion of public policy. Equity and welfare become crucial. Government is about social justice, policy about redistribution. The alleged efficiency of markets may need to be weighed against the rights of communities or against the national importance of maintaining a viable steel industry. Public policy should define and achieve social goals and not just administer the spaces left by unregulated capitalism.

This debate among practitioners about the realm of 'public policy' is reflected in much of the international academic literature. Most texts define public policy analysis as examining the role of politicians, bureaucracies and corporations in making decisions which affect our lives. Some academics focus on institutions, others on process. Many American public policy writers concentrate on the huge US defence and social programs introduced during the last three decades by presidents and legislatures. The much used introductory text by Anderson (1984), for example, describes Washington decision makers and federal institutions, with special attention to the budgetary process. Many standard American works are interested in developing methods of quantification and measurement for evaluating the effects of legislative programs.

British texts, on the other hand, demonstrate little interest in evaluation techniques. Authors prefer to tie public policy concerns to broader social theories. The work of Ham and Hill, as a case in point, stresses that the policy process 'cannot be assessed independently of analysis of the distribution of economic and political power within political systems' (1984: 20). Ham and Hill emphasise theories of the state, models of bureaucracy and the consequences of agency discretion. Analysis remains abstract, rather than dwelling on the specifics of policy formulation within a particular society.

Australian academics occupy a range of positions. Though the term 'public policy' has been fashionable since the early 1970s, there has been no consensus about what constitutes a 'policy' or 'decision', no single accepted method of inquiry, and little agreement about the boundaries of a field called 'public policy'. What there has been since the 1960s, however, is a recognisable shift in emphasis in academic studies from public administration to public policy, from institutions to processes, from bureaucratic behaviour to the content of decisions.

Forward (1974) was one of the earliest Australians in print to employ the term 'public policy'. Introducing a series of case studies, he noted new interest in the way policies are formed. There were, however, inevitable problems of definition. Forward began with the proposition that public policy equals actions taken by governments. Strictly speaking though, public policy must be policy which affects the public. As Forward recognised, this includes the actions of private citizens and corporations, for 'even when an area of activity is left entirely in private hands the very act of leaving it alone can be a deliberate policy of the authorities' (Forward 1974: 2). Thus 'any serious analysis of questions about public policy quickly expands into a discussion about politics in general and society as a whole' (Forward 1974: 5).

Spann and Curnow remained somewhat sceptical about whether a new field of 'public policy' had indeed emerged. They noted that some of what passed for the study of public policy was 'by no means new' and seemed 'indistinguishable from what earlier was termed the study of "government" or of "public affairs"' (Spann and Curnow 1975: 456). Nevertheless, they saw some scope for developing three important strands in public policy analysis: models of policy making at a macro level, examination of policy content, and the development of techniques to evaluate and improve the content and process of government policy. They warned, however, against attempting to construct grand theories of public policy; 'to encompass the reality of public policy making in one systematic, interactive and operational whole', they suggested, 'is probably beyond the wit of man. We "satisfice" in our conceptual frameworks as well as in our administrative behaviour. Our models simplify reality and reduce to manageable proportions that which seemed unmanageable' (Spann and Curnow 1975: 460).

Such doubts about any integrated theoretical basis for public policy contrasted with Emy's 1976 hopes for a conceptually unified approach to policy problems. Emy wanted public policy analysis to be concerned with more than narrow technical or economic issues. His interest in public policy stemmed from a strong sense of crisis, a perspective shared by many European social theorists writing about the legitimacy and fiscal difficulties of the contemporary capitalist state. Emy spoke of a 'prevailing disillusionment, the feeling that culture and institutions cannot cope with the problems of post-industrial society' (Emy 1976: 3). He identified a central tension between the policy options chosen by experts and the 'irrationality' of politics; public policy must be normative, seeking to address the crisis, and to make the policy process more 'rational' through techniques, structures and understanding. In studying the substance and process of decisions, analysis must have 'policy relevance' (Emy 1976: 22).

The findings of the Royal Commission into Australian Government Administration were also published in 1976. Established by the Whitlam government but reporting to the Fraser ministry, RCAGA offered a comprehensive portrait of a large and complex public service facing sudden contraction after decades of post-war prosperity and expansion. In its arguments, findings and volumes of supporting material, RCAGA revived Australian debate about public administration and set the agenda for work on understanding and improving the local policy process.

Many RCAGA themes were taken up in 1979 by Hawker, Smith and Weller. Following Heclo's definition of policy as applying to something bigger than particular decisions, but smaller than general social movements, Hawker et al. chose to focus on central institutions and the 'proximate' policy makers, those closest to the actual making of decisions. They noted five major influences on the shape of public policy identified by international literature—social and economic conditions, prevailing ideas, institutions and individuals, technical and analytical procedures and general theories about the way policy is made. These influences can be considered as different levels of analysis; they are not necessarily contradictory, nor mutually exclusive. General social theories, however, can 'offer descriptions of differences in certain policy outcomes and correlate these with social and economic conditions' but 'cannot go much further' (Hawker et al. 1978: 11). As Self would later note, theories seeking to explain politics are inevitably limited, partial, and time and space specific. 'It may be a great intellectual nuisance (although possibly a practical benefit) that social phenomena have multiple causations to which precise weights cannot be assigned; but if that is the state of the world, it had better be recognized' (Self 1985: 8).

Hawker et al. differed from Emy not only in their insistence upon, and practice of, example over speculation in public policy analysis, but in their attitude towards politics. While Emy saw politics as irrational, Hawker et al. argued that politics had its own essential logic; they questioned whether technical expertise and rationality are necessarily synonymous. Emy saw the role of the discipline as improving the techniques of policy making, while Hawker et al. were more sceptical about any overall 'rationality'; 'rational for whom?' they asked. Though individual actors might behave rationally in their own interest, policy formulation is a process shaped by the deliberate and the unintentional, without a necessary cohesion. Power is unevenly dispersed, authority fragmented and policy making uncertain, complex and intermittent. Nevertheless, the authors felt this pluralist view of the processes of government did not commit them to a world of complete disorder and confusion. 'Far from it. To assume that no individual or institution is omnipotent is not to say that processes are random. Governments and departments may be able to achieve some ends by purposive action, but influence is unevenly distributed' (Hawker et al. 1979: 23).

Hawker et al. noted various possible levels of public policy analysis, and then made a pragmatic decision to concentrate on central government institutions. In 1981 Encel, Wilenski and Schaffer expanded this focus to include policy formulation on the fringes of the formal structures of government. They noted not just the difficulties of defining something called 'public policy', but the considerable problems of tying down its key unit of analysis, the 'decision'. A decision, they argued, is rarely a single uncontested event.

Viewed by different actors in the process, a government decision carries different meanings and different implications. What to one actor may seem to be the the definitive statement of government views may, to another, appear in a different context as a marginal and ambiguous shift. Even when it is quite clear that an important decision has been taken, argument over its meaning and the way it should be implemented can re-open many of the issues to the point where it again becomes difficult to pinpoint where in the process the critical commitment in government resources took place (Encel et al. 1981: xv).

Because decisions are rarely discrete events which can be separated from a long and sometimes disjointed policy process, Encel et al. were not optimistic about the prospects for 'rationality'. Decisions, they said, ultimately require a choice between clashing values.

The difficulty for 'rational' policy making is a theme taken up by Weller (1981). He noted the poor record of 'managerial' solutions to government financial problems. Public program and zero-based budgeting, three-year forward estimates and other experiments of the 1970s had failed, suggested Weller, because their advocates did not understand the processes of implementing policy, the complexity and interrelatedness of government action, or the problem of multiple consequences from any single action. The advocates of managerial models forgot about the role of politics, as though governing required only the application of techniques learned from a public administration textbook.

So Australian studies of public policy have embraced numerous approaches, foci, methods and findings. Within the rubric of public policy Hawker et al. have conducted detailed examination of central government institutions, while Emy pleaded that public policy analysis should deal with the broader questions of 'planning, social control, accountability, rationality, bureaucratic power, knowledge-based politics, budgeting and organisational design ... its tacit concern for the question of political rationality marks a revival of the Aristotelian conception of an architectonic approach to politics, a theoretical science dealing with the practical construction of political orders' (Emy 1976: 19).

Approaching Public Policy Analysis

A variety of techniques have been used in public policy analysis. Much of the earliest (and best) work in Australia has been through case studies published in monographs and journals. From Encel's investigations into intrigue surrounding extensions planned for the Sydney GPO, to Gray's work on the termination of Medibank, case studies provide valuable descriptions of the actions of politicians, the value systems of bureaucrats and the role of institutions and custom in the policy process (Encel 1981; Gray 1984). Many emphasise the randomness of outcomes—as though, within the structures we build, chance makes our history.

There are problems, however, with proceeding solely through example. Case studies are generally concerned with policy change and discontinuity rather than policy maintenance (Smith 1977: 262). They rarely examine structures which are stable. At their best, case studies can throw a broader light; at their worst they do no more than build detail upon detail, signifying little.

Two other strategies for public policy analysis, which in part overlap, are institutional and process studies. Institutional studies examine the workings of a particular organisation, asking about its procedures, environment and influence. The Painter and Carey study of interdepartmental committees (1979), and Warhurst's examination of the Industry Assistance Commission (1982), fit these categories. Institutional studies often incorporate case studies as illustrations of the way systems work and seek to place an organisation within the broader structures of government.

Process studies appear in two forms. One version examines the influence of interest groups on policy outcomes over a long period; Heclo's analysis of the development of social policy in Britain and Sweden (1974) is a skilful example. The other approach traces the policy process within a single institution over time as Whitwell does in his study of the Australian Treasury (1986). In documenting the development and application of a policy, process studies may call on Lasswell's sequential model (1963) suggesting seven stages of decision making: intelligence, recommendation, prescription, invocation, application, appraisal and termination. The process approach has been refined by British writers such as Hogwood and Gunn (1984).

This diversity of approaches suggests that public policy is not a discipline with a well mapped-out field and consensus about problems and assumptions. Rather it is a method of analysis requiring an amalgamation of political, legal and economic judgements which are not the easy or unchallenged preserve of any one academic discipline. Not disciplinary, then, but necessarily multi-disciplinary. Public policy as

Public Policy as method must draw together the threads of policy activity, with studies of the development and content of policies, the processes which shape decisions, and the institutions which influence choices. Analysis must look to insights from a range of approaches and avoid being confined to the narrow concerns (or jargon) of any one approach. As Heclo has argued, 'the point of distinguishing policies from programs, decisions, social movements and intentions is to suggest that policy is not a self-evident, independent behaviour fact. Policy acquires meaning because an observer perceives and interprets a course of actions amid the confusions of a complex world' (Heclo 1974: 4).

If public policy is the choices (intended and unrecognised) acted upon within a society, then public policy analysis becomes a method for disentangling those decisions, for seeing why issues arise on the agenda, and how they are resolved. Public policy analysis therefore requires us to 'puzzle out' (to use Heclo's apt phrase) the processes and limits of the state and to assess the relative influence on outcomes of politicians, bureaucrats, interest groups, organisational structures and economic forces.

To understand the events of October 1982, for example, a public policy study would need to explore the economics of the steel industry, government policy toward protection and tariffs, the advice of the public service and interest groups, legal constraints on Commonwealth intervention, the strategies of business and politicians, and the electoral implications of retrenchments.

The factors which persuaded the Fraser Liberal government not to get involved in 1982 must have weighed differently with the Hawke Labor ministry a year later when it agreed to protect BHP through a steel industry plan promoted by Senator John Button. The difference may reflect an electoral commitment, changes in the world market, greater representation for threatened workers through the government-ACTU Accord, or an agreement with BHP. It was, however, a political decision, and a reminder that underlying all public policy choices are political interests. No matter how much decisions are proposed by experts, legitimated by learned tribunals or justified on the grounds of economic or technical rationality, policy is above all about politics.

Hence Aristotle's master science is necessary (but not sufficient) for analysing the policy process. A policy—or demand for a policy—can be studied through a variety of useful frameworks, from law to organisational theory to sociology. Better policies may be proposed or judged using the instruments of econometrics, the insights of social welfare case studies or the experience of bureaucrats. These cannot explain, however, why a particular policy has been adopted or ignored. For this we must turn to the supposed source of 'irrationality'—politics, that endless disagreement about priorities, resources and principles.

So public policy analysis involves observing politics, and tracing how economic and social forces, institutions, people, events and circumstance interact. It offers a way of exploring how policies were chosen, and a method for judging their impact.

Recent Approaches

From general discussions about the nature of decisions and administration, Australian academics have begun to focus on particular policy arenas. From Corbett (1965) on the airlines, to Brennan and O'Donnell (1986) on issues in child care, writers have asked how—and in whose interest—specific policies have been formulated. Many studies have taken up the issue of implementation, noting that policy decided within the central institutions of government is not necessarily reflected at the delivery point. All these studies have been concerned with the structures and practices which make Australia different.

This book is also concerned with particular Australian practices. The international public policy literature provides important concepts and arguments from diverse theoretical traditions; but what is true for America or Britain does not necessarily hold for Australia, and it can be frustrating to learn only from overseas texts. Ideas need to be tested against Australian experience.

To describe the local policy arena and processes, to explore the interplay between people and institutions, and to emphasise the continuing role of the political, this book moves from the general to the specific across two levels of analysis. Simeon (1976: 556) has characterised this approach as a policy 'funnel of causality', moving from the broadest possible scope to detailed concern about a particular policy or participant. In Simeon's formulation, the funnel begins at its broadest point with the socioeconomic environment, moves to questions of power, culture, ideology and institutions, narrows again to the policy making process, and finishes with specific public policies. The funnel technique embraces case, institutional and process studies to approach its subject from a wide range of perspectives. A funnel technique assumes that different explanations are required at different levels as the analyst's perspective moves closer and closer to the specific.

At the macro level this book begins with the role of the Australian state, the extent of the public sector, and the roles of central bureaucrats, parties and interest groups. This is more than setting a context. It raises questions about why some sorts of policies are chosen and others excluded, before the second half of the book asks how certain policies are determined and implemented.

A macro approach emphasises that public policy analysis must not neglect the role of 'economic forces acting upon and through the state' (Head 1983: 34). It also conveys the complexity for many policy arenas arising from Australia's federal arrangements; the division of power between the Commonwealth and States produces quite different institutions and patterns of choice than those, for example, of unitary Britain. In exploring the significance and consequences of federalism for public policy the impressive Canadian literature is of particular value (see for example Doern and Aucoin 1979; Doern and Phidd 1983; Jackson et al. 1986). The impact of federalism cannot just be assumed away, as some writers do, by asserting that in Australia the state can be considered as 'the national government and public service' because state power is 'increasingly centralised in these bodies' (Theophanous 1980: xv).

The second level of analysis in this book focuses on specific areas of policy formulation and implementation. It begins with theories of decision making. Though problematic, these suggest some common patterns in the way ministers, bureaucrats and organisations make and evaluate choices. Application comes through examining several key Australian policy fields—the economic, industrial and social.

These cases indicate the frequent complexity and fragmentation of the policy process in Australia. They lead into a final section commenting on the prospects for 'rational' policy making, decisions made according to technical, expert criteria rather than through political contingency. In such rationality lies hope for co-ordination, planning and considered choice. This book, however, emphasises the centrality of politics, rather than technocratic rationality, in shaping Australian public policy. Economics, engineering or law may provide the arenas, concepts and arguments for 'rational' choice, but the political process—and only the political process—can determine who wins. Indeed, the annexation of the term 'rational' is itself an attempt to bestow, or deny, legitimacy for particular policies. The limits to government action arise then not from an inability to appreciate what would be the 'best' policy, but from structural and electoral constraints. With these the book concludes.

Many of the policies which affect people in a liberal democratic capitalist society do not emanate from government. As Forward noted in 1974, public policy writ large is more than the actions of politicians. Home loans and interest rates decided by private banks affect public policy, as do the decisions by foreign companies to invest—or withdraw —capital from Australia. What governments do, therefore, is often decided in civil society, outside the immediate scope (if not the reach) of the state. We have sought to capture this complexity, while focusing on the decisions and processes of the public sector. For if public and private are intertwined, to analyse one is inevitably to evoke the other.

Further Reading

Anderson, James E. (1984) *Public Policy Making* 3rd edn, New York: Holt, Rinehart & Winston.

Doern, G. Bruce and Phidd, Richard W. (1983) *Canadian Public Policy* Toronto: Methuen.

Emy, Hugh V. (1976) *Public Policy: Problems and Paradoxes* Melbourne: Macmillan.

Ham, Christopher and Hill, Michael (1984) *The Policy Process in the Modern Capitalist State* Sussex: Wheatsheaf Books.

Hawker, Geoffrey, Smith, R.F.I. and Weller, Patrick (1979) *Politics and Policy in Australia* University of Queensland Press, chs 1 and 10.

Heclo, Hugh (1974) *Modern Social Politics in Britain and Sweden* Yale University Press, ch 1.

Simeon, R. (1976) 'Studying Public Policy' *Canadian Journal of Political Science* 9, 4, pp. 548–580.

Part 1

ACTORS
AND
INSTITUTIONS

2
The State in Australia

American car manufacturer Henry Ford once criticised the comparatively activist role of the state in Australian society. Australia, he suggested, had become 'socialist' because the railways were built and run by governments. Though perhaps overstated, Ford's observation highlights a fundamental truth about Australian public policy. Australia began as a colony which depended on the state to establish a European society in an unknown continent. The activities, commitments and responsibilities of the public sector were crucial to developing an economic order in the antipodes. This was never the minimalist state advocated by classical liberal doctrine. Rather, the state in Australia was 'centralised, omni-competent and authoritative' from its earliest formation (Aitkin 1983b: 176).

This activist state mobilised public resources for private gain. While other capitalist societies sought to follow a 'free' market path to development, the public sector in Australia strategically intervened in the economy from early colonial days. The local state took actions probably considered outside the ambit of legitimate public intervention in Britain. In Australia the state would adopt a crucial role in national development.

By the early twentieth century Australian commentators shared Ford's concern about 'statism' leading toward 'state socialism' (Eggleston 1932; Hancock 1930). Politicians and administrators were prepared to use the state in innovative ways to achieve immediate and self-interested ends such as establishing social or economic infrastructure. The state borrowed capital to supplement private investment and satisfy sectional interest claims. In this sense 'state socialism' implied, as Ford had meant, that direction and control over society's resources was being gathered in public rather than private hands. In retrospect, however, this 'socialistic' verdict is misleading and analytically inadequate in a number of respects.

Our survey of the state in Australia includes an analysis of its structure—what the state is and does, its historical development, its important interventions, the fragmented nature of the Australian state

15

and the limits and possibilities of its impact on outcomes. Rather than offer a precise definition of the state, about which no general agreement exists, it is more useful to begin with a description of the main functions and roles of the contemporary Australian state, for examining the pervasive role of the state is crucial to understanding public policy in Australia.

The Structure of the Contemporary State

The concept of a 'state' is not synonymous with the 'public sector'. While the two terms are often used interchangeably, the notion of a 'state' has a wider set of meanings than the people, institutions and practices usually understood as the 'public sector'. Each term assumes a particular analytical focus and raises a different set of questions. The notion of the public sector, for example, is a descriptive category derived largely from economic theory (Lane 1985). It assumes that what is not public is private, so that one sector could 'crowd out' the other. It also refers to the institutional framework of government administration, public commercial activities and state-run utilities.

Conversely, the notion of the state is drawn from philosophical and political theory. Conceptual concerns rather than descriptive categories sustain much discussion of state theory (Carnoy 1984). While the public and private dichotomy is commonly understood—if also much criticised—state theories often rely on a much less clear distinction between the state and civil society. In analytical terms the state is an agency of control, social order and cohesion, legitimacy, socialisation and economic intervention. This suggests that the issues separating the terms 'state' and 'public sector' are not simply matters of preference nor, as is often believed, mere code words for radical or conservative standpoints. It is inappropriate to consider accounts which use the term 'the state' as subscribing to radical politics, while those which use 'public sector' as conventional or liberal—pluralist. Instead, both terms more appropriately specify different theoretical concerns and levels of analysis. The state and public sector are different animals. While government is only part of the state, the public sector cannot be as easily subsumed into this general category.

As well as distinct traditions, different levels of analysis distinguish theories of the state from those of the public sector. State theories tend to analyse at a high level of generality, while public sector discussions examine specific processes or institutions. General accounts seek to capture the state as an overarching power structure within society (Connell and Irving 1980). Theoretical coherence assumes paramount importance; writers may rely on selective evidence to substantiate their claims (Frankel 1983). More partial public sector accounts, on the other hand, dwell on the details of government or department practice. They rarely take up issues raised by the general theories (Curnow and Wettenhall 1981; Painter and Carey 1979). Instead, they contrast particular insights against comparable literatures. Case studies provide the mainstay of this approach, though innovative work is appearing in public policy debates which steps outside the narrow concerns of institutional analysis (Lloyd and Troy 1981). These issues are taken up in the following chapter on the Australian public sector.

The Institutions of the State

Though the state is clearly more than a collection of buildings and officials, analysis begins by identifying the institutions which constitute the state apparatus. This approach indicates the organisational scope of the state and provides an approximate guide to its essential functions (cf. Miliband 1973; Deutsch 1986).

1 The elected representatives, meeting in a parliament established by the Australian constitution, provide the legislative arm of the state (Crisp 1978). From the parliament are drawn the ministers of state. Meeting in cabinet and with the head of state, ministers act as the executive (Jaensch 1986). These central actors maintain legitimate political authority within the state. The institutions of parliament and cabinet provide forums for policy-making discussion and considerations, and act as arbiters of rival interests throughout society (Encel 1974).

2 Second are the non-elected administrative departments of state. Included in this public service category are the central departments of Treasury, Finance, Attorney-General and Foreign Affairs, and the welfare and social-oriented departments such as Housing and Construction, Immigration, Social Security, Health, Education, and Aboriginal Affairs. Since the 1960s the range of government departments has increased to embrace 'quality of life' concerns including the environment, arts, culture, sports and recreation. These administrative organisations are the technical service of the state responsible for policy implementation (Spann 1973). Departments of state also provide considerable advice on policy formation, and so influence government decisions. The prerogative to implement government policies may result in control over outcomes.

3 The judiciary and courts provide the third tier of institutional decision making. The High Court arbitrates on all constitutional matters brought before it, setting limits to the powers of the Australian state. Other specialist judicial bodies and tribunals include the Arbitration

Commission, family courts, the Human Rights Commission and the Australian Broadcasting Tribunal. Although approved and at higher levels appointed by governments, the judiciary retains an independence from government and administration. While some critics regard the operations of the judiciary as an ideological process sanctioning the actions of the state (Playford 1972; Theophanous 1980; Therborn 1978), others note the important role of the courts in representative liberal democracies based on a capitalist economic system. Legal constraints qualify the actions of the other sections of the state and may serve to prevent the emergence of more arbitrary and despotic forms of government. The Australian judiciary performs a public policy-making role in interpreting and enforcing laws.

4 A significant section of the state enforces public order and defends territory. The armed forces act as external enforcers of state power. They provide the state with security and with coercive options at home or abroad. Domestically the armed forces are the final supporters of any regime's monopoly of coercive power. Internal enforcement agencies include the surveillance agencies, police and investigative forces, and other enforcement bodies such as prisons and detention centres. Police powers may extend to inspection and regulatory bodies, from meat inspectors to casino licensing boards.

5 Since 1901 the state in Australia has been divided vertically between the Commonwealth and the six States. This makes the Australian state not a unitary hierarchy but a loose federation based on regional power at the State level with certain limited functions centralised at the Commonwealth level (Sharman 1975; Aldred and Wilkes 1983). Australia has not one but seven state apparatuses with an eighth—the Northern Territory—about to emerge. These regional States provide additional layers of power, with levels of the state interacting through conflict, co-operation and opportunist politicking. At the lowest and most restricted level of state action, local government bodies function as service and regulatory agencies directly within communities.

6 State trading enterprises comprise a further acquired function of the state. Commercial state enterprises include the Commonwealth Bank, Australian Airlines, Telecom, Australia Post, the TAB, Medibank Private, the railways, utilities and electricity suppliers. Some of these state enterprises, such as Qantas, were created by the nationalisation of private enterprises, but most were originally established by governments. The creation of Australian state enterprises did not usually rest, however, on socialist thinking. Some exist to modify or compete with the private sector as, for example, do Australian Airlines or the Commonwealth Bank. Others were established to stimulate further private sector expansion by the provision

of guaranteed, and often subsidised, state services such as railways, roads, electricity and water supplies. Here the government acted as developer by providing necessary infrastructural services. Contrary to the assertions of some economists, many state trading enterprises produce considerable profit on investment (cf. Caves et al. 1981).

7 The state has also established a plethora of regulatory bodies, statutory authorities, and boards commissioned for specific purposes. This diverse group includes the Australian Broadcasting Corporation, Industries Assistance Commission, Human Rights Commission, Wool Corporation, the universities and regulatory boards for products such as potatoes, eggs and wheat. While these statutory authorities may ultimately be responsible to a minister or parliament, they are for the most part corporate bodies and autonomous in their operations (Wettenhall 1983). Indeed, many regulatory boards are more precisely described as semi-state institutions, for a sizeable portion of their membership and income come from the private sector.

8 Finally, if the state is conceived in the broadest sense, other less obvious institutions may be regarded as state sponsored or as semi-state organisations. Examples include the parties, pressure groups, the establishment church, sections of the media and, because in Australia registration with a tribunal is required, even trade unions. These semi-state institutions represent the margins of state policy-making and policy implementation. The state has influence on, or even some control over, institutions which might otherwise be considered as elements of civil society.

The Size and Authority of the Australian State

How large is the state? Assessments usually rely on quantitative criteria, including state use and transfer of resources, the percentage of gross domestic product channelled through state institutions, the number of employees within the public sector, measures of the state's productive capacity, or its legislative and program outputs (cf. Rose 1984; Aitkin 1983b). Such criteria provide approximate indices of state size, and allow comparision over time between nation states.

There is, however, no agreed formula for calculating state size (Taylor 1983). One measure, used by the international Organisation for Economic Cooperation and Development (OECD), is based on estimates of central government outlays. This suits unitary systems such as New Zealand, but is less accurate for federal systems, because the emphasis on central control of outlays tends to neglect activity within the States. Calculating gross state outlays for a federation such as Australia requires that central disbursements be augmented with regional (State level)

Figure 2.1 Schematic structure of the Australian state

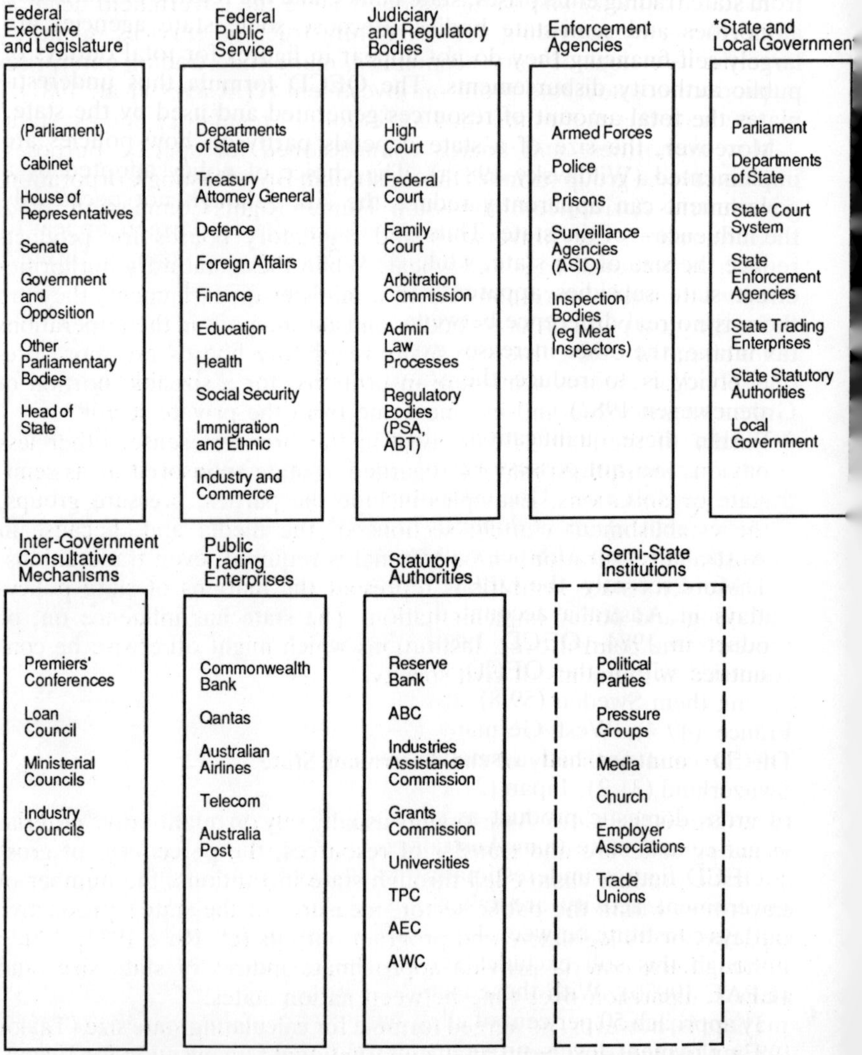

Federal Executive and Legislature	Federal Public Service	Judiciary and Regulatory Bodies	Enforcement Agencies	*State and Local Government
(Parliament)	Departments of State	High Court	Armed Forces	Parliament
Cabinet	Treasury	Federal Court	Police	Departments of State
House of Representatives	Attorney General	Family Court	Prisons	State Court System
Senate	Defence	Arbitration Commission	Surveillance Agencies (ASIO)	State Enforcement Agencies
Government and Opposition	Foreign Affairs	Admin Law Processes	Inspection Bodies (eg Meat Inspectors)	State Trading Enterprises
Other Parliamentary Bodies	Finance Education	Regulatory Bodies (PSA, ABT)		State Statutory Authorities
Head of State	Health			Local Government
	Social Security			
	Immigration and Ethnic			
	Industry and Commerce			

Inter-Government Consultative Mechanisms	Public Trading Enterprises	Statutory Authorities	Semi-State Institutions
Premiers' Conferences	Commonwealth Bank	Reserve Bank	Political Parties
Loan Council	Qantas	ABC	Pressure Groups
Ministerial Councils	Australian Airlines	Industries Assistance Commission	Media
Industry Councils	Telecom	Grants Commission	Church
	Australia Post	Universities	Employer Associations
		TPC	Trade Unions
		AEC	
		AWC	

* State structures replicate much of the Federal structure

KEY: PSA - Prices Surveillance Authority
ASIO - Australian Security Intelligence Organisation
AEC - Australian Electoral Commission
TPC - Trade Practices Commission
ABT - Australian Broadcasting Tribunal
ABC - Australian Broadcasting Commission
AWC - Australian Wool Corporation

and local outlays not derived from the centre, as well as with profits from state trading enterprises, state banks, and the returns of marketing authorities and semi-state bodies. Because some state agencies are largely self-financing they do not appear in figures for total outlays of public authority disbursements. The OECD formula thus underestimates the total amount of resources generated and used by the state.

Moreover, the size of a state depends partly on how policies are implemented (Wildavsky 1985a). The choice of policy adopted by a government can apparently reduce the size—though not necessarily the influence—of the state. Thus tax concessions for farmers appear to reduce the size of the state, while providing the same support through direct state subsidies apparently increases state outlays. In practice there is no real difference between the two strategies; one reduces the tax intake, the other increases expenditure. Yet on paper the effect of one policy is to reduce the state, on the other to expand it (cf. Groenewegen 1982).

Within these qualifications about the accuracy of measurements, Australia does not possess a particularly large state, though one which has grown over time. One estimate puts the Australian public sector at 22.4 per cent of gross domestic product in the 1930s, 25.9 per cent after the war, and 37.8 per cent by the late 1970s (Groenewegen 1982: 15). More recently, the OECD has calculated that central government outlays in Australia accounted for 33.4 per cent of gross domestic product in 1984 (OECD 1986). At least seventeen other capitalist countries within the OECD group possessed a larger central state, among them Sweden (59.8), the Netherlands (56.5), Denmark (58.0), France (49.4), West Germany (44.2) and Britain (44.9). Only four OECD countries had a smaller state than Australia—Spain (31.8), Switzerland (31.2), Japan (27.1) and Iceland (26.4). With 36.9 per cent of gross domestic product as state spending the United States had a larger central state than Australia (cf. EPAC 1985a).

OECD figures underestimate total state activity. When all levels of government activity are taken into account, Australian government outlays constitute between 41 and 43 per cent of gross domestic product, although this still excludes semi-government commercial enterprises (EPAC 1985b). With these included the total size of the public sector may approach 50 per cent of all declared economic activity in Australia.

Employment levels provide a further indication of the size of the Australia state. In 1985 the Commonwealth, States and local levels of government employed 1.7 million people or 32 per cent of a total workforce of 5.4 million (ABS 1986). This proportion has noticeably increased in recent decades. While in 1966 around one in four employees worked for the public sector, by 1987 this had reached one in three. Moreover, if those not in employment but receiving government pensions or benefits as income maintenance are included, then over 4.3 million Australian individuals/households rely on government for their main source of income.

Quantitative factors, however, are not a reliable guide to the importance of the state. The measurement of resources or workforce is not a calculation of the authority of the state, its spheres of responsibility or its ability to make and enforce decisions (Rose 1984). While many commentators imply that a growing state has concomitantly increased its power, authority and responsibilities, a persuasive argument can be made that state power has been compromised by increased size and organisational complexity. Authority may have been fragmented, with interests inside and beyond the state able to veto key choices. After 1983, for example, the Hawke government found it useful to engage in corporatist-type arrangements with business and unions. It recognised that state policy or government intervention was ineffective without endorsement and commitment from powerful sectional interests. 'Big government' is not necessarily 'big brother' (Wilenski 1983). Size is not a good indication of the effective authority of a state.

Relations Between the State and Society

The state is not a monolith with a cohesive and uniform set of policies. Because it is divided into institutions which sometimes pursue conflicting directions, the Australian state is a 'hydra-headed' complex of organisations which may only rarely work in concert (McFarlane 1968: 2). Contradictory or divergent state policies reflect the disjointed and sectional problems which emerge from the structure of society. Each state agency is addressing a particular constituency, not striving for coherence across the whole state. State policies are generally partial policies, expedient solutions to aspects of particular problems.

For some problems the state has insufficient control to achieve solutions (cf. Hood and Wright 1981). In applying Keynesian principles of economic management, for example, the Australian state can determine fiscal and monetary policy but has little influence over other economic factors, such as investment levels or capital movements, on which Keynesian prescriptions rely. States are also faced with 'wicked problems' which defy definition let alone solution. What 'problem', for example, is addressed by health policy? The state could put aside an almost limitless budget for health services, though at the cost of other, perhaps more productive, public projects. No matter how much money is put into health, however, there will be experts to proclaim that the state is not doing enough, that people are suffering from a heartless policy, that still more resources are required for a really 'effective' health system. Alternatively, it will be argued that the state should subsidise private health provisions. For such dilemmas, the essential questions for the state become: what problems are posed, who has control over the agenda and, given an infinite choice, to which problems should the state respond?

The Functions and Roles of the State

Just as size is not a reliable measure of influence, so too describing institutions is not necessarily a guide to the actual or potential functions of a state. Explaining what states can do is integral to the controversy between competing analytical approaches.

Nevertheless, most accounts agree that the state performs a number of vital functions and roles. All states seek to preserve their community, and so are involved in security, defence, law and order, foreign relations, and trade access. States also wish to maintain social order and cohesion, for no economy can operate effectively where class antagonisms, popular dissent or conflict perennially disrupt the system. Therefore, the state must defend the prevailing economic relations, the interests of business, and the social groups controlling economic resources. To perform these roles, the state seeks to preserve itself and guard its own and society's interests.

Beyond these basic functions, the activities of western states were acquired with the development of capitalist society. A welfare role emerged as social obligation passed from class to the state, and as representative institutions based on universal suffrage allowed articulation of a broader range of social interests. Keynesian prescriptions of state intervention and economic management emerged when the 'failure of the market' presented societies with severe economic depression and mass unemployment. Separated from immediate economic interests, with a revenue base of its own, the state became the only organisation able to counter cyclical phases and stabilise economic activity. As economic downturns have re-emerged, the state has assumed responsibility for crisis management and industry renewal. The state has also sought to promote the position of particular economic interests within the local economy. The Australian state, for example, has traditionally protected domestic manufacturing, largely through tariffs. Other industries also received state inducements as forms of indirect protection, including the rural industries, mining and the tertiary sector.

Theories of the State

Different theories of the state emerge from contending frameworks. Theoretical explanations of the state rely in many cases on the values and objectives of the investigator to identify what is important, what claims are being substantiated, what 'world view' is adopted. Some theorists, particularly conservatives, adopt an 'organic' view of the state as the 'body politic', its parts so interconnected that any change will have implications for all society (Huntington 1981). Liberals see the relationship between the state and the citizenry as one ideally based on a contract relation. They tend to favour a minimalist state which will least interfere with individual rights (see Withers 1983; James 1985; Crozier 1979). Socialist and anarchist writers often characterise the state as a coercive structure (Mandel 1975; Held et al. 1983), although others have concentrated on hegemony and legitimacy in the maintenance of state power (Offe 1984; Poulantzas 1978; Pierson 1984; Clark and Dear 1984).

In general, theories of the state are marked by controversies over the purposes of the state and the appropriateness of analytical tools. The state may be seen as a set of political institutions operating in relation to 'civil society' (Nordlinger 1981). Other writers, however, emphasise the state as an agency of social power, or as an instrument of class rule (Miliband 1973, 1977). Some stress the economic functions performed by the state (Lindblom 1977, Gough 1979; Holloway and Picciotto 1978), while a further group concentrate on the state's role in co-ordination and conflict resolution through specific policies or political arrangements (Berger 1981; Cawson 1985).

The state also receives greater attention in some historical periods than in others. At particular times the state has been considered important because of its role in marshalling a society's development. In other circumstances the concept may be considered redundant if the state appears of less consequence. The Australian colonial states of the 1880s and 1900s have attracted considerable analysis because of innovative state 'experiments' conducted throughout those years (Reeves 1969; Metin 1977). By contrast, the Australian state of the 1950s, with few exceptions (Encel 1960; Simms 1982), has been less studied or debated.

Clearly, then, the concept of the state ebbs and flows over time. As one recent survey noted,

some 'old-guard' political scientists like David Easton have seen this renewed interest in the state as a retrograde step: 'The state, a concept that many of us thought had been polished off a quarter of a century ago, has now risen from the grave to haunt us once again'(Easton 1981: 303). Others however see a focus on the state as a means of coming to grips with one of the essential parts of post-war advanced capitalist democracies, and as a way of going beyond the constraining assumptions and dogmas of both liberalism and Marxism that have coloured political analysis in both traditions [Head 1984] (Galligan 1984: 82).

The 'state' is a concept not only inherently difficult to define, but also characterised by historical phases of interest. It is not the state *per se* that is more or less important, but the changing analytical concerns which mark an academic discipline.

Contrasting Approaches

Comparative reviews of theoretical approaches to the state are widely available (cf. Held et al. 1983; Head 1983a; Gold et al. 1975; Jessop 1982; Crouch 1979; Carnoy 1984). Such surveys provide detailed and sophisticated assessments of the competing claims. Often reviewers separate classical theories of the state from modern controversies. The classical theorists work largely within the traditions of liberalism, conservatism and Marxism (Head 1984). Yet many of the classical theorists (Smith, Locke, Mill, Rousseau, Burke, Hegel, Marx, Lenin, Weber) did not principally address the subject of the state; later advocates have tended to further develop premises or theoretical positions not made explicit in the original texts.

In classical debates, liberal political theory was normative, asserting that civil society rested on individualism, private property, and a minimalist state (cf. Macpherson 1973; Friedman and Friedman 1980). Conversely, Marxist theory remained ambiguous, torn between explaining the organising capacity of the state and the class nature of its exercise of power (Urry 1981; Offe 1984).

More recently, pluralist theory has addressed the state indirectly, claiming that institutions of authority respond to group pressure (see Dahl 1967, 1978; see also Parkin 1980; McGregor 1968; Emy 1974). At its extreme the state could be portrayed as so enmeshed in contradictory demands and responsibilities that it is rendered unable to move. Such critiques led to arguments that governments were 'overloaded'—committed to financing so many different interests and programs that they could no longer raise sufficient funds to maintain all their activities (Birch 1984). The overload thesis assumed a certain prescience as the economic crisis of the 1970s continued to confront the state with fiscal limitations (cf. Crozier et al. 1975; Howard 1984; see also Crouch 1983 and Manley 1983).

Neo-Marxists emphasise the role of state activity in supplying the conditions, infrastructure and support for the private sector. In subsidising exports, providing tax concessions for small business, or controlling wages, the state aids 'capitalist accumulation' (Wheelwright and Buckley 1975–1983). One of the strengths of neo-Marxist analysis has been to demonstrate the extent to which the state can transform an economic structure while operating within that system (Tsokhas 1984; Beresford and Kerr 1980). This approach has been concerned to explain changing patterns of organisation within capitalism and, indeed, to question what capitalism may now mean for societies such as Australia with such extensive state sectors. The levels of state intervention, patterns of regulation, legitimacy, state welfare, conflict resolution, economic management and planning, labour regulation and social structuring remain topics of considerable debate in neo-Marxist literature (cf. Simms 1983; Miller 1986; Therborn 1986; Offe 1984).

Since the 1970s, corporatist analyses of state arrangements have been much discussed in Europe and to a lesser extent in Australia (Grant 1985; Loveday 1984). Corporatist theories point to state intervention based neither on liberal–market nor bureaucratic mechanisms but on bargained group consensus. They identify an interpenetration of the state with the economic producer groups of organised business and labour. This corporatism is variously interpreted as interest intermediation, functional pluralism, tripartism, consultative policy directions or a process of extra-parliamentary policy making (Panitch 1980; Lehmbruch and Schmitter 1982). While a precise definition of what might constitute a corporatist state remains elusive, the Australian experience of economic and tax summits, industry councils and planning bodies has seemingly opened a range of potential theoretical and empirical possibilities (cf. Loveday 1984; Stewart 1985; McEachern 1986).

Alternative Approaches

Beyond these ideological accounts, there are at least four other significant descriptions and explanations for the fundamental roles performed by a state. These focus on the political nature of the state.
1 An *administrative approach* defines the state as the institutions and
  practice of public power. Government departments, agencies and
  the public sector become the central focus for analysis (Spann 1973;
  Curnow and Wettenhall 1981). State policies evolve incrementally,
  shaped by the logistics of public sector administration (Nethercote
  1982).
    Some accounts in this tradition present the administrative state as
  a phenomenon of technical rationality, virtually devoid of politics.
  The public service is outside party politics, an efficient machine
  available for whoever controls government. Others, more plausibly,
  regard administrative and institutional arrangements as explicitly
  political, influencing both policy inputs and outcomes. Bureaucracy
  becomes a central focus for policy formation and implementation,
  part of the institutional 'pressure cooker' environment of state decision
  making. Analysts seek to ensure bureaucratic efficiency and effectiveness, responsiveness and accountability, and the application of administrative 'rationality' to the practice of public policy. Pluralist or
  Weberian theoretical approaches predominate in this approach,
  though not without critics (cf. Kouzmin 1983).

2 The *instrumentalist view* identifies the state as the agent either of the capitalist economy or of interest groups. In some accounts the state is reduced to economics, with policies determined in the economic 'base' and transmitted to the political superstructure for implementation (Playford 1972). Less mechanical Marxist accounts present the state as an instrument for the conduct of class rule, with dominant factions able to control the agenda through a cultural hegemony. Classes struggle for control of the state.

Elite theorists also pursue an instrumentalist understanding of the state. The state is viewed as a bureaucratic instrument imposing the necessary order to satisfy elite interests (Higley et al. 1979). Instrumentalist accounts may also rely on corporatist or modified pluralist notions in which organised interests determine the dimensions and policy concerns of the state. Each of these theoretical strands suggest that the state is in some way tied to structural forces in society and enjoys only limited independence of action. Public policy becomes a response to pressures from the economy or from private interests.

3 The state can also be characterised as an *agency of system maintenance*, with a measure of autonomy from both the economic base and from dominant interests or class factions. Here the state performs a comprehensive political role, guaranteeing social order even where this entails acting against major interests within the economy. At the broadest level the state may function as a system of domination. Conservative, functionalist, structural-Marxist and hegemonic accounts each insist that the state is motivated by the longer term concerns of civil society. The system requires a sufficiently independent state to ensure its continued survival (Jessop 1982; Frankel 1983).

4 Other state-centred accounts are more sensitive to the *political dimensions* of the state. Realignments of power, coalitions and alliances, populism and the building of cultures, political cleavages, leadership, decisions and reponses are factors in these explanations of state policies (Skocpol 1980). Politics provides room to manoeuvre, space that can be strategically explored, possibilities available to leaders, policy processes and organisational dynamics (cf. Galligan 1986a: 244−65). Politics becomes the state qua state, with the state 'acting for itself' (cf. Evans et al. 1985; Nordlinger 1981; Therborn 1986).

The Development of the State in Australia

The Australian nation began as British military and penal settlements. This contributed to a legacy of colonial 'statism', of authoritarian

administrations which took upon themselves responsibility for establishing a local economy and extending European settlement. Even
colonies which relied on free settlers rather than convicts, such as
South Australia, still considered that their economic survival as frontier
societies rested on a strong and innovative local state.

The Australian state which emerged was not a 'nightwatchman' state
limited by the concerns of liberal political philosophy. Local land
owners and commercial interests did not seek to avoid state interference;
rather, they saw the indigenous state as an instrument for economic
development. Public and private elites coalesced with colonial administrations. The state promoted the local establishment, and the local
establishment encouraged the state, until private and state power were
systematically interlocked. Politics was a struggle for control of the
state apparatus, a recognition that the resources of the colonial state
could be used for private ends. Pervasive state intervention, encouraged
by private interest, characterised these frontier societies.

Colonial Liberalism

By the mid-nineteenth century Australia's development could be characterised as 'colonial liberalism' (Butlin 1983). Familiar liberal institutions
such as parliament, citizenship and individual representation were established, as was democratic participation through voting and political
rights. Yet this pragmatic 'liberalism' did not adhere to the orthodoxy
of small government, balanced budgets and private entrepreneurship
based on personal liberty. Rather, 'colonial liberalism' was a hybrid,
for the earlier practice of state intervention continued. The state protected the establishment of Australia's emerging 'marsupial capitalist'
economy, just as it later protected endangered species of fauna (Wanna
1981; see also Brugger and Jaensch 1985). The prevailing liberal culture
still accepted that state intervention was essential for economic
development.

The 'colonial liberals' were developers operating as part of, or in
tandem with, the machinery of state (McGhee 1967). They saw the
state essentially as the vehicle for public works based on borrowed
funds, an institution securing British capital for infrastructural investment (Butlin 1959; Galligan 1984). The state would overcome the
barriers to development. In these years before the Labor Party existed,
parliamentarians were almost all land holders, employers, professionals
and business owners who professed liberalism but encouraged statism.
While other nations recall their *laissez faire* past, the important concerns for Australians were always about the most appropriate projects
for an interventionist state.

Federalist Integration

The 'colonial liberal' states were regional entities (New South Wales, Victoria, Queensland, South Australia, Western Australia and Tasmania) with separate political economies. The decision to federate was motivated by a desire for nationhood and a concern to co-ordinate certain functions of government (La Nauze 1972). The colonies chose to come together under a constitution which sought to combine the American federal structure and the British 'Westminster' system (Lucy 1985; Thompson 1980). This agreement was shaped not just by legal considerations but also by economic concerns. Colonial negotiators represented the administrative, landed, commercial and professional interests already established within the colonies. Such representatives were concerned to ensure that a federal administration did not interfere too dramatically with existing interests, including economic and social concerns. Hence they wrote a constitution which limited central power and sought to curb the emergence of a dominant national government away from their regional economic bases (Patience and Scott 1983).

Following federation the States retained many of their rights of self-government while the new central administration worked with a set of limited but important powers. From 1 January 1901 the Commonwealth assumed legislative responsibility for defence, foreign policy, taxation, trade and commerce, custom duties and tariffs, a range of state enterprises, immigration, currency and banking. Regional States retained functions not specified in the formal constitution. This gave them significant space to manoeuvre, for many implicit powers could be exercised at the State level. Thus the new federation constrained the central state while leaving the States with considerable scope to pursue separate policies within their own territories.

Interest Protection and Sponsored Intermediation

The Australian state which emerged during the first years of the twentieth century moved from colonial statism to a more general concern for interest protection and adjudication (Butlin 1983; Emy 1974). The economic vulnerability of Australian industries encouraged producer groups to 'syndicate' for common advantage (Encel 1960); powerful interests joined to urge a system of 'protection all round' (Shann 1948). 'Syndical satisfaction' was encouraged by the boom–bust character of Australia's economic development, with cyclic fluctuations and expansionary swings from industry to industry (Miller 1954; see also Nevile 1981; Catley and McFarlane 1983). The power blocs of the manufacturing sector, finance, the major mining groups, parties and the trade unions all supported local protectionist policies. For some commentators this led to the Australian state sponsoring 'historical compromises' between sectional interests (cf. Shann 1948). State policy shifted from priority for infrastructural development to concern with the relationships or arrangements between organised interests.

One important extension of state intervention was the establishment of compulsory industrial arbitration to institutionalise relations between capital and labour and to regulate the labour market. Arbitration allowed the adjudication of rival interests, for state intervention at the federal and State levels restricted the scope for private determination of industrial relations. Legislation required the registration of trade unions, introduced minimum and basic wage levels, enforced state determinations in disputes and regulated many of the terms and conditions of employment.

To promote 'protection all round', the state introduced tariffs to assist the economic expansion of domestic interests, particularly the emerging manufacturing sector. Tariffs were available to employers who could claim some hardship or who provided award wages set down by state arbitration. It also formed part of a broader state policy of import substitution and government revenue raising.

Responding to pressure from workers and liberals, the Australian state also gradually extended its creed of protection to social welfare support. Most benefits were provided on a 'residual' basis (Castles 1985), for this minimal welfare state was intended to provide charitable relief and base entitlements rather than to redress market inequalities. Public policy nevertheless responded to demands for social justice based on claims for fair wages, land access, the right to work, and the maintenance of income through pensions and unemployment benefits (Macintyre 1985). Indeed some have argued that Australian policy-makers established a 'wage earners' welfare state', in which protection for the wage earner with a family was the cornerstone of state policy (Castles 1985). Those sections of society not included in this wage earners' welfare state, such as single parents, non-wage earners and Aboriginal people became social 'losers' while organised interests 'won' greater state safeguards (cf. Matthews 1980; Macintyre 1985)

As part of its creed of protection, the state actively encouraged the incorporation of interest groups. In particular, the state established a range of commissions, tribunals, regulatory and licensing bodies to resolve conflict through interest representation in state agencies. The state interposed itself between the major classes of capital and labour, between sectors of capital—rural, finance, mining and manufacturing—and between social groups over welfare issues. An already interventionist state became the adjudicator of conflicting interests (for recent public policy case studies in this vein, see Scott 1980).

International Pressures on the Australian State

A chronology of the Australian state highlights the considerable influence of external factors on internal development. During the last thirty years in particular, the Australian economy has been increasingly integrated within a world system. International pressures inevitably constrain Australian state policies, as does the significant British, American and Japanese investment and control of property and resources within Australia. Some argue that this has turned Australia into either the fifty first State of the United States (McQueen 1982), or a 'client state' of the major transnational enterprises (Crough and Wheelwright 1982).

While it is easy to overstate the significance of external pressures, international integration has created substantial constraints for national policy-making. During the Great Depression, for instance, overseas banks successfully pressured governments to adopt policies of contraction, rather than default on international loans. In recent years large domestic and foreign speculators have made it extremely difficult for the national government to regulate key elements of the economy, including currency and interest rates, trade balances and investment levels. The Australian state must deal with multinational enterprises which are often conglomerates larger than itself in terms of revenue and international influence. They are part of the world economy which affects Australia's exports and trading links, as capital and the labour process are increasingly organised on an international scale.

These external challenges confront the state with an overarching set of problems to which it has few answers and very limited influence. International pressures undercut the traditional role of a state with sufficient power to mediate domestic interests within a frontier capitalist economy.

'New Interventionism'

During the present long economic recession the state has vacillated markedly over policy directions (cf. Hughes 1980; Kasper 1982; Catley 1983). Rival economic policies advocated inflation first or employment first strategies, and argued over the optimal role and size of government. Whatever policy option was tried, however, two significant features of state intervention remained constant. The size of the Australian state did not generally decrease during the 1970s and 1980s; indeed, despite the rhetoric, it continued to expand. Second, state interventionism was not constrained but tended to be redirected in intent and effect.

Perhaps most significantly, this redirection included greater business and labour links with the state (Marsh 1983a; Beilharz and Watts 1983). Though business always had contact with the state, the present downturn led to a consolidation of relations at a formal level over macro economic and industry policies. Labour, on the other hand, while linked through state regulation of labour relations, rarely enjoyed close consultation with the state over policy directions. This may in part be a reflection of the dominance of non-Labor parties in federal government. After 1983, however, the ACTU leadership was able to channel their policies into the deliberations of the Hawke government. The 1980s have thus witnessed a renewed debate about the relative impact of business and labour organisations on state policy (Ewer and Higgins 1986; Singleton 1985; McEachern 1986; Palmer 1986).

This recent integration of the state with dominant private interests has been characterised as a 'new interventionism'. Several OECD nations have adopted similar state policies—the promotion of strategic state policies to stimulate economic growth, a reliance on 'guided' market forces including 'deregulation' initiatives by the state, and the introduction and co-ordination of industrial policies to preserve established industries, facilitate change and generate new industry expansion (OECD 1983a). An important concern of 'new interventionist' policies is long term employment maintenance, sometimes referred to as 'positive adjustment programs' (OECD 1983b; Jones 1983).

In Australia new interventionist initiatives have included the deregulation and reregulation of banking, the floating but surreptitious regulation of the Australian dollar, and the use of guided market policies to achieve government objectives. The accords with the union movement have tightened the links between union leaders and the state, and incorporated unions within state economic strategies. State 'plans' for the steel and motor vehicle industries have employed new interventionism strategies for industrial restructuring, rather than relying solely on previous patterns of protection through subsidy and tariffs.

New interventionist policies assume a changed perception of the nature and role of the state. The state has pursued a more sensitive intermeshing with the private sector in its policies about regulation, the provision of assistance, government services, privatisation and the presence of the state in economic joint ventures with private consortiums (Head 1986). Many people now demand that state intervention be justified by results, with the criteria based on private sector measurements of success using cost−benefit accounting.

New interventionism, however, has not been pursued without opposition. The 'new right' has argued that 'big government' favours labour over the needs of small business. They interpret these policies as pro-union and pro-corporate developments which support continued government expansion. Farmers crusading with the National Farmers' Federation, for example, want preferential policies which do not require the preservation of trade union influence nor significant tax costs to the farm sector. New interventionism, with its policies of 'economic rationalism', has been the cause of political struggle in Australia. It has been supported by advocates of continued selective state intervention, and opposed by those concerned that these Labor government policies preserve trade union power and cut across the traditional access of some interests to the policy process (West 1984; Nurick 1987).

The Australian State

This historical survey suggests six important functions of the Australian state (cf. also Wolfe 1977).

The State as Developer

A fundamental role of the Australian state involved the active promotion of economic and social development. The state used public sector resources and overseas borrowings to induce economic expansion. This involved the state in providing infrastructure, organising investment projects, subsidising industries and joining partnerships with private developers.

The State as Protector

The defence of a spectrum of local interests has traditionally occupied much state activity. Statutory authorities and agencies were established to protect sectional groups, interests were represented in the policy process, and welfare provisions introduced as protection for the social order.

The State as Regulator

State regulation covers most areas of economic and social behaviour such as business, labour, migration, social commitments and entitlements. Regulation allows the state to reduce uncertainties, provide acceptable bases for social interaction, impose restrictions, implement enforceable standards and monitor or control particular sections of society (Tomasic 1984).

The State as Arbitrator and Distributor

The high level of state involvement in the adjudication of interests is a characteristic of Australian public policy. Arbitration and marketing or producer boards have guaranteed income levels for business and labour producers. As part of the state's role as arbitrator, it redistributes resources. Through taxation, charges and duties the distributive state transfers income from one group to another. State distribution is not only from taxpayers to non-taxpayers, but also from consumers to business, industry to industry, and from the middle-aged to the young and old.

The State as Organiser

The Australian state performs the important role of organising productive and social relations in civil society. This includes attempts by the state to organise economic performance and capital accumulation (Offe 1984). The state is involved in organising the structure of society, particularly through policies designed to encourage social integration, such as with the welfare state, educational provisions and migration.

The State as Producer

The Australian state as producer supplies infrastructure, public utilities and services. Public enterprises tend to stabilise private sector economic activity. Where the state undertakes production it generates employment, guarantees essential services, provides necessary inputs and affects subsequent consumers by subsidies, transfers, price determination, quality standards and structural capacities. The state enters production not only because the private sector is reticent, but also to establish influence over the industry or to extend economic controls.

The Limits to State Interventionism: the Fragmented State

Though the Australian state has at various times acted as developer, protector, arbitrator, distributor, organiser and producer, it is not a monolithic organisation carefully following single policies which move slowly but inexorably toward fixed goals. The danger in analysing the state is to give it the appearance of life and certainty, to find hidden logic in its actions, or motivations separate from the intentions of those who make, or are affected by, state policy. For the state is above all a fragmented set of institutions and individuals with roles that are often contradictory, responding with varying effectiveness to competing class and sectional interests (Head 1986; Galligan 1986a). As a complex body which generates and modifies public policy, the state operates with largely undetermined limits and possibilities of action. State activity establishes the parameters for the processes of public policy, the impact of policy decisions, the scope for leadership, the technical details of policy implementation and the formation of administrative networks. These processes in turn can change the shape and functions of the state. The policy process and the state become difficult to separate as each defines the other.

Constraints on state intervention arise from the economic structure of Australian society and from the influence of an international economy. As the recession drags on, Australian public policy may follow the experience of other debtor nations, for whom credit comes only through accepting the directions of an agency such as the International Monetary Fund. Such might be a logical conclusion of increasing integration in a world economic order.

The federal structure of Australia creates multiple state administrations and means state intervention can be unco-ordinated and overlapping (Sharman 1980). As a consequence, state policies which follow the path of least resistance pass for co-ordinated state policy. The Australian constitution preserves this fragmented structure, provides the ground-rules, and creates an institutional framework for power plays between different levels of the state (cf. Rydon 1975; Groenewegen 1976; Burke 1984; McMillan et al. 1983; Aldred and Wilkes 1983). These internal state divisions reduce the coherence of state policy and often make policy deliberations subservient to departmental or intra-governmental disputes.

In a capitalist economy, state intervention is the politics of the feasible. It both responds to and reshapes society. Intervention continually re-establishes the bounds of state politics, renegotiates the limits and outcomes of state action, and opens new avenues for future directions, struggles or modifications. State intervention is extensive but imprecise. While the Australian state has continually been active in the provision of economic inducements, state policies toward welfare and social services, after a period of early innovation, were retarded and spartan when compared with Western Europe. The Australian state was not interventionist across the board, but remained selective about its areas of activity. There are no fixed limits to the extent of state intervention; different capitalist nations display markedly different patterns.

Though Australia emerged with an activist state, this state was not large by international standards. Australia has not been a nation of 'big government', but a society using the state sector primarily to promote economic development. Public policy reflects this role of the state as developer, protector, arbitrator, distributor, organiser and producer. It has been determined by the interests, parties, and class groups competing for access to the state, anxious to influence the choices of an emerging, middle power, peripheral economy.

Further Reading

Butlin, N.G., Barnard, A. and Pincus, J. (1982) *Government and Capitalism* Sydney: Allen & Unwin.

Galligan, Brian (1984) 'The State in Australian Political Thought' *Politics* 19, 2, pp. 82–92.

Head, Brian (1983) 'State and Economy: Theories and Problems' in Brian Head (ed.), *State and Economy in Australia* Melbourne: Oxford University Press.

Simms, Marian (1983) 'The Political Economy of the State in Australia', in Alexander Kouzmin (ed.) *Public Sector Administration: new perspectives* Melbourne: Longman Cheshire.

3

The Public Sector

Born a penal colony in the age of liberalism, European Australian society was always marked by an activist state. Though its citizens quickly acquired the rights and practices of parliamentary democracy, they did not seek a reduction of public intervention. From colonial statism to the new interventionism, the Australian state was encouraged to operate as developer, protector, regulator, arbiter, distributor, organiser and producer.

Why has the Australian state always been so involved in civil society, so bound up in national economic development? Competing explanations highlight the role of local capital and labour syndicates, corporatist tendencies in decision making, or the influence of the bureaucracy in promoting a central role for the state. Whatever their disagreements, all these perspectives agree that the Australian state has not been a neutral umpire which followed the liberal creed of minimal interference beyond defence, law or the provision of basic welfare. This is a useful finding which invites investigation of the specific form of the Australian state, the way it operates, and the process by which political ambitions are translated into bureaucratic action.

Public policy seeks to explain how, why and to what extent particular policies are adopted. To do so the discipline must demonstrate some macro understanding about the context and operation of the state. Hence the importance of apparently abstract debates about the state, and of historical and political economy approaches to state actions. There is, however, no single, accepted, adequate theory of the state employed in the public policy literature; most case studies can be claimed as support by several competing paradigms, and much analysis avoids the thorny question of explaining the local form of state intervention either by omission or by taking it as given.

If a broader understanding remains implicit and incomplete, it may be that public policy has not read back its own findings. For there is much to be learned from the institutional and administrative approach to the state, a tradition which begins not with broad theoretical constructs but from the day to day details of a particular government. 'Public administration' has often been criticised for its alleged narrow

37

focus and positivist approach to the institutions and processes it studies. Early proponents of public policy, eager for academic and market difference, distanced themselves from the older tradition and spoke of focusing on social structures rather than administrative minutiae. The debates within public administration circles about the optimal forms and structure of government were seen as irrelevant during the recessions of the 1980s, when changes in intervention were accompanied by cutbacks and discontinuities in government administration. Yet the differences between the fields were perhaps exaggerated, for what happens within a state is clearly crucial to public policy explanations. It is this public administration tradition which can supply important links between specific government policies and general state theories.

Public administration emphasises 'middle range' questions. It focuses on the government agencies, bureaucracies and quasi-official institutions which comprise the 'public sector'. R.S. Spann's *Government Administration in Australia* (1979), for example, examines the structure and functions of government, policy, personnel management and industrial relations within the public service, and issues of co-ordination, accountability, budgeting and reform. This is an agenda different only in emphasis from the interests of public policy studies, one which concentrates on structure rather than outcomes. For though they risk becoming description rather than analysis, public administration studies pose important problems for state theories. Much of the literature suggests that government is rarely a machine which efficiently translates into practice the decisions of elected officials. Delivery is not always reliable, for policy can be derailed by the bureaucracy, altered in implementation or perhaps negated by other government agencies. Turning intent into state action relies on the structures and processes identified by public administration studies but not always discernable in top-down models of the state.

Policy outcomes are influenced by the specific forms and practices of a public sector, so broad pictures of the Australian state must accord with an understanding of how people, processes and institutions interact. A viable discipline of public policy must link these two levels of analysis so that each reflects upon the other. From debates about the state, this chapter turns to some of the concerns of public administration. It explores how agencies transfer resources, the effect of fragmented institutions, the problems of popular control and the implications of bureaucratic norms and practices.

The Role of Government

With economic recession and new interventionism, debate about the role of government has shifted. Australia's public sector is now often portrayed as a dead weight on prospects for economic revival. A curious ambivalence has emerged—a traditional distrust of bureaucracy, yet continuing expectations that governments should provide a wide range of services. Some Australians readily blame 'big government' for the deteriorating state of the economy even while they demand better roads, business incentives from taxation, subsidies to promote production and government protection from overseas competition. Manufacturers criticise state intervention in the market yet petition government to impose wage freezes and protect local industry. Farmers vote for avowedly free enterprise parties, yet expect subsidised fertiliser, fuel and research, and strict regulation of farm production and exports. Organisations arguing that 'politics should be kept out of sport' nevertheless lobby governments to provide new stadia and playing fields. Everywhere the state, and the public sector it embraces, are cast as both villain and white knight. When politicians advocate privatisation of trading enterprises, reduced personal tax at the expense of state functions and less involvement in arbitration and regulation, the public sector appears under siege.

With central government outlays at around 32.8 per cent of gross domestic product, the Australian state is not large by OECD standards. Yet by the mid-1980s, the leadership of both Liberal and Labor parties had accepted as economic orthodoxy arguments that the public sector was too large, too costly, and must be reduced as a necessary condition for renewed prosperity. Austerity cuts began as early as 1974. By the time of the Review of Commonwealth Functions (RCF 1981), known as the Lynch 'razor gang', pruning exercises had became part of the normal Commonwealth and State budget rounds.

This seeming consensus about the need to 'roll back the state' is a response to a general fiscal crisis. Recession, slow growth and mounting debt have reduced the capacity (or at least the enthusiasm) of most western nations to sustain historically large public sectors. Cut backs promote, and reflect, the breakdown of bi-partisan agreement on Keynesian economic management principles. For some critics, government itself—and not just its policies—is the cause of economic malaise. The conservative rhetoric of the late 1980s asserts that big government creates high taxes and unfavourable interest rates, destroys initiative, and redirects capital from the private to the 'unproductive' public sector of the economy (see for example Nurick 1987).

There is, of course, a sleight of hand in many of these arguments. Despite 200 years of state intervention to provide infrastructure for business, such critics imply that the public sector does not contribute to economic growth, that governments take but do not give back. Stretton has noted that the familiar attack on the welfare state emphasises the taxes people pay, but not the collective goods they receive:

Why don't we ridicule such childish tricks by responding in kind? It would be just as easy to perceive only the goods we get from the public sector and the prices we pay to the private sector. 'God Bless The Public Sector' we could say as we salute the flag each morning, 'it gives us Australia's freedom and independence, and all our individual rights. It gives us law and order and public health and fire brigades and, as far as mortal man can, it keeps our shopkeepers honest. It gives us super highways and shady suburban streets and charming cobbled lanes. It feeds and cares for us in sickness and old age. It gives us the science that makes our economy grow, the education that makes us aware and skilful, and most of our highest culture. By contrast with that wonderful productivity, all that the parasitic private sector does is to demand our money. They've got prices on everything we touch, from necessities to luxuries. You can't walk into any shop or supermarket or service centre in the land without the brutes demanding money. And what for? To line the pockets of foreign shareholders and fat-cat bureaucrats in the multi-nationals. The private sector is now taking more than half the national product—more than half the hard-earned income of every one of us! Capitalism cannot survive bloodsucking on that scale—it is time to call a halt, reverse course, return to sanity'. It would be no sillier than the opposite nonsense we put up with every day (Stretton 1980: 21).

In defending the concept (though not necessarily the specifics) of the Australian welfare state, Stretton warns against simplistic notions about public services. He points to the role of government not just in redistributing income to support the less well-off, but in providing the conditions for economic prosperity. A public sector does more than just displace private activity; as the public administration literature notes, numerous state agencies are employed to transfer resources between groups and to promote private capital accumulation.

The Public Sector as Subsidy

The competence of public officials and their organisations is often compared in unflattering terms with the private sector. Governments are assumed to be characteristically inefficient. The large annual losses of some public-owned railways provoke predictable warnings about government waste, while the substantial profits of public-owned Telecom or the OTC draw accusations of excessive charges and poor services.

As one public policy analyst noted, 'the argument that private firms are more efficient than public corporations is based on assertion rather than analysis. Such evidence as is available is largely anecdotal rather than scientific' (Howard 1986: 14). The functions of government and business often cannot be compared. Many public functions 'such as law and order, public health regulation, economic planning, have few or no close parallels in the private sector' (Spann 1979: 22). Public agencies incur costs not imposed on business—they must be financially and operationally accountable to a minister, must conform with legislation such as the Public Service Act, and are open to scrutiny from parliamentary committees, administrative law and freedom of information legislation. Public accountability requires extensive records and elaborate written justifications for most decisions. The public sector must conform to all the auditing and reporting requirements imposed on business, and then work to an additional set of responsibilities not imposed on private sector competitors.

For public functions such as customs or immigration, there is no market mechanism to allocate resources or determine priorities, and no simple criteria for success. Profit and loss are useful measures of efficiency for business (at least those which are not monopolies, or protected by tariffs, or sustained through government contracts, or operating as part of cartels). The balance sheet is a less reliable guide to the performance of many public sector agencies. Politicians use the public sector to subsidise the private (Stretton 1977). The roads, railways and ports employed by business to transport their products, the education and training of their workers, the communication networks between branches and often their venture capital, export assistance and protection from international competition—all are supplied by governments and funded if need be through general taxation.

Further, State and Commonwealth governments cross-subsidise services of direct benefit to consumers, farmers and industry in smaller centres. Electricity, rail, gas, water, postage and telephone authorities support outlying areas through profit from metropolitan services. Telecom is not asked to produce the cheapest possible telephone service between Sydney and Melbourne, and then allowed to ignore all other potential consumers. Rather, it is required to ensure a relatively inexpensive telecommunications service across the nation, and so give all Australians access to affordable telephone connections. Telecom's 'efficiency' must be judged within these constraints.

Much of the public sector, then, is involved in subsidy and redistribution. Transfer payments represent some 75 per cent of Commonwealth outlays. Resources are directed from urban centres to the countryside, from New South Wales and Victoria to less populated states, and frequently from PAYE taxpayers to business. Concessional rail and electricity rates, for example, have been used by State governments to lure industry and mining to invest; the public-owned railways become a form of hidden subsidy, with costs paid from more profitable lines or from general tax receipts. The annual 'losses' of the rail system are thus an unreliable guide to the quality of its management or the application of its workforce.

Attempts to remove this redistributive function are likely to meet with bitter opposition from sectional interests. Selling off large state utilities, the British practice of 'privatisation', has been much discussed in Australia. Advocates argue that monopolies such as Telecom have little incentive to run efficiently, and so become wasteful. They assert that the introduction of competition would ensure efficiency and so cheaper services (see for example submissions to Davidson Committee 1982; Albon 1985).

The defenders of Telecom note that cross-subsidies depend on continued monopoly status. Faced with private networks, Telecom could only remain viable by retaining high volume Sydney—Canberra—Melbourne connections while closing down unprofitable lines to rural areas and distant States. Cheaper services for some would come at the cost of equality of access (Reinecke and Schultz 1983).

The privatisation debate thus becomes a clash of economic and social objectives. Should the market be the only mechanism for allocating resources, or should Australians use their public sector to redistribute wealth, to subsidise farming, industry and employment, and to provide equal and fair national services?

Sections of the ALP have been captured by the rhetoric of 'economic rationalism', and the Hawke government pursued policies of new interventionism. Privatisation, however, has made little inroad into Labor thinking. State Labor governments, particularly in Western Australia, have been more inclined to experiment with 'hybrid' public ventures combining government and private capital. At a national level, the ALP seeks to reduce government expenditure but recognises that much of its constituency works in manufacturing or the public sector, and benefits from state intervention. In general Labor administrations have accepted the existing framework of supporting social services and economic activity through the public sector. Whatever the alleged economic benefits, large scale privatisation is rarely seen as an appropriate social policy.

The choice is perhaps more problematic for conservative politicians. Liberal Party rhetoric emphasises reduced government involvement in the economy. In practice, however, many Liberals find it difficult to support privatisation. Capital city business interests are often enthusiastic about privatisation proposals for Telecom, Australia Post and Australian Airlines. They sense prospects for lower costs and increased choice. Should state agencies be sold off as monopolies, there may be opportunities to buy into established, profitable utilities.

Business people from smaller centres, however, along with farmers represented in the National Party, are less enthusiastic. An end to cross-subsidies protected by state monopolies would cost them money. A redistributive public sector works to the advantage of outlying States and, whatever the philosophical commitment to small government, will be defended.

Mapping the Australian Public Sector

Redistribution is a primary, but not the sole, function of the departments, statutory authorities and courts operating within the public sector. There is a range of rationales for particular agencies, from economic management to social development. Writing about the similar institutions of Canada, Jackson et al. (1986) suggest a typology of domestic policy areas. This produces a map of the public sector, for each policy areas requires agencies for implementation, and often government departments for monitoring.

The Jackson map indicates a series of arenas for policy formulation. Around each agency are the pressure groups, clients and opponents forming a 'policy community'. Agencies are co-ordinated through the annual budget process in accord with government macroeconomic policy. In practice, however, this map indicates the terrain of bureaucratic disputes. Each agency seeks to preserve its budget allocation through lobbying, competing with other agencies or mobilising the policy community if continued support looks threatened. These myriad state agencies may only rarely work in concert.

The division of state functions into particular agencies can be quite arbitrary, reflecting the immediacy of the problem addressed, the strength of lobby groups demanding intervention or the prevailing understanding of an issue at the time of agency formation. Thus in Canada and Australia there are a number of state departments and agencies dealing with women's issues; these are located in different parts of the map depending on the time and reason for their creation. Pensions and supporting benefits for women, support programs in child care and maternity leave are the concern of social policy agencies. Prohibiting sexist bias in advertising or the media is the province of more recently established departments in accord with quality of life policies, while responsibility for equal opportunity laws and programs rests with central economic bureaus (see Sawer and Simms 1984; Goodnow and Pateman 1985).

Such multiplication of agencies indicates the diverse pressure for government action, and the numerous—perhaps contradictory—

44 *Public Policy in Australia*

Figure 3.1 A typology of domestic public policy areas

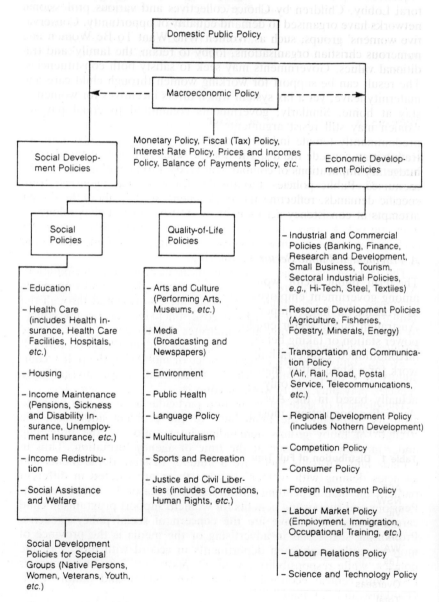

Source: Jackson et al. 1986 p.569

objectives of policy. Feminist organisations such as the Women's Electoral Lobby, Children by Choice collectives and various professional networks have organised to demand equality of opportunity. Conservative womens' groups, such as Women Who Want To Be Women and numerous christian organisations, lobby to retain 'the family' and traditional values. Governments may seek to satisfy both constituencies. The result can be support for working women through child care and maternity leave, yet a tax system which offers incentives for women to stay at home. Similarly, governments committed to equal pay for women may still resist arguments about making equal the wages of predominantly female industries and other professions. The administration may concede the disparity in incomes but fear the public sector budgetary implications of comparative worth increases for groups such as nurses. Public policies and their agencies are often reactions to specific demands, reflecting the push and pull of politics, rather than attempts at consistency across all state organisations and programs.

A Fragmented Public Sector

The term 'public sector' would be misleading if it implied unity of task among government employees. Public servants tend to be caricatured as working in huge, impersonal, Orwellian offices. Yet the typical Australian public sector employee is more likely to be stationed in a power station or taking bets in the Bundaberg TAB than working in an airconditioned Canberra building. Over 60 per cent of public servants work for a State rather than Commonwealth government. Even at the Commonwealth level, only 27 per cent of federal public servants are actually based in the Australian Capital Territory (ACT); like the Australian population, most public sector employees work and live in State capitals.

Table 1   Distribution of Full Time Commonwealth Public Servants

		%
ACT	48 035	27
NSW	40 255	23
Vic	36 866	21
Qld	17 791	10
SA	13 318	7.5
WA	10 552	6
Tas	3 657	2
NT	2 499	1.5
Overseas	4 151	2
Total	177 124	100

Source: Public Service Board *Annual Report* 1985/6:168

The public sector is a disjointed grouping of public servants, institutions and functions, divided between three levels of government, and distributed across a bewildering array of departments, statutory authorities, public companies, utilities and municipal services. At various levels of government it embraces colonels, ambassadors and road sweepers, institutions from Qantas to shire councils, and buildings from parliament house to the local bus shelter. The Australian public sector is complex and dispersed. Generalisations from the 'big government' debate about 'efficiency' or 'effectiveness' must therefore be treated with caution, for what is true of Telecom may not be valid for the Egg Marketing Board or for the Department of Veterans' Affairs.

This complexity reflects both the extent of state functions and institutional arrangements which create multiple centres of power. Fragmentation begins with the division of the public sector between levels of government. Commonwealth, State and local administrations all operate services which require permanent, specialist bureaucracies. Table 2 shows the 1980 composition of public employment.

Table 2   Public Sector Employees As A Percentage of the Workforce

Level	Number	% of Workforce
Commonwealth		
Australian Public Service	148 600	2.9
statutory authorities	248 700	4.9
defence forces	71 200	1.4
Subtotal	468 500	9.2
State	988 700	19.4
Northern Territory	13 900	0.3
Local government	130 200	2.6
Public service total	1 601 300	31.4

Source: McCallum 1984: 87

This division of the public workforce between levels of government is a consequence of the federal arrangements laid down in the Australian Constitution Act of 1900. Alfred Deakin proudly noted the intention of the founding fathers to erect a 'constitutional edifice which shall be a guarantee of liberty and union for all time to come, to the whole people of this continent and the adjacent islands to which they shall learn to look up with reverence and regard, which shall stand strong as a fortress and be held sacred as a shrine' (Jackson 1985: 244). Unfortunately the edifice was constructed before the advent of mass communications, national transport systems or a universal social security network. This constitution is a snapshot of the late nineteenth century, reflecting the interests of the colonies in restricting the powers of any federal government.

Because the constitution is nearly a century old, it mirrors the power structure and concerns of a very different era. The result is a document which can now seem to insist on a somewhat arbitrary division of powers between a Commonwealth government and State capitals (which in turn devolve responsibility to local councils). Section 51 of the constitution details the functions which States were prepared to cede to the Commonwealth. Some seem appropriate in establishing a national approach to defence, foreign affairs, uniform weights, currency, customs and migration, interstate business and legal matters. Others, however, are the outcomes of deals between colonial politicians keen to preserve State power bases. The federal government is made responsible for communications, but the States keep railways and road systems. The central administration is given power over taxation, but the States retain education. These are not rational divisions of responsibility. The constitution creates ambiguous federal and State jurisdictions, all enshrined in a document which can only be altered with extreme difficulty.

As Gough Whitlam observed, the cost of federalism can be company and union laws which change from State to State, overlapping advisory committees and professional accreditations, multiplication of ministers, duplication of services, unco-ordinated facilities, dispersal of skills, replication of State bureaucracies, delays in signing international treaties and dissipation of resources. 'The ability of the Australian people to use the political process to guarantee for themselves a secure economic future', argues Whitlam, 'is jeopardized by a political structure that is outdated, reactionary and resistant to change' (Whitlam 1983: 48).

The Divisions of Powers

In a unitary nation such as New Zealand, a single government controls the budget process. Centralised allocation of money enables some coherence in dividing responsibilities, and so reduces the possibility of redundant overlaps. The power of the purse becomes the instrument of co-ordination.

In a federation it is more difficult to reach agreement on a division of powers, particularly if the ambiguities of responsibility are further complicated by tax arrangements. Originally the Australian States levied most charges. If a State government introduced a new program, then it had to raise taxes itself, and face the electoral consequences. This is no longer the case. State governments can now spend other people's money. Wartime measures adopted in 1942 introduced uniform national income and company tax administered by Canberra. Though States retain a range of taxes, levies and charges, they must now rely on an annual handout from the federal government to support expensive social services.

As a result, the tax system has become a continuous process of cross subsidies and transfers, often cutting across the responsibilities outlined in the constitution. Though education belongs to the States, much of the money for schools, colleges and universities is provided by Canberra. This gives the federal government a reason to be involved in education policy. It creates potential for intergovernmental fighting and can prevent effective accountability. For if each politician can blame another at a different level of government, then who is to be held responsible for any service inadequacies?

To resolve inevitable conflicts over powers and tax receipts, the constitution established a High Court. The justices of this bench can examine laws passed by Canberra and decide whether the legislation falls within federal jurisdiction. Important federal policy has been struck down by the High Court—from bank nationalisation legislation in the 1940s, to taxation law in the 1980s. The High Court thus provides another forum for politics. Unlike Britain, where the Houses of Parliament are the final arbiter of all disputes, Australian jurisdictional arguments are handed to lawyers for resolution. In a nation where a constitution rather than parliament is sovereign, politics and policy often proceed through litigation (Galligan 1987).

So the constitution is a basic cause of public sector fragmentation. Decisions made in the nineteenth century are still accepted as binding on the Australian policy process. While ostensibly clarifying the division of power, the constitution in fact invites occasional reproduction of functions at national and State levels, provokes disputes over jurisdiction, is the cause of ambiguity in accountability and responsibility, and allows lawyers to pronounce judgement on the acceptable scope of government activity.

There is a mechanism designed to allow adaptation, the referendum provision. Yet only eight times since Federation have a majority of Australians in a majority of States agreed to change sections of the constitution. Australians must be happy with federal arrangements, ignorant of its implications, or too conservative to alter the familiar.

The complex division of powers ordained by federalism make it difficult for any administration to implement coherent policy. Essential functions may be controlled by another level of government dominated by a rival party. How can a federal government formulate plausible macroeconomic policy, for example, when the constitution has been interpreted to deny Canberra power to set prices and wages, or the right to nationalise industries? Similarly, how can Australians expect cogent fiscal measures when the power to levy some taxes, such as personal income tax, rests with the federal government, but important State and payroll taxes belong to seven different States? When a government's power is fragmented then so, in consequence, will be its policies. (For a discussion of Commonwealth—State financial arrangements see Mathews 1983.)

Further, electors can play off one administration against another. If the Commonwealth government refuses to fund a childcare centre, then pressure groups move to the State level or even to their local council if need be. In a nation where elections are frequent and hotly contested, one level of government can be lobbied to provide a service refused by another. Those who hope to 'roll back the state' may be thwarted by federalism, for reductions at one level of the public sector may only encourage demands for expansion elsewhere.

Government Control of the Public Sector

The pattern of government is the same at the federal, State and local level. Elected officials preside over a professional public service. This bureaucracy is organised into divisions, each with responsibility for a specialised function, often working from buildings some distance from the sites of formal power. At State and Commonwealth levels there is an important further division of public sector institutions into government departments and statutory authorities. While departments operate under the direct control of a minister and can be altered or abolished at any time, statutory authorities are established by law and designed to be independent of government though accountable to parliament. Much administration and policy formulation is under the direct control of a minister, while the control of public companies and utilities is less direct. These departments and statutory authorities are the institutions most frequently studied in public administration, and most frequently identified as influencing policy outcomes (see Spann 1979, Weller and Jaensch 1980, Weller and Grattan 1981).

In examining such institutions, a central concern is the issue of power. Who is servant and who master can be difficult to distinguish, for the growth of the public sector introduces a curious paradox: though government has expanded, this has not produced a corresponding rise in the power and influence of politicians. Rather, the increased complexity of the public sector, and the transfer of many functions from direct ministerial supervision in departments to statutory authorities under less stringent scrutiny, may have reduced government influence in some policy areas. In principle parliament controls Telecom (and the other approximately 240 federal statutory authorities). In practice, 94 000 staff make Telecom the nation's single largest employer and a major investor in local industry. Telecom's industrial relations and capital expenditure decisions thus have a major impact on the labour market and the economy, as will its programs of overseas borrowing and technology transfer.

The policy process, then, works both ways. Government needs some control over Telecom in the interests not just of telecommunications policy, but because of the wider social and economic implications of Telecom decisions. On the other hand, technical and operational expertise reside within Telecom, and government necessarily relies on advice from this statutory authority in policy formulation. Further, Telecom's legislation allows it some discretion in implementing broad government objectives; Telecom management is sensitive to government policy but keen to pursue its own agenda. Finally, other agencies and interests are involved in Telecom decisions. The unions and the federal Arbitration Commission, for example, are significant influences and potential constraints on Telecom actions.

The result is not so much parliamentary control as *negotiated policy*. Major public enterprises, utilities, the ABC and universities, all seek to maintain their distance from direct government supervision. Each will balance organisational goals against outside demands for particular policies. The logic of organisational self-interest may work against attempts at central co-ordination. Because much of the Commonwealth and State public sectors comprise semi-autonomous institutions which can negotiate policy or even resist government directive, many of the day to day managerial decisions of the extended state have moved beyond the immediate control of politicians. A fragmented public sector, offering significant independence to key organisations, can be neither easily controlled nor marshalled in pursuit of a single set of macro policies.

Though government departments may have less opportunity than statutory authorities for independent action, they too are accused frequently of eluding control. Theorists have warned that, though intended as an impersonal apparatus, a public bureaucracy can become a special and privileged group within the state. Bureaucrats are perceived as pursuing their interests by maintaining and extending their administrative domain, of coming to believe in their own superior objectivity in interpreting the national interest free from party bias, and of exercising their power, based on knowledge and experience, under a cloak of secrecy (Beetham 1974: 72).

In a world dominated by public servants, elected masters may become irrelevant. As Whitlam observed, 'politicians exercise power if they are in the majority party, but public servants do so the whole time. A person who has been head of a government department for twelve years has achieved more than most ministers ever do'. Unable to impose their will or to master the technical complexities of portfolios, ministers could be reduced to making speeches, opening fetes and placing their departmental line before cabinet when required.

Australian public administration and political science literature suggests, however, that not all ministers are mediocre, nor can all public servants agree on what would be best for their department (Hawker et al. 1979; Weller and Grattan 1981). More importantly, the interests of different State and federal departments do not co-incide, but frequently clash; compliant ministers necessarily reflect these divisions when speaking to cabinet. The bureaucracy's ability to dominate policy outcomes can be constrained by the competing interests of politicians, by the alternative advice of ministerial staff or by the outside scrutiny of parliament, pressure groups and the media. Politicians may ignore the advice of their bureaucrats. When Malcolm Fraser resigned from the Gorton government, he accused the prime minister of ridiculing 'the advice of a great public service unless it supports his view'. As prime minister himself, Fraser used the public service astutely, asking for more details when he was unsure about possible outcomes, finding alternative sources of information, and restructuring divisions and departments to suit better his aims and wishes.

There is, in short, continuing tension between governments and their agencies. The bureaucracy may be too internally divided to effectively dominate a government, even if still too powerful to be totally dominated by all ministers. Outcomes are not a foregone conclusion. They reflect issues, organisations, personalities and skill.

Underlying attempts by elected officials to impose control over policies and institutions are problems of fragmentation as the state develops within the arbitrary divisions imposed by federalism. There has been

proliferation of government agencies, and growth of many different centres of power and initiative. It is misleading to suppose that government (any more than business, or education, or religion) marches steadily toward unification and centralisation. In many respects countries are becoming more pluralistic and harder to govern from the centre, not easier (Spann 1979: 13–14).

Bureaucratic Politics

With limited control over the public sector, politicians have difficulty co-ordinating policies and programs. Cabinet and Parliament—the central institutions designed to ensure coherence—will be discussed in the next chapter. The Westminster system, however, is faced with a 'policy vacuum' when departments and ministers can find no way of resolving policy conflicts or collectively dealing with important areas of overlap (Painter and Carey 1979: 116). Some cooperation between levels of government is common, particularly in non-controversial areas. There are mechanisms such as interdepartmental committees to enable cross-agency discussions. Yet there remain significant problems for politicians who seek to impose unity of purpose and agreement over objectives. Bureaucrats can frustrate the design of politicians.

Unlike statutory authorities, which can appeal to legislation as legitimation for their actions, government departments have no enabling Act, and no specific goals articulated by parliament. Some overlapping of concerns, if not functions, is hard to avoid. Duplication of advice and programs is not necessarily wasteful; it can produce useful alternative sources of advice and more avenues for clients, though an agency which offers options only to have them rejected by a minister is likely to suspect the 'interference' of other bureaucrats.

Arguments between departments over functions, resources and authority are frequent—demarcation disputes which pit agency against agency, and so leave bureaucrats less able to dominate the policy process. Size is an unreliable guide to influence. At the Commonwealth level, the important policy departments are small and based in Canberra, while the large line departments are spread through the States, implementing the programs of government. For example:

Table 3   Full Time Staff of Some Commonwealth Departments

Department	Canberra based staff	Total staff
Aboriginal Affairs	312	792
Attorney General	1 246	3 311
Defence	5 236	30 615
Education	922	1 877
Employment and Industrial Relations	1 071	9 632
Finance	880	1 167
Health	1 443	4 397
Primary Industry	820	3 325
Prime Minister and Cabinet	489	505
Public Service Board	575	804
Social Security	1 588	16 336
Trade	400	432
Treasury	594	614
Veterans' Affairs	798	12 748

Source: Public Service Board *Annual Report* 1985/86: 171–172

Crisp classified bureaucratic politics within the Commonwealth public service. His complex schema distinguished between externally imposed divisions and disputes arising from interaction with departments. From outside the bureaucracy, Crisp noted that departments may disagree over orders coming down from the minister or party officials, may take sides in factional disputes, be influenced by sectarian, trade union or client priorities, or be caught in demarcation disputes arising from federalism. From within the bureaucracy, he observed politics arising from departmental empire building, over qualifications and the claim to expertise, between general administrators and professionals, from the gender based division of labour and over industrial issues arising from employment within the public service. Despite the multiple divisions, however, he concluded that the Commonwealth public service coheres and operates in a manner which does not put internal disputes before all other concerns (Crisp 1972: 309).

Nonetheless, one of the key internal divisions arises because public servants adopt the perspectives of their departments. On any major issue a large number of departments and agencies prepare position papers reflecting their particular concerns. Ministers are briefed accordingly, and the eventual cabinet debate reflects these diverse viewpoints.

So where public servants stand on an issue depends on where they sit (Allison 1971). Departments tend to be insular, to develop their own world view and a corporate loyalty which can make each agency suspicious of all others. Government departments may also identify with, and become protective of, their clients. The Department of Primary Industry, for example, is sometimes accused of speaking for the farmers, and the Department of Social Security of becoming an advocate for welfare beneficiaries.

Overlaid on these divisions of interest are inevitable arguments about resources, particularly between departments which control money (such as Finance and Treasury) and departments which spend it (such as Education, Housing and Social Security). All bureaucracies within the public sector look after their own interests and seek to defend their influence. Bureaucratic divisions are thus inevitable, and often important in policy formulation; 'to disregard the crucial roles that institutions play in transforming ideas into policy or in manipulating the environment to their own advantage would be as foolish as to disregard the importance of individuals as they jostle for advantage' (Hawker et al. 1979: 284).

Co-ordination

The public service is a set of institutions created to serve the needs of governments. Institutions, nevertheless, can sometimes develop a life of their own. In Britain the original state departments—the Foreign Office, the Colonial office and the Treasury in particular—have long histories, recognised traditions and a reputation for pursuing their own policies whatever the government in power. Politicians must mediate between these great 'ships of state' (Juddery 1974).

Australian public service structures are more fluid than those of Britain. Departments can be dissolved and reconstituted to suit a ministry's need. In 1982, for example, the Fraser government required an additional portfolio for a demoted cabinet minister. Cabinet hived off sections of the the Departments of Defence and Industry and Commerce, and combined them to form a new Department of Defence Support. These expedient institutional arrangements built in structural rivalries between two agencies of the state. Defence Support complained that it was not getting adequate financial information from Defence, while Defence argued that its Support did not fully understand military priorities. If these departments had been forced to work together over a long period, they may have defined their spheres of responsibility and resolved the constant bureaucratic disputes which plagued their relationship. The bureaucracy, however, is structured by ministerial imperative. When the subsequent Hawke government no longer required an additional portfolio, the junior ministry was reabsorbed within the Defence Department.

Splitting and remaking departments reduces their capacity to build long-term interests and alliances. It provides advantages for those older institutions which have managed to remain relatively stable, though few departments are able to avoid entirely shifts in function and location.

Concerned about the arbitrary division of functions, a series of government reports have argued for measures designed to improve 'co-ordination' by reducing the tensions within the public sector (see RCAGA 1976, Reid 1983, Dawkins 1984). Indeed, the last ten years have seen a Commonwealth Royal Commission into government administration and an investigation of the public service in every State. As the chairman of the Commonwealth Public Service Board, Peter Wilenski, noted wryly, however, 'at the end of the 1970s it seemed fair to characterise the preceding decade in Australia as one of administrative reform commissions and inquiries rather than as a decade of actual reform' (Wilenski 1986: 166).

Most of these reports recommended the use of central agencies and increased planning to co-ordinate the public sector. Intended to ensure uniformity of bureaucratic practice and coherence in the policy process, departments of the prime minister or premier have been expanded, departments of finance or budget management have been established, and the traditional influence of public service boards has been eroded.

The Department of Prime Minister and Cabinet in Canberra, and its equivalent Premiers' departments in the States, service the cabinet, prepare agendas, distribute policy proposals, and review all cabinet submissions before they go to a meeting of the ministry. Deftly used, this department can allow the prime minister to exert considerable influence on policy proposals from other departments, though often at the cost of resentment and accusations of interference from other ministers.

Traditionally, governments relied on the Treasury to monitor public expenditure and to provide policy options on economic matters. As the key advisor on budgetary measures, Treasury was able to influence government priorities and to assess the claims of other departments. A small unit, with an ideological commitment to economic modelling and neo-classical prescriptions, the Treasury was frequently accused of offering only narrow and 'orthodox' advice. Indeed Treasurers such as Jim Cairns complained bitterly that their department would not provide a range of options, nor take seriously policy alternatives outside its own 'line'. Since 1976, the specific scrutiny of budgetary proposals has been taken from the federal Treasury and given to a new Department of Finance. The Treasury is now one of several economic policy advisors (see Hawker et al. 1979: ch 9; Whitwell 1986). The routine budgetary assessment of program proposals is now performed by the Department of Finance, which advises the government on the merits of each department's claim for resources. Finance enables government to consider alternatives and to impose reductions across the public sector, though at the cost of lengthy disputes between Finance and almost every other agency.

The emphasis on budgetary agencies has reduced the influence of Commonwealth and State public service boards. These co-ordinate the functions, terms, conditions and structures of the public service. They attempt to ensure the minimum of waste or duplication between departments and to implement government policy about administration procedures. With a new emphasis on reduced government spending, however, and the application of more flexible public sector management principles, the work of public service boards has been significantly reduced. While the federal board has been used to institute reforms to the structure of the Commonwealth public service, particularly the introduction of a senior executive service, governments in Australia are moving toward abolishing their boards. They have been replaced by separate agencies concerned with public service appointments, appeal procedures and controls over public sector spending.

Such changes reflect new trends toward smaller government. They also acknowledge that the introduction of co-ordinating agencies did not eliminate bureaucratic disputes. Central agencies disagree. They have different, incompatible aims, overlapping jurisdictions and may battle for influence over policy. During the 1970s, for example, the Commonwealth Treasury argued with the Department of Prime Minister and Cabinet. Treasury asserted a right to maintain its monopoly on economic advice to cabinet, while Prime Minister and Cabinet sought to offer alternative options. When Malcolm Fraser, annoyed with Treasury's refusal to co-operate by providing alternative policy suggestions, split its functions by creating a separate Department of Finance, he presented the move as a means to greater co-ordination, telling the House that 'the changes are essentially designed to provide for more effective management of the business of government, and to strengthen the government's decision making processes'. As Crisp noted, however, 'a more common, if less official, explanation was that the Treasury was divided to reduce its power and influence' (Crisp 1978: 452).

Given struggles for power, institutional jealousies, and a policy formulation process involving so many competing interests and people, 'cabinet and the central co-ordinating agencies have great difficulty in drawing together the threads of policy and in doing much about the muddle and confusion of policy making' (Hawker et al. 1979: 282).

A Talent for Bureaucracy?

Fragmentation, limited co-ordination and departmental rivalry influence how the public sector translates the ideas of politicians into bureaucratic action. Yet much of the work of government agencies is directed toward policy maintenance—the routine redistribution and application of resources, carried out by departments and statutory authorities with reasonably clear and uncontested objectives. For the public sector is more than an arena for current projects—it is embodied policy itself, the repository of past decisions, a set of people and structures organised according to earlier policy choices. This is history given form, able to shape—and to circumscribe—the possibilities for new policies.

The Australian state has long been involved in economic and social life. It has built dams and highways, subsidised industries and farmers, educated generations and later paid them pensions. From birth in a public hospital to burial in a council cemetery, public sector institutions have been pervasive. To maintain these organisations and their varied functions, the state has required a large workforce.

Australia inherited many traditional notions about state administration from Britain. The public service should be neutral, it should carry out the wishes of the government, and remain accountable through a minister to parliament. With hierarchy, specialisation, impersonal rules, entrance and promotion by examination, specified duties and a collective memory through files, the various colonial and federal bureaucracies have resembled Weber's 'legal—rational' ideal type, an effective organisation operating within legally prescribed limits (Weber 1978). They have been characterised by independent, non-ministerial control of recruitment and employment conditions, recruitment by merit, incremental advancement, permanent structures, advancement on the grounds of efficiency and seniority, protection against indiscriminate dismissal, a promotions system ensuring justice, a guaranteed system of retirement and pensions, and opportunity for movement within and between departments (Wiltshire 1975: 105).

While European theorists argued about the inevitability of rule by officials, Australian writers questioned whether government bureaucracies were capable of implementing the ambitious schemes of local politicians. Not all observers were convinced that a legal—rational structure and practices necessarily ensured competence.

Arguments that Australian government bureaucracies might be ineffectual or prone to bad judgement were particularly unsettling for a society relying so heavily on its public sector for social and economic development. Writing in 1930, W.K. Hancock was particularly sceptical about the ability of the public service to promote talent or use technical expertise. He argued that the best available talent (which Hancock's generation assumed would be male) was not recruited to help economic planning, but drawn into the school and university systems as teachers. This left as administrators people perhaps not capable of unravelling cause and effect or imagining economic effects. Australians, said Hancock, have always assumed that economic problems are simple. Accordingly, they have resented 'those classifications and rewards which suggest that some men have a higher class of intelligence than that of the majority. Democratic sentiment applauds the sound argument that every office boy should have a chance to become a manager, and perverts it into a practical rule that no one shall become a manager who has not been an office boy'. By luring away technical experts into teaching, 'the State has most ingeniously contrived that its system of democratic education shall not embarrass the public services by introducing into them resplendent talents' (Hancock 1930: 141–142).

Hancock wrote when the balance of power remained with State governments. The Parliament House in Canberra had been open only three years, and his examples of 'state socialism' and unimaginative administration were drawn primarily from Victoria and New South Wales. During the next generation the focus of government shifted, and a Commonwealth public service developed to implement decisions reached in the national capital. The number of full time federal public servants grew from 28 916 in 1930 to 173 014 in 1986. By 1958 A.F. Davies was prepared to argue that an impressive and broadly engaged Australian bureaucracy had emerged:

The characteristic talent of Australians . . . is for bureaucracy. We take a somewhat hesitant pride in this, since it runs counter not only to the archaic and cherished image of ourselves as an ungovernable, if not actually lawless, people; but, more importantly, because we have been trained in the modern period to see our politics in terms of a liberalism which accords to bureaucracy only a small and rather shady place. Being a good bureaucrat is, we feel, a bit like being a good forger. But in practice our gift is exercised on a massive scale . . . Of course, the pervasiveness of bureaucracy is a feature of most industrial societies, and its spread, which has been slow and steady, has its roots not only in developing technology, but also—and especially in its political application—in the modern demand for security and equality. Australian appetites have merely been in a general way larger and coarser than the average, and much more concentratedly political. It is on the supply, rather than the demand, side that Australia has really scored: in particular by the construction this century of a national government machine, which, thoroughly professional at the core, is nevertheless neither invidiously recruited, nor authoritarian in outlook, but even able, in an odd way, to draw nourishment from its envelope of representative democracy (Davies 1958: 3).

In 1967 Caiden asserted that the Commonwealth public service had become 'Australia's most important social institution and the largest single employer and investor' (Caiden 1967: 27), even if its adminis-trative style lagged behind other western nations, and its bureaucrats occasionally appeared 'old-fashioned, conservative, narrow, provincial and uncritical' (Caiden 1967: 3). He wrote of the difficulties for a Commonwealth public service which must 'grapple with the country's problems, particularly those arising from State narrow-mindedness' (Caiden 1967: 10).

The concern expressed by Hancock that the public sector might be prone to systematic and expensive error because it lacks technical expertise was challenged by R.S. Spann. Pointing to the influence of professionals within the bureaucracy, to the complexity of public sector decisions, and to the role of ministerial decisions—rather than administrative error—in many public sector mistakes, Spann argued that it is the politicians who make dubious choices; governments have been regularly tempted into large-scale errors such as the Ord river scheme 'by considerations of political necessity or prestige' (Spann 1979: 25). Ministers want to make their mark quickly, said Spann, and can do so by announcing large, expensive public works projects—with the knowledge that they are unlikely to be around to take the blame later. This might suggest that the efficient rule of bureaucrats is being interrupted by political 'irrationality'.

The Public Sector, the State and Public Policy

The Australian public sector comprises the people, organisations and functions of government. These are divided into departments and statutory authorities, scattered across different levels of government, and often embroiled in bureaucratic disputes. Australian structures and policies have been shaped by a number of factors. The tradition of state-led development, plus shared taxation powers, produce a tense federalism with sometimes competing levels of authority. Imported British traditions of Westminster government encourage the public service to see itself as impartial, able to serve the government of the day without fear or favour. The electorate, meanwhile, has learned that it can play off local, State and federal administrations. 'Inefficient' public services become hidden means of subsidy, as the public sector responds to the demands of multiple interests.

The result is a public sector perhaps too fragmented to dominate the policy process, but with powerful institutions able to advocate projects and influence ministers. It includes departments and statutory authorities which provide many of the services which have created an Australian society (even if one with divided loyalties to States, territories and a nation). It is a public sector so involved in the economy, and so committed to providing resources and infrastructure, that it is often intertwined with the private sector to which it is so frequently, and unflatteringly, compared.

These institutions, processes and ideological disputes are the subject matter of public administration literature. Read back, they suggest that any mechanistic or structural metaphor for government is inadequate. The output of a machine can be reliably predicted. Its parts do not argue among themselves but work in a preordained sequence. The effects of intervention, however, are not always those anticipated. No theory of the state can assume that a machinery of government is available, willing and reliable, for any leadership or policy; nor are structural needs and interest demands automatically translated into state action through appropriate administrative arrangements.

Further, departments and agencies become the arena around which pressure groups compete. They are the focus for, and embodiment of, policy demands. Because such groups have specific demands, and are more interested in their own cause than in overall government coherence, they encourage a contradictory state. A health department may promote anti-smoking campaigns even while an agricultural agency is subsidising the production of tobacco. Each is responding to its own constituents and objectives. The state is not necessarily consistent in policy directions; Australian governments, and the agencies they create, can simultaneously pursue contradictory proposals.

These difficulties of co-ordination reflect the discretion given to state agencies. Policies are often vague statements of principle; effect is determined through implementation. Politicians may lack the technical expertise to question bureaucratic practices. Central agencies may not have the administrative clout to interfere, particularly if a policy is enacted through a statutory authority with independence guaranteed by law. The state can resemble a loose confederation of relatively autonomous agencies, each carefully defining and protecting its function, collectively circumscribing the capacity of any elite to impose total control over the system.

Finally, the finding that bureaucratic bargaining and disputes affect state action requires public policy analysts to indicate what they mean by 'politics'. What is this ghost in the machine, working within but able to change the structure of the state, played out in microcosm in each government office, and at large across society?

Public policy tends to work with a limited definition. Politics is disagreement about priorities, resources and principles. More particularly it is action, from persuasion to violence, designed to influence outcomes. Implicit is a rejection of social or economic determinism; to argue for the importance of politics is to believe that we make our own history, though not necessarily within structures we would choose. Politics animates the institutions and processes; perhaps more importantly, politics is also the space between these, an arena in which are played out the fights over direction, the struggles over money and control, the disputes about what to do next. It is a space which leaves room for leadership and manoeuvring, an activity which affects its constraints, so creating a complex relationship.

Figure 3.2

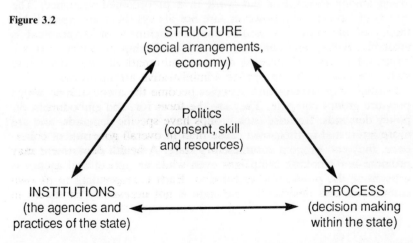

STRUCTURE
(social arrangements,
economy)

Politics
(consent, skill
and resources)

INSTITUTIONS
(the agencies and
practices of the state)

PROCESS
(decision making
within the state)

Theories of the state tend to investigate the broader rules of structure
formation, emphasising the influence of economic forces and their
respective interests. Public administration investigates the specific institutions which embody the functions and policies of the public sector.
Public policy is concerned with politics. It seeks to understand what
actually happens within that space called the state. Politics is the
process by which the structure, process and institutions are brought to
a decision or outcome. It is an endless activity; while politics operates,
all decisions are provisional.

Further Reading

Lucy, Richard (1985) *The Australian Form of Government* Melbourne:
Macmillan, ch 14.
Reinecke, Ian and Schultz, Julianne (1983) *The Phone Book: the future of
Australia's communications on the line* Melbourne: Penguin, ch 12.
Spann, R.N. (1979) *Government Administration In Australia* Sydney: Allen &
Unwin, ch 1.
Stretton, Hugh (1980) 'Social Policy: has the welfare state all been a terrible
mistake?' *Labor Essays 1980*, Melbourne: Drummond.
Weller, Patrick & Grattan, Michelle (1981) *Can Ministers Cope? Australian
federal ministers at work* Melbourne: Hutchinson, ch 4.

4
Policy at the Centre

An activist state has produced a diffuse and fragmented public sector. For the politicians occupying the formal positions of authority the problem becomes, how can the full weight of governmental authority be thrown behind a unified and coherent set of objectives when power is dispersed between multiple centres and myriad agencies? Given the internal divisions of the public sector and the competing interests of the bureaucracy, are elected decision makers of any significance? Who if anyone can provide coherence and direction to government?

In the responsible government model, power rests with the prime minister, cabinet and senior officials. These are the proximate decision makers at the centre. In combination their control should range across all government activities. Certainly the media pay close attention, attributing to the ministry a capacity to direct the fortunes of the country. Governments are as often given the name of the leader as of the party, to emphasise the importance of individuals. This assumes that ministers and senior officials have the capacity to make and direct public policy. The impact of leaders on policy, however, should not be taken for granted. Governments cannot always make the decisions they would like, or be certain their choices will be implemented. Proximity to the institutions of government is not necessarily access to power.

The Westminister Model?

Australian government is based on the Westminster system. This indeterminate set of principles, implied but not specified in the constitution, sets up lines of responsibility for decision making and implementation. Ideally, public servants are responsible to ministers. Ministers are responsible to parliament, and parliament answers to the electorate. There are also clear delineations of function. Ministers are responsible

62

for determining policy, for deciding what the executive will do. Non-partisan public servants implement policy and serve all elected governments with equal loyalty and dedication. An informed parliament authorises expenditure and legislates in response to executive proposals. Parliament may scrutinise government behaviour, but it does not directly govern.

The notion of parliamentary sovereignty views the legislative body as the supreme authority in the land. Ministers can be held accountable, parliament can control the actions of the executive, and it can use control over granting funds to require the redress of grievances. The temporary and responsible ministers appointed by parliament provide direction because they have specific policies they wish to pursue and can direct the permanent and non-partisan public servants.

These notions about the process of government must be unpacked to understand how practice differs from the model. The assumptions of Westminster responsible government oversimplify Australian parliamentary life. Parliament may be seen to be sovereign, yet many other levels of power qualify or bypass parliamentary government. Some writers have suggested that parliamentary politics may have survived only because they are conducive to the development of a particular capitalist economic system that requires legitimacy within a private economy (Jessop 1978; Theophanous 1980).

These views posit a limited scope for parliament, but do not suggest that parliament has become irrelevant. On the contrary, parliament remains one of the most important institutions within Australian society. It enjoys specific powers and responsibilities not shared by other centres of power.

Recording criticisms emphasised by conventional political science literature, Parker has suggested that the Australian system of responsible government can be better understood as the 'Westminster syndrome'. Ministers must be responsible for what is done or proposed by themselves or those under their authority. Officialdom must have expertise to implement policy without fear or favour. There is, however, no clear-cut division of labour between minister and public servant; the dichotomy between 'politics' and 'administration' is false, for both politicians and bureaucrats are involved in each. The only requirement is that in all decisions the elected minister should have the last word. Finally, the lines of accountability run from the public servant through the minister to cabinet, parliament and ultimately—and only by that route—to the people (Parker 1978: 349–53).

This Westminster syndrome emphasises the leadership role of ministers, their relationships with public servants, and the links of the executive to parliament. This study of the proximate decision makers therefore considers the role and sovereignty of parliament and the capacity for government direction. To do so it must examine the role of ministers, their relations with the public service, the capacity of cabinet and the influence of the prime minister. The central focus is on who, within these inner circles, has the capacity to shape crucial decisions.

This model of parliamentary responsible government is duplicated at the State and Commonwealth levels, though ministers in State capitals have very limited scope for manoeuvre; their choices are bounded by a limited jurisdiction and the pre-eminence of federal government in many policy arenas.

Parliamentary Government

Functions of Parliament

The Australian form of parliamentary government is explicitly based on British practices; indeed the Australian constitution is not a declaration of independence but an Act of the British parliament. The basis of parliamentary control is power over the purse. A government stays in office for as long as it has money. Funds are voted by parliament, so leaders can govern only if they gain and retain the support of a majority of members in the House of Commons in Britain, or the confidence of the lower houses in the State and Commonwealth parliaments in Australia. Should the supply needed to carry on the business of government no longer be assured, the leader must resign.

An Australian federal government and its State counterparts are put to the test twice each year with votes on supply bills. In Canberra appropriation bills are put before the House in May, and the budget in November. Control of the parliament, however, is more than maintaining supply. A government could not govern unless it won most parliamentary divisions.

The advent of disciplined parties competing for state office ensures greater continuity of government. The majority party forms a government with the 'confidence' of the House. Only in 1929, 1931 and 1941 have federal governments been defeated by desertions within their own ranks. Similarly, State governments are rarely brought down by internal divisions, though the Labor split of 1955–1958 forced State ALP governments to surrender the treasury benches mid-term. Normally governments can be assured of a solid vote in the lower house. This has significant implications for any traditional model of ministerial responsibility based on parliamentary sovereignty. When particular cabinet ministers are under challenge in the parliament, however much at fault they may be, the party closes ranks behind them. Disciplined voting has reduced the danger of defeat for governments in the lower house. Ministers are now responsible to the party leader. Parties and not parliament are the contemporary forum for accountability (Thompson 1984; see also Reid 1984; Lucy 1985).

'Party' has therefore reduced the most obvious capacity of parliaments to determine who should govern on a day-to-day basis. The parliament, however, still performs important functions in providing legitimacy and a forum for debate (Therborn 1978). The election of the lower house is the mechanism for determining who will form a government. A majority of seats—and not the total vote—determines which party will control the parliament and so form the executive.

Further, parliament trains leaders. At both federal and State level ministers must be a member of a house of parliament, though section 64 of the constitution allows for temporary appointment to Commonwealth portfolios. A minister must usually develop a reputation as a competent parliamentarian to ensure promotion. Question time—in those chambers where it is not gagged by government numbers — provides some test of how well ministers have mastered their briefs. Parliament thus acts as a leadership proving ground.

Parliaments also retain their authority over expenditure. Where this procedure is routine, it still provides legitimacy for government actions. Where it is not, such as when an opposition controls the State upper house or the federal Senate, passing the budget bills becomes a major political exercise. Rejection may trigger an election.

Similarly, parliament's function of legislating can be more than symbolic. Legislation has become more extensive and more involved in the details of the social and economic life of the community. Parliamentary debates on bills may be ritualistic, but they can on occasion show up the motives or incompetence of a minister. Amendments are common and often significant, particularly if a hostile upper chamber seeks to frustrate a government's legislative program.

At the federal level, a new emphasis on scrutiny through parliamentary committee has led to greater ministerial and bureaucratic accountability. Some committee inquiries, such as those into securities and exchange in the mid–1970s, and into the activities of the Asia Dairy Corporation under Ian Sinclair's ministry, have been embarrassing and detailed. Parliamentary committee reports, however, reflect limited time, expertise and range; they cover only a few areas of the extensive government administration.

Victoria and New South Wales have followed, or even anticipated, federal use of parliamentary committees. State governments in Queensland, however, strenuously avoid the scrutiny of a public accounts committee; they recognise that an effective committee system may prove a significant constraint on executive action (Coaldrake 1985; Uhr 1982).

The most significant departures of Australian parliaments from the British model have been the retention of powerful State upper chambers and the creation of a Commonwealth Senate as a veto point. This Senate has the power to delay or amend legislation; it can even, as the events of 1975 illustrate, force an election for the lower house. Each State has equal numbers in the Senate, so providing disproportionate representation for less populated States. This loaded franchise, and a voting system which enables independents or small parties to gain representation, makes it unlikely that any major party will have the numbers to control the Senate. A Senate without a consistent majority should be able to act as a States' house and a watchdog on government activity. The Senate, however, operates not as a weapon of parliamentary scrutiny but as a party house. Oppositions and independents use their numbers to extract concessions from governments or to grandstand by denouncing unpopular bills.

The continuing need for money and legislative authority ensures a significant role for parliament in the formal process of politics. Ministers prepare extensively for question-time because they can be asked about anything within their portfolio and because their credibility depends on good performance. Parliamentary motions of no confidence can provide occasions of great tension. Morale within government may depend on its dominance over the opposition. Prime ministers with Whitlam's skilful repartee or Fraser's dogged persistence can ensure confidence within government ranks. Premiers may fail to persuade and so be overthrown from within their own ranks.

Parliament, however, does not rule or even decide what will be done. Many important decisions, such as the investment and employment decisions of business, are made outside the formal political arena entirely. Within the institutions of government, parliament can influence policy, but its agenda and legislation are the prerogative of the executive, decided by cabinet or by the governing party. Debate now centres around whether parliament can still hold the individual minister, or the cabinet as a whole, to account (for broader treatment see Solomon 1986; Jaensch 1986).

Ministerial Responsibility

Ministers are responsible to parliament for the actions of their departments. They are required to explain their policy to parliament, to account for the activities of their officials and, if mistakes have been made, to take remedial action and avoid further errors.

Various writers have sought to define ministerial responsibility. Spann (1979) draws a distinction between role responsibility for a particular task, and answering for all functions of the department. Parker (1976) argues that ministerial responsibility is concerned with ensuring that ministers and public servants are answerable to parliament for their actions. Thynne and Goldring (1981) identify five different meanings of the term 'responsibility': task responsibility for doing a job, appropriate responsibility in acting sensibly, accountability responsibility to someone, cause responsibility in not doing harm, and blame responsibility in taking the credit or the opprobrium. For each of these distinctions there are case studies which suggest a difference between ideal and practice. Clearly, conventions about ministerial responsibility are open to interpretation by politicians. The operation of ministerial responsibility varies depending on circumstances and expediency. There is not, and cannot be, a set of clear principles to be objectively applied.

In almost all cases, Australian politicians have not resigned their portfolios whenever a mistake is made, though such demands are invariably heard from the opposition. As a former minister noted, ministerial responsibility in practice means that 'the Minister is responsible to Parliament for his Department to explain, and where error is shown, he takes the corrective action. He will only resign if the Prime Minister believes it is for the good of the Government but in most cases that simply admits error and, party conflict being what it is, admission of error is more serious than the error itself' (Garland 1976: 24). The final judgement is therefore an electoral calculation. Does the government have more to lose from toughing it out, or from cutting the minister loose? Thus whether an individual resigns may reflect no more than the importance of the minister, the strength of their factional alignment or their public profile.

The 'principle' of ministerial responsibility for the action of officials must be separated, however, from more frequent crises of ministerial propriety. Ministers are held responsible for their personal actions, and may be asked to resign or to stand down until their behaviour has been examined. The sacking of Senator Withers by Fraser for involvement in an electoral redistribution, the removal of Mackellar in 1982 and Young in 1984 for breaches of custom regulations, and the sacking of Cairns and Connor for misleading parliament in 1975—these were all resignations resulting from personal, not official, behaviour.

Resignations for ministerial impropriety, however, follow the same pattern as punishment for ministerial lapses; they are based on an electoral judgement. What are the costs and benefits of holding a minister responsible? Will forcing a resignation create a long-running problem or, as with the Lynch decision to stand down in 1977, end a dispute immediately? Is a royal commission report too dangerous to ignore? Will the failure to pay duty on a television set or a paddington bear cause electoral damage if ignored? Pragmatic rather than constitutional issues decide.

Leaders are reluctant to conclude that a minister should go; all ministers have supporters and so any removal has electoral costs.

Ministerial responsibility is a convention which operates only when it accords with political judgement. Typically, ministers go when others decide for them. Parliament in these instances is less important than the leader and the cabinet. For in parliament, party discipline will ensure the ministers survive, whatever the indignant arguments of the opposition.

Collective Responsibility

Collective responsibility is less a constitutional principle than a tactical necessity. It requires that cabinet presents a united front, for public support evaporates when a government appears divided and unsure of its policies. Collective responsibility is premised on the belief that ministers who fail to hang together will hang separately.

The practice of collective responsibility is a matter of convenience. At the federal level, National (Country) Party ministers have openly disagreed with the policy of coalition governments; McEwen disputed the 1967 decision not to devalue the currency at the same time as Britain, while Doug Anthony led a revolt against another devaluation decision in 1971. In both cases Liberal prime ministers accepted the disagreement without public reprimand. Labor ministers are always permitted to debate openly during national party conferences, and can exercise their right within this forum to challenge government decisions.

During the Whitlam government, ministers were permitted to appeal to caucus. Should they be overruled in cabinet, ministers could take their case to the meetings of the parliamentary Labor party. This was in part a break of the traditional notion of collective responsibility that required all ministers, whether involved in the decision or not, to support in public all decisions of the government.

The Whitlam interpretation followed from the assumption that caucus is part of government. The Hawke government, however, returned to a more traditional practice of collective responsibility. Cabinet considered the matter at its first meeting. It decided that all cabinet ministers, and all ministers outside the cabinet co-opted to discuss a particular item, were committed to the cabinet decision, even in caucus. Later it agreed that ministers not involved in the decision could disagree in caucus. This compromise was reached to accommodate Stewart West, a left-winger who could not support a government decision on uranium but who wished to remain a member of the outer ministry. The Hawke interpretation totally changes the meaning of the convention. Indeed the *Cabinet Handbook* had to be rewritten, carefully, so that rules conformed to practice. The alteration confirms that collective responsibility is inevitably liable to prime ministerial interpretation (Weller 1983; 1985b; *Cabinet Handbook* 1983: 3).

The remnants of parliamentary sovereignty have now largely been replaced by the disciplined party system (Starr et al. 1978; see also Jupp 1982). Australian ministers are responsible to the prime minister or premiers in cabinet, and thence to the party. They need no longer fear the censure of at least the lower house, though parliament remains the centre of political theatre and the testing ground for establishing credibility. Much of the power formally vested in parliament has in fact passed to the party, to a strengthened executive and to an enlarged bureaucracy. Australian parliaments in the States and in Canberra retain their antiquated procedures, at times as form without content. Parliament does not govern; indeed it cannot even exert a daily influence. To understand who decides, therefore, the focus must perhaps turn from the institution of parliament to that of the political core: the executive. Indeed, an important question for state theory is the extent to which state managers can influence state policy and outcomes. What capacity do ministers have to direct the formulation and direction of policy?

Cabinet versus Bureaucratic Direction?

Perceptions of ministers in parliamentary systems have largely been shaped by the British comedy *Yes Minister*. A mediocre politician is manipulated by clever public servants who retain control of the policy process, obfuscate about their administrative responsibilities, and surreptitiously avoid parliamentary scrutiny. The moral is clear: power rests not with ineffectual elected officials, but with the permanent career bureaucracy.

Yes Minister succeeds as caricature because it plays on long standing concern that a democratic regime will come to be dominated by its public service (Weber 1978). Like parliament, ministers may retain the trappings but not the substance of power. In the world of parody, skilful bureaucrats can even elevate the bumbling Jim Hacker to the prime ministership. Australian public servants, however, do not share identical interests. They are as much frustrated as any politician by the fragmentation of the public sector. Indeed only elected officials close to the centre have any prospect of imposing substantial control on the operations of government, for only cabinet has the jurisdiction and clout to make decisions across the whole range of government activity.

The Selection of Ministers

Ministers must be members of parliament. State members may continue some involvement in their former occupation. Canberra, however, sits on dusty limestone plains a long way from most industry or legal chambers. Since distance makes it impossible to combine a business and a political career, institutional politics is full time. Increasingly too, people enter parliament at a younger age. Many become career politicians, spending their working lives in parliament (see King 1979). Outside experience—and certainly outside success—is rare. On the other hand, success as an academic or a lawyer is not necessarily an indication of likely success as a minister. There is no apprenticeship for the position; a person can only succeed in the job.

Prime ministers cannot simply choose the most competent twenty-seven people as ministers. In a federal Labor cabinet, all ministers are elected by the parliamentary caucus. Elections may be strongly contested, as in 1972, or they may be settled entirely by agreement between the factions, as occurred in 1983 and 1987. Labor prime ministers then have the responsibility to distribute portfolios, determining who gets which job.

The selection of ministers by Liberal leaders is also constrained. They must take account of any coalition with the National Party, the pressures for ministers in the Senate, the need to ensure that every State has at least one representative, and factional pressures from the left and right of the party. In effect a Liberal prime minister can probably only leave out one or two senior people, and only has a real choice of the one or two most junior ministers. Malcolm Fraser learned the cost of exercising prime ministerial prerogative when he excluded Don Chipp from his ministry in 1975. A disgruntled Chipp left the Liberal Party to form the Democrats. For the last three years of the Fraser era, Chipp kept control of the Senate from his former coalition colleagues.

Portfolios may be distributed for a range of reasons. The prime minister may wish to maintain a balance between parties, to protect particular jobs from effective opposition critics in one house by giving it to a minister in the other, to ensure that important posts go to senior ministers, to quieten potential dissidents or backbench critics, to direct policy along particular lines through appointing a sympathetic or malleable minister, or to reduce or increase attention on a policy area. Putting together a cabinet is like fitting together a jigsaw. The last piece has to fit, even if it seems illogical (Weller and Grattan 1981: ch 2).

The Roles of Ministers and Officials

Ministers must perform multiple roles, and this makes previous success in business or at the bar a poor guide to likely success with a portfolio. Ministers must perform in parliament and cabinet, act as head of department, maintain their party position, look after their local electorate, deal with the media, travel and somehow maintain a private life.

Ministers are therefore not exclusively concerned with the formulation and implementation of government policy. Their other responsibilities seldom leave more than 50 per cent of the working day for departmental business. During elections or at times of crisis departmental supervision may be put aside for more pressing concerns. A minister is not a full time departmental supervisor, and so relies on bureaucrats for policy advice and program monitoring. Departments become expert at keeping an unenthusiastic or preoccupied minister out of trouble.

Ministers seldom have administrative experience. By contrast departments are headed by officials whose careers have been spent in the public service. Senior bureaucrats have access to long-standing expertise in policy areas, files explaining earlier choices, and a capacity to influence the options or items put before the minister. The balance of time and expertise, particularly when ministers first take over a new department, must be tilted towards the officials.

Who makes a government decision frequently depends on the type of choice in question. Former British cabinet minister Lord Boyle identified four major types of decisions made by government. Major decisions, often interdepartmental, involve ministers who must defend their own turf. More technical decisions are usually settled by public servants, who operate with confidence that they know the minister's mind. A minister may of course become involved and make it a major political decision, but 'he will never have the time, let alone the knowledge, to turn all category 2 decisions into category 1 decisions'. Then there are specific decisions arising out of parliamentary debates, deputations or correspondence. These flow from the representational aspect of politics, and are the responsibility of the minister. Finally there are decisions involving the detailed applications of rules. These are usually taken by public servants without ministerial involvement. Yet 'for every act of a public servant, a minister has to answer in parliament' (Boyle 1980: 7−8).

Boyle argues that a good minister is one who becomes more, rather than less, involved in the second category, for such detailed, technical decisions are often likely to be important. Ministers who do not get involved cede power to public servants (Boyle 1980: 7−8).

Public servants want ministers who are hard-working, briefable, consistent and who, most importantly, can achieve results in cabinet. It is frustrating for career bureaucrats when incompetent ministers destroy months of work by failing to carry cabinet with a well defined proposal, simply because they lacked clout or failed to read and understand their brief.

The importance of cabinet as the decision making forum explains why a minister who is 'captured' by the bureaucracy is of little use to a department. A minister who can be easily controlled by an experienced permanent head may equally be unable to win in cabinet where public servants cannot attend and get the minister out of trouble. Ideally, departments would prefer to be represented by an 'ideological captive', a competent minister who accepts the department's general line, is persuaded of its correctness, and has clout in cabinet. A department such as Treasury will place considerable emphasis on 'educating' a minister, inculcating 'proper' values and a highly defined world view.

Ministers are expected to shape the policies of their departments. Should the policy directions be acceptable to the officials, administrative life can be harmonious. If ministerial directions clash with the agenda of the public service, then conflict occurs. A minister will require considerable stamina and ability to persuade the department to reassess its priorities. As Richard Crossman noted about his experience as a British minister, 'the point of a manifesto is not to persuade the voters. The point of a manifesto is to give yourself an anchor when the civil service tries to go back on your word' (Hawker et al. 1979: 39).

Public servants are obliged to argue strongly against proposals which they consider unwise, even if they are contained in a government's party platform. The bureaucrats must point to the likely consequences. Public servants learn, however, that some ministers are capable of standing firm, and expect their decision to be implemented. According to one bureaucrat, 'to object once is obligatory, twice is necessary, three times is suicidal' (Weller and Grattan 1981: 83).

Given different levels of decisions, varying degrees of competence and interest, and a constant interplay for influence between departmental objectives and the imperatives of elected officials, it is impossible to assert that ministers or public servants do, or should, bear sole responsibility for the initiation of policy. Some proposals come from the party platform, others from the department, while many are thrust onto the agenda by a determined pressure group. The process is about argument and negotiation as minister and public servant discuss and refine a policy before it is sent to cabinet.

Thus the structures of decision making leave scope for considerable manoeuvre by the individuals holding the elected and administrative posts of government. In part the balance between particular ministers and public servants depends on the character of individuals. Both have institutional advantages that they can use, and each has problems—a lack of expertise and time, or no access to cabinet. The minister is concerned that proposals are financially viable, ideologically consistent and electorally rational. Public servants seek decisions which are administratively consistent, operationally rational and preserve departmental influence. When ministers hold firm—provided they care—they will get the last word. Bureaucrats, however, implement the choice, so the decision process does not end with a cabinet vote. The ministerial–

official relationship is always one in which personal and institutional factors intersect.

Cabinet: Structure and Capacity

Cabinet is the fulcrum of government, the place where political, economic, bureaucratic, social and international pressures all intersect. Membership is the summit of most politicians' ambitions, for cabinet has the potential to wield tremendous power. It determines the general strategy of government. It decides what legislation is to be introduced and which programs or policies are adopted. It arbitrates between ministers and between departments, and provides a ministerial perspective on departmental submissions. Cabinet must cope with sudden crises, control parliament, and make appointments. Above all, it must ensure the government's electoral survival. So cabinet is not about the careful choice between technical alternatives. Rather it is an arena where the criteria of politicians, rather than a set of rational precepts, operate. This central decision making body is surrounded by an air of mystery. The weight given to its pronouncements is enhanced by the secrecy of its processes.

Bagehot (1966) described cabinet as the buckle linking the legislature and the executive, the pivot around which government revolves. If a government is to work well cabinet must operate effectively, but it does not always do so. Cabinet is often short of time. It is faced with a mass of detailed information and piles of paper, may be plagued by factions and often has great difficulty maintaining any broad perspective. Endless crises mean cabinet is seldom master of its own agenda.

It is difficult to convey the sheer amount of work which cabinet must complete. Between May 1974 and September 1975 Labor ministers considered 662 papers and made 1125 decisions. During the Fraser government, cabinet took close to 19 000 decisions—about ten decisions every working day for seven years. Many were incidental, but some required voluminous detail, such as submissions on the size of the deficit or the implications of new programs. Even while these were being considered, new submissions piled up, waiting for approval (Kelly 1984: 61). The average cabinet minister appears in studies as an overworked generalist with little detailed knowledge of his or her portfolio, fighting a losing battle to stay on top of the paperwork and the conflicting demands on their time. As one minister noted, 'the sheer volume is quite enormous. It's nothing to cart two linear feet of cabinet documents to cabinet' (Weller and Grattan 1981: 111). With twenty or more items scheduled for each meeting, another minister admitted that he read only 10 per cent of cabinet submissions thoroughly

—'and if anyone claims to read more he is lying' (Weller and Grattan 1981: 110).

The workload pressures fall not just on cabinet, but on departments. The complexity of government, and the interrelatedness of many functions, require each agency to assess the implications of the various decisions required by departments, statutory authorities, foreign governments, the military, pressure groups and the parliament. Under Fraser, for example, 'the public service creaked, groaned and staggered ... the head of the Prime Minister's Department, Sir Alan Carmody, dropped dead; his successor Sir Geoffrey Yeend paced himself and took sick leave' (Kelly 1984: 47).

Fraser may have been an exceptional cabinet taskmaster, but his furious pace is now built into Australian government decision making. The pressure results from the staggering range of cabinet's responsibilities; this group of twenty seven people are responsible not only for key decisions about the public sector and government transfers, but must oversee an extensive network of government agencies, confer with the States, and devise strategies to stay in power. Ministers must then sell their policies to their parties and the electorate, placate the various interest groups and supporters making demands and somehow also find time to run their departments and keep in contact with their local constituents.

The workload is exacerbated when the quality of cabinet is uneven. If ministers are generally mediocre, an extra burden will fall on those senior, experienced and able ministers who must carry their less talented colleagues. Under consistent pressure for policy decisions, they must keep the cabinet coherent while not losing perspective on the significance of particular issues or the sensitivities of the electorate.

Cabinet is a committee, and all committees are noted more for the frustration they engender than for their decisiveness. What is unusual about this particular collective enterprise is the expectations aroused by the mystique. Cabinet is continuously involved in trying to resolve crises, manage the unmanageable, routinise the extraordinary, systematise the disorderly, co-ordinate the incoherent and calm the passionate. It is not surprising that its capacity is more limited than legend asserts.

Agenda

The agenda for cabinet is officially drawn up by the prime minister or premier, acting with the advice of officials from their department. In theory the setting of the agenda gives the leader great authority. At times it does, but this can be exaggerated. Many items come to cabinet as a matter of course, including major policy issues, proposals involving employment or large expenditure, items requiring legislation or amendments to legislation, proposals that have a considerable impact on relations between different levels of government, and senior appointments. This list suggests guidelines, however, rather than binding commitments to collective consideration of particular categories of problems. What is finally discussed by cabinet depends, in part, on what the leader wishes to discuss, and in part on how far ministers need the support of cabinet for their decisions.

Prime ministers and premiers can, with the agreement of the responsible ministers, consistently keep items off the agenda. During the Whitlam government, foreign affairs were never debated in cabinet. The prime minister preferred to make international policy by himself or in conjunction with the minister; he did not consider it the business of colleagues less well-informed than himself. On the other hand, other items may be forced onto the cabinet. Strikes, international crises and the budget inevitably come before the cabinet for discussion. Electoral importance and sensitivity decide whether items appear on the agenda. Should general agreement exist on a resolution, the problem will not be discussed exhaustively by cabinet. Time is too valuable for that.

Ministers constantly complain that they are overworked. Under Fraser there was an attempt to dispose of some issues by giving the minister of finance greater independent authority. Other ministers complained, however, when more autonomy for Finance affected their department's programs and new project bids. The subsequent Labor administration came to office with a 'machinery of government' plan to prevent ministerial overload by delegating responsibility. Yet within three months of becoming prime minister Bob Hawke was already commenting on the time-consuming pressure of meetings, and much of the plan was discarded.

There are at least three compelling reasons why the work pressure on cabinet and the ministry has not been reduced. First, as a senior minister admitted, 'a collective decision will always have a chance of being better than an individual decision' (Weller and Grattan 1981: 135). Besides, decisions taken on occasion without cabinet approval have later come unstuck, and have subsequently required cabinet consideration.

The second reason for unrelenting pressure reflects cabinet's role as a clearing house for government business. Cabinet decisions are regarded as authoritative in interdepartmental struggles, and public servants need specific authorisation for their actions. Formal decisions are the currency of government administration.

More importantly, however, is the desire of ministers for collective authorisation of their actions. Once a decision is taken, cabinet is locked into support, and a minister can proceed with some confidence. As a senior Liberal put it:

> I find it hard to believe that the good government of a country needs as many cabinet or cabinet committee decisions as it gets. But, on the other hand, as matters do come before cabinet it is one way of making sure that all ministers understand what is happening and what it is about. It gives the minister the reassurance of his cabinet colleagues and it is important therefore for the cabinet system and for cabinet solidarity if ministers have been part of a decision (Weller and Grattan 1981: 136).

Many cabinet decisions are in fact first discussed or even taken by cabinet committees, whose membership and terms of reference are settled by the prime minister.

Under Fraser, for example, the monetary committee made many of the decisions about the exchange rate and other economic management matters, while the foreign affairs and defence committee kept security matters to itself. Under Hawke an elaborate and formal committee system considers numerous items and reaches preliminary decisions; these are then forwarded to cabinet for noting and ratification.

As well as the committee system, leaders usually gather a group of senior ministers to discuss electoral and parliamentary tactics. Fraser created his co-ordination committee as part of the formal cabinet system; as a consequence its decisions had a formal status. Other prime ministers and premiers use more informal 'kitchen cabinets'. As consultation is crucial to maintaining the leadership, all heads of government rely on an inner, often floating, group with whom they can discuss problems.

Cabinet as a Decision Making Forum

Cabinet is often regarded as a fairly inefficient forum for making decisions. So it is in many ways; ministers are busy, the range of topics is immense, the workload is heavy and technical questions are difficult. Yet cabinet must fulfil many roles at once, so procedures which facilitate one purpose may hinder another. Though it is difficult to categorise all the manifest and latent functions of such a complex institution, its activities will at least include acting as a clearing house, as an information exchange, as arbiter, as decision maker, as co-ordinator, as guardian of the strategy and as source of legitimacy.

Though many decisions are actually made by cabinet committees or by bilateral meetings of ministers, these choices are then reported to cabinet. Here the cabinet performs as a clearing house, giving formal authority to decisions and keeping other ministers aware of what is happening.

Cabinet is also an information-exchange. No minister can be expected to know all that is going on in government. Information papers, taken to cabinet for noting, let colleagues know what is particularly important or is likely to have electoral implications.

Disputes within governments are inevitable, so cabinet must act as arbiter. Some ministers want more money for programs, while the minister of finance and the treasurer will argue for restraint. Departments and their ministers argue over jurisdiction. Cabinet must make decisions about which minister wins, and which loses.

Cabinet is a decision maker. Often proposals made by bureaucrats may be technically sensible, but tactically insensitive. Cabinet members, even without detailed or expert knowledge, need to look for the pitfalls and draw out any dangerous electoral consequences that might follow.

As the centre of government, cabinet is a co-ordinator. Public sector functions are diverse; there is always a danger that two or more departments are tackling the same problem from different angles or that some policies are inconsistent. Cabinet is the main forum in which those tensions can be reduced.

Further, cabinet is the guardian of the strategy. Ministers almost inevitably come to cabinet to fight for their department's interests. That is a proper role; after all, if the minister for education does not argue the case for expenditure on schools or universities, no one else will. The effect, however, can be tunnel vision. Working so hard in one area it is difficult for a minister to keep the broader picture in perspective. It therefore becomes the responsibility of the chair to maintain the balance between the general and the particular. Putting an item before cabinet is a means of ensuring that the proposal meshes with overall government objectives.

Finally, government acts as legitimator. It gives authority to those state actions and decisions taken during its term of office. In a broader sense, cabinet is also part of the state apparatus which legitimates social arrangements of power and resources. In times of financial crisis, cabinet has to work out the viable trade-offs; it will want to provide concessions to disadvantaged sectors and classes, yet maintain economic development.

Because cabinet functions in all these areas at once, it is subject to diverse pressures. It must avoid becoming entrapped in detail, yet know enough to prevent unnecessary duplication. Cabinet acts as both a battleground between competing interests and a conciliator in drawing together the threads of a coherent strategy. Individual policies must fit within an integrated economic strategy, so ministers must relate specific items arising from their departments with government strategy. They must strike the right balance between pressures, for cabinet as a collectivity gets no assistance. It alone is responsible for its decisions.

The Budget

Competing pressures on cabinet reach an annual peak with the budget. Though the processes of budget formulation are almost continuous for public servants, ministers become involved at one or two crucial moments. Their intervention is crucial. In deciding where to allocate resources, cabinet is stating its priorities. When more is spent on education and less on defence this reflects government preferences, even if ministers have not explicitly chosen between the two areas.

In the federal sphere ministerial involvement in budget formulation begins in March; as State budgets are predicated on federal decisions, their budget process will be tied to Commonwealth consultation. In Canberra the cabinet first considers three-year forward estimates. These inspired guesses from departments about their likely capital and recurrent needs are collated by the Department of Finance and the Treasury. A cabinet committee concerned with expenditure review then assesses the three year estimates and recommends cuts. Departments and central agencies are allowed to review their program bids in the light of those committee decisions, and to submit revised estimates. When the Department of Finance and the spending department can settle on a figure, these are called 'agreed bids'; when they still differ, they are 'disagreed bids' and are sent to cabinet for arbitration.

The meeting of the federal budget cabinet lasts a week, usually in July. The treasurer will first provide submissions outlining economic forecasts, estimate the likely deficit, and recommend the levels at which departmental expenditure should be held. Once an overall strategy is agreed, each department's claim is considered in turn. Most of the debate concentrates on the disagreed bids. The amount may be small— in 1977, disagreed bids totalled only $8 million in a budget of $26 000 million—but they are often strenuously contested. At the end of the week, proposals for raising additional revenue are considered. Sometimes this is done by cabinet, but more often a small committee or even just the prime minister and the treasurer will fix the final details (for discussions of the budget process see Weller and Cutt 1976; Wiltshire 1975; Spann 1979; Hardman 1982).

Decision making by cabinet in its budget deliberations is generally ad hoc, incremental and sequential. Each case is argued by itself, using the previous year's figure as a base. Settled items receive little attention, though ongoing programs inevitably take up most of every year's budget. There is little scope for other than marginal change (Wildavsky 1979).

The way in which budgets are formulated and the discussions in budget cabinet increase the advantage of information. Only the prime minister, the treasurer and the minister of finance will have a clear overview of strategy and possibility; in combination they will likely be unbeatable. Other ministers have to read, understand and absorb 150–200 submissions for budget cabinet, and only receive briefings from their departments on those items with an impact on the portfolio. In cabinet debate, ministers do not start with equal opportunities; it is difficult for a minister for social security or education to prevent cuts to their departments when opposed by determined, well informed, senior government figures.

Prime Ministerial Government?

For the last twenty years British practitioners and academics have debated whether the power to make authoritative decisions has passed from the cabinet to the prime minister. It is argued that prime ministers have seven great advantages: the power to hire and fire ministers, the power to set the agenda, structure and process of cabinet, control over the machinery of government, leadership of a disciplined party and thus control of parliament, centralised control of access to the media, extensive personal patronage, and the personal support of a large bureaucratic machine (See Crossman 1963, 1971; Mackintosh 1977). Others argue that prime ministers are limited by their colleagues. The system of government in Britain, said one observer, 'cannot really be called prime ministerial government, nor can it be called cabinet government. The right term is ministerial government' (Jones 1985: 72).

What can be said of Australian leaders? Inevitably any prime minister is often powerful in determining choices and outcomes. Personal style influences the approach to the job. Some prime ministers may be interventionist and autocratic, others weak or indecisive. Few learn to delegate authority; most gather as much as possible to themselves. Nonetheless all prime ministers must work within certain confines, dictated by possibility, institutional structure, legal requirement and historical convention.

Prime ministers are not always master of their own fate. The circumstances of their ascendancy will partly define their authority. Whitlam in 1972, Fraser in 1975 and Hawke in 1983 were inevitably more influential than anyone selected in the circumstances faced by McMahon in 1971. Power within the party room, cabinet and bureaucracy can be more easily exercised by a leader following an electoral victory than by a prime minister elevated to control of a divided, listless and often mutinous crew.

So prime ministerial power is neither given nor unchangeable. It is not applicable in all circumstances. It varies, even within the course of one premiership. Most prime ministers reach the position because they have superior political skills; they must keep using them to stay there. Menzies, Whitlam and Fraser were often able to get their way in cabinet because they were the most hard-working, the best informed and the most able of the ministers. Hawke, on the other hand, backed his lieutenants on most policy initiatives. Hawke based his government on a wages and incomes policy agreed with the trade union movement. His major concern therefore was to protect the strategy; within the constraints of the accord, Hawke did not seek to override his ministers on many policy issues.

Australian prime ministers owe their position to parliamentary colleagues. Elected by the party room, they can—and have been—removed by a party vote. As John Gorton discovered, no prime minister can afford consistently to ignore or alienate colleagues. As long as Fraser kept winning elections comfortably, he was supported. Once opinion polls suggested that he might lose the 1980 election, his grip on the leadership came into question. He won and became again secure within the party room. When Fraser finally lost in 1983 he resigned from the parliament, knowing that in a party vote he would inevitably lose the leadership. With his departure former ministers began recounting their brave stands against the dominant Fraser; while he was leader, however, only a few colleagues were prepared to publicly criticise his policies or style of government.

Prime ministers are likely to be influential in those areas where they intervene. Because what they do is newsworthy, prime ministers dominate the headlines. This gives the illusion of prime ministerial involvement in all major issues, though in fact media coverage touches on only a small part of government activity. Many routine decisions are taken by ministers; in doing so they set important policy precedents and exercise considerable discretionary authority. There is a danger in equating government with crisis, for crises emphasise the role of prime ministers rather than the collective process of most government choices.

However talented the individual, there remain important structural limits to the power of prime ministers. They are constrained by limited time and information, by the need to maintain support within the party, by electoral fortunes and the demands of major pressure groups. In particular they must depend upon their cabinet colleagues. Though usually the most important minister, this does not make the position of prime minister all-powerful. Despite the ponderous pronouncements of editorials and pundits, Australian government has yet to become presidential (Weller 1985).

The Collective Problem

These threads of prime ministerial, ministerial and bureaucratic power can be brought together as dimensions of the collective problem. This puzzle asks how a group of ministers, each with a departmental view to put, each with a range of roles to play, can combine to develop a collective strategy for government direction. Government decision making tends to be fragmented, ad hoc and sequential, while careful plans require long term commitment to objectives, understandings about what resources will be available, and agreement on priorities and timetables. A government strategy requires clear, unambiguous objectives and a firm unrelenting policy.

Yet politics is never so simple. Governments are trying to deliver on a wide range of fronts. They can never be certain of the effect of their policies, for unanticipated consequences may swamp deliberate change. What is a suitable strategy one day may be unacceptable soon after-wards. Flexibility can be seen either as breaking promises or as refusing to adhere to outmoded commitments in a fluid situation. Yet if decision making is often reactive and inevitably segmented, how can governments find collective directions, and so assert some policy coherence on a diffuse and divided public sector?

One way to impose consistency might be to hire expert advisors. Such a staff could survey the whole range of government activity; free of the constraints and demands which prevent serious consideration of complex issues, they could produce recommendations for the over-worked cabinet. This procedure was tried between 1970 and 1983 in Britain with the Central Policy Review Staff, and in Australia between 1972 and 1975 with the Priorities Review Staff. They were to provide the cabinet with comments on departmental submissions, to give advice on government strategies, and to undertake analyses of particular troublesome policy areas.

Policy review offices did not change the way governments operated. Ministers listened to reports about urgent problems but were not interested in hearing that long term aims were not being immediately fulfilled. Further, ministers resented reports which criticised their own departmental claims. They were prepared to restrict the access of the Priorities Review Staff, to accuse it of playing bureaucratic politics, or simply to ignore its recommendations when they were not convenient. The Priority Review Staff was abolished when the Fraser government came to power (Boston 1980).

So the problem remains: if governments are to have any impact, if they are to exercise power, then they must be able to reach and enforce collective decisions. To make viable choices ministers require information. The pressures of office, however, restrict the possibilities for extensive participation. If experts, the party or the parliament are to offer advice about an overall strategy, to whom should the information flow? Should agendas and issues be the concern of already overloaded ministers, the problem of influential but unelected officials, or the prerogative of the leader as the only person with the power and prestige to maintain a sense of governmental direction?

Blondel has advocated a collective solution for Britain. He believes that cabinet governments need 'a group at the very top which, though composed in part of some of the ministers, must also include men and women who, together with the leader, are primarily engaged in policy-making and co-ordination . . . the group at the top must remain collec-tive' (Blondel 1982: 233). Other British observers have sought to strengthen the individual authority of the prime minister. Hoskyns (1983) and Berrill (1980) want increased bureaucratic support to provide prime ministers with greater information and scope for action. Dell (1980: 40–44) seeks to replace collective responsibility with the concept of 'collective purpose' and to strengthen the centre of government in its relations with the departments. Hoskyns, Dell and Berrill are all practitioners of politics. They must be aware that whatever the public image, leaders have considerable difficulty imposing strategic direction on government.

In Australia, the prime minister and State premiers already have the advantage of a bureaucracy able to provide policy advice. The Depart-ment of Prime Minister and Cabinet in Canberra was used to great effect by Fraser, and with less urgency by Hawke. The question be-comes whether advice to the cabinet should come from career public servants or from party appointees in some policy unit. In a review of their performance in government, the Liberals argued for greater out-side assistance (Valder 1983). Yet the problem remains how an outside group meeting at irregular intervals can effectively assist a government with its daily problems. Whatever the consequences for collective responsibility for decisions, full time partisan appointees have become an important and influential part of the advisory process in Australia (Walter 1986). These minders always assist the individual. There have not been serious attempts to restructure the collective decision making processes of government.

Leaders and proximate decision makers matter. They are important because they determine the allocation of public sector resources. Their strategic location makes them the only group able to impose some coherence on government policy and direction. Yet problems remain for those at the centre making collective decisions. Resources are limited, demands are overwhelming and choices constrained by social and economic factors beyond the immediate control of government.

Valuable effort is expended trying to co-ordinate multiple agencies, and to maintain any purpose amid the confusions of politics.

A government cannot institute long term strategic plans. The variables are not sufficiently predictable, the process of implementation uncertain, constitutional power too dispersed, the economy too uncontrollable, the times rarely settled. The best a collective cabinet can achieve is the determination that one central plank—the reduction of the deficit under Fraser, the accord under Hawke—be the criterion against which other policy proposals are judged. Policies can at least be made consistent with a central objective, even if not always with each other.

So those at the centre offer—at best—limited direction for government; politicians can use collective processes and institutions to coax some influence over the actions of government and public sector. Influence, of course, is not necessarily control; the effect of public policies can not always be explained by the intentions of their authors. Politics is more than individual actors in co-operation or competition, and government more than the 'rational' choices of particular leaders.

Further Reading

Hawker, Geoffrey *(1981) Who's Master, Who's Servant? Reforming Bureaucracy* Sydney: Allen & Unwin.

Nethercote, John (ed.) (1982) *Parliament and Bureaucracy* Sydney: Hale & Iremonger.

Solomon, David (1986) *The People's Palace; parliament in modern Australia* Melbourne University Press.

Symposium (1985) 'Strategic Leadership in Modern Government' *Canberra Bulletin of Public Administration* 12, 2, pp. 77–134.

Weller, Patrick (1985) *First Among Equals: prime ministers in Westminster systems* Sydney: Allen & Unwin.

Weller, Patrick and Grattan, Michelle (1981) *Can Ministers Cope? Australian federal ministers at work* Melbourne: Hutchinson.

Wilenski, Peter (1979) 'Ministers, Public Servants and Public Policy' *Australian Quarterly* 51, 2, pp. 31–45.

5

Parties and Pressure Groups

'Which side are you on?' sang the demonstrators as delegates pushed through the crowded foyer and into the conference room. With the meeting back in session, a vote was taken. Each delegate moved to one side of the auditorium or the other, calling aye or nay as they did so. Demonstrators booed, while the media sat in silence, counting. The final vote was fifty three in favour and forty six against.

The occasion was the July 1982 National Conference of the Australian Labor Party. The motion before the chair was moved by Victorian State Secretary Bob Hogg. It sought to modify an existing policy strongly opposing the mining and export of uranium. The demonstrators, some holding banners, one dressed as a skeleton, personified the anti-uranium movement, while observer chairs were occupied by representatives of business associations, foreign governments and trade unions. This tableau neatly and publicly illustrated the players in policy formulation.

Organisations make a significant contribution to the distribution of influence and the circulation of policy ideas. Groups advocate solutions for public problems—whether through the discrete lobbying of business councils or the more public displays of farmers and conservationists. Groups pressure parties, governments and departments on behalf of their members. Examining the role of such organisations in the policy process, the academic literature identifies two major types of political organisation: political parties (Jaensch 1983: 12–16) and pressure groups (Matthews 1980).

Political parties with genuine claims to achieving majority support are broad coalitions of sectional interests. This is their electoral strength and their policy making weakness. While a coalition of support enables a party to win elections, it creates problems in reconciling the conflicting preferences of members. Such parties are bound together by mutual support for a very broad set of principles; they accept that only through acting collectively can they become the government. Members may disagree on a particular issue, but necessity keeps them together. A divided party will not win office.

Each of the major Australian political blocs—the Australian Labor

Party, and the Liberal and National Parties—is a collection of sectional interests with differing views on policy (Starr et al. 1978; Parkin and Warhurst 1983; Costar and Woodward 1985; O'Brien 1985). All are federal parties, based on autonomous State branches representing regional interests. As collections of interests, parties are made of formal or informal factions. The ALP has three officially organised factions, usually known as the Right, Centre Left and the Socialist Left. The factions are based in the State branches, though they are increasingly organised at the national level (Lloyd and Swan 1987). The Liberal Party is divided informally along a number of axes—between the 'wets' and the 'dries' on economic policy, between the liberals and the conservatives on social policy. Though the smaller National Party is generally homogeneous, there are still contesting perspectives on policy between the Queensland branch and the federal party, and within State branches.

Australian parties are divided by gender. This often leads to separate organisations for women within parties and to competing views on policies. The National Liberal Women's Conference, for example, supports anti-discrimination legislation while the party as a whole does not (Women's Electoral Lobby Seminar 1977; see also Sawer and Simms 1984). There are also differences between the metropolitan and rural wings, often represented by separate conferences within the party. Indeed all parties embrace a diversity of interests and are divided on philosophy, region, gender, locality and perhaps on other criteria such as ethnic background and union affiliation. Such differences create internal party disputes based on shifting coalitions around sectional interests, issues and individuals.

Only a small percentage of the Australian population are members of political parties. Yet nearly all Australians are members of an 'interest' group (Matthews 1980; Warhurst 1985). Certainly the representation of almost every Australian is claimed by one or other pressure group. The churches 'represent' the eighty per cent of the population with a religious affiliation. Trade unions represent the organised fifty five per cent of the workforce. Women's groups claim to speak for the female majority. Membership of such pressure groups is large and rising. Over half a million Australians are said to be members of conservation groups.

Pressure groups are, by definition, partial and often narrow. Yet even these relatively tight coalitions of interests do not always agree on objectives or tactics. Trade unions differ among themselves, feminists fall out, right-to-lifers quarrel bitterly over tactics. Pressure groups seek to influence—but are also consumed by—politics.

Although they are different types of organisations, there is considerable overlap between political parties and pressure groups. Key individuals often operate across several organisations. Members of small business lobbies also are likely to be active in the Liberal Party. Indeed each of the major parties owes its creation to a sectional interest. The ALP grew out of the trade union movement, the National Party (originally the Country Party) emerged from farmers' organisations, and the Liberal Party was founded by groups mainly representing the urban business community.

Parties and Policy Making

Government action hinges on party policy. Almost all candidates elected to parliament are endorsed by parties. The candidate's individual opinions do not matter, for they are bound to follow the party philosophy expressed by the platform. During the campaign the party leader will make a policy speech setting out their priorities and approach to the current agenda. Once elected, governments can claim a mandate for the policies they espoused during the campaign. Their performance is judged at a subsequent election, and the process is repeated.

So parties determine governments, and a government is assessed by the policies of its party. Political parties have become an integral part of the policy process. They have constant access to the parliament to ventilate ideas. The media accords their representatives, above all others, the space to pass judgement on contemporary issues. They contain some of the best known individuals in the country. Parties, with their financial resources, have access to the best marketing and policy expertise in the country (see Mills 1986). The issue agenda is largely set by the political parties. Hence party debates on issues such as uranium become crucial, for only with party support can a proposal become government policy. Individuals and pressure groups use political parties as a channel into the policy making process.

Party Platforms and Policy Speeches

The Australian Labor Party's 1984 platform is a book of 258 pages organised into twenty seven policy fields. The platform is a comprehensive document. It seeks to contain the party view on every issue of importance, for it officially represents 'short and long term aspirations of the ALP' (ALP 1984). This platform is the result of party conferences held every alternate year since the turn of the century. Each version builds on the preceeding platform, making policy formulation a cumulative, incremental process.

The Liberal Party's 1982 federal platform is a somewhat shorter document of fifty six pages covering thirty seven separate fields. It is approved by Federal Council, though as a set of recommendations rather than as binding commitments. The Liberal Party believes that final responsibility for policy formulation must remain with the parliamentary wing and State branches. Indeed the reader is advised that since 'various sections are interdependent, the document should be studied as a whole. It should also be read in association with the Divisional Platforms of the Party which deal specifically with matters appropriate to the Divisions of the Party'. The Federal Council sees the platform as 'the statement of essential principles based upon the Liberal philosophy' (Liberal Party 1982).

Each party's platform is determined by vote of a national conference or council (Hutchinson 1982, 1985). These conferences have become public events. Excerpts are televised, current affairs reporters linger around the doorways, academics offer learned opinion or themselves scout for gossip. Yet often the sound and fury serves only to legitimise private agreements already made between factional leaders.

Motions do not simply appear during proceedings. Before the conference meets a series of policy committees review sections of the platform; their recommendations and draft revisions are then put before the conference. Such policy committees are made up of party members, including members of parliament (MPs), nominated by State branches for their interest or expertise. Usually the committees are dominated by full time politicians, for MPs have staff to do research and gold passes to travel to meetings. When Labor is in office, policy committees are important arenas for ministers to ensure that the government's preferences become official party policy.

Policy committees work incrementally, beginning with the existing platform. If the party is in power, then ministers may bring ideas which originate with their departments. Ideally some proposals will come from the party faithful, in the form of motions passed by local and State branches. Few of these suggestions, however, last the distance. Electoral imperatives, not branch suggestions, usually shape the choices of policy committees.

A party in opposition does not have access to the advice of the bureaucracy, and may have few ideas about a policy field. Professionals become important, though they offer proposals which are not constrained by the problems of implementation. While the Liberals were in opposition during the Whitlam years, pressure groups put in considerable time and resources to 'capture' key policy committees. In a celebrated case, shadow Liberal social security spokesperson Don Chipp was won over by the social welfare lobby in 1975, only to be left out of the next Liberal ministry by Prime Minister Fraser.

New party policies reflect changing public attitudes and the presence of influential individuals with strongly held views. Don Dunstan described the long struggle of ALP activists during the 1950s and 1960s to shift the party from its 'White Australia' policy (Dunstan 1981: 90–92, 98, 126). In the years before 1972 Gough Whitlam worked hard to revise or create ALP policies on cities, education, health, welfare and foreign affairs (Freudenberg 1986). Staffers, MPs and outside experts were drafted into committees to prepare new ALP positions on numerous issues. Some of these professionals, such as Troy in urban affairs and Scotton and Deeble in health, followed Whitlam into government as public servants to assist in implementing the program.

The prominence of the anti-nuclear movement, and the success of the Nuclear Disarmament Party in 1984, led the Liberal Party to develop a separate policy on nuclear disarmament. In their years of opposition during the Hawke government, the Liberals were also pressured by groups such as the 'new right' to adopt more conservative, market policies. Tensions emerged between 'ideological captives' and those Liberals who feared the electoral consequences of shifting from more moderate, traditional policies.

The party platform is meant to be an important statement of principles, especially within the ALP. The National Conference has resolved that 'the programme for each 3 years of a Labor government will continue to be drawn from the platform' (ALP 1984). From within the party there was considerable criticism of the Hawke government for disregarding—even sneering at—the platform. Yet very few people, even party members, know or care what is in the document. It is holy writ only to a select band of activists. The party platform is consulted only by journalists, public servants in relevant departments and leaders of pressure groups.

What matters to a larger public is the policy speech, which seeks a mandate to govern. These are written for a party leader to declaim over television, and rely on slogan, general promises and emotion. They are designed to win an election. Kim Beazley senior quipped that in the Whitlam cabinet room the 'platform is the Old Testament, the policy speech is the New Testament' (Freudenberg 1986: 130). Whitlam's 1972 speech was written by Graham Freudenberg, who recalled

> . . . the task was essentially collating, organising and editing the mass of material produced in the previous six years. But I was under no illusions about the principle purpose of the task. It was to produce the most effective possible document to clinch the 1972 elections (Freudenberg 1986: 131).

Because policy speeches are designed to win elections, they are often seriously flawed from a policy perspective. They posture, avoid detail and minimise bad news. They promise—to spend money on new programs, to cut taxes, to abolish or create departments and agencies.

Such pledges have served their use once the election is over, though occasionally governments may seek to observe their commitments. Whitlam's 1972 speech contained over 120 promises, and the prime minister reputedly ticked off each one as it was achieved (Bilney 1986: 22). More often, however, promises only harm a government. Circumstances change, finance is unavailable or the policy proves to be ill-considered. Such pledges can return to haunt an administration. The opposition and media continually point to broken promises. This was the case with Fraser's 1977 commitment that unemployment would fall, and with Hawke's 1983 vow not to introduce a capital gains tax.

Problems in Party Policy Making

Making policy through a party platform and policy speech can lead to serious errors of judgement. As Lloyd observed about the ALP platform:

> Put together section by section on the floor of the Conference, the platform is riddled with internal inconsistencies. It contains more than 250 individual commitments, most of them ill-defined, incapable of expression in effective implementation programs, and impossible to cost accurately. The document lacks any semblance of 'ways and means' or even of rudimentary priorities. The most dedicated readers of the ALP platform in recent times have been the party's political opponents who have analysed the document and exploited its cost implications and lack of rational organisation (Lloyd 1983: 244).

Party policy is guided and constrained by basic principles and by the balance of factions within the organisation. Coherence can be more illusory than real, though principle may also greatly restrict proposals. Experts in a particular field may come under considerable pressure to conform with prevailing party ideological beliefs. The Liberals under John Howard, for example, accepted industrial relations policies which were opposed by Ian Macphee, the frontbencher with greatest experience in the field. If they override the professionals, parties may adopt policies too far from the 'middle ground' to be implemented once in government.

Party policies rarely specify priorities. They assume that proposals can be honoured during a government's term of office. Yet without a timetable there is no mechanism, other than the floor of the conference or the speech writer's head, to ensure co-ordination of policy proposals. Pledges may conflict because they originate with different factions. There may be insufficient time or resources to implement each element of the policy, forcing governments to choose between commitments.

Constructing policy is even more difficult for an opposition without access to bureaucratic advice, accurate costings or the lessons of implementation. Opposition proposals, when vetted by governments, invariably involve spending unrealistic amounts of money. Not only are the proposals inflated by electoral pressures, but each set of policy proposals must be put forward in a vacuum. Co-ordination of proposals and timetables is difficult for a party out of office. Oppositions do not want to alienate any support. On the maxim that 'oppositions don't win office, governments lose it', their best strategy may be to remain noncommittal about policy. The practical difficulties of testing proposals outside the context of government can combine with the expediency of vagueness to produce an opposition with few clearly defined proposals (Marsh 1976). In any case, oppositions recognise that party policy is prone to be outdated. Economic circumstances change more frequently than conferences meet. A party may win an election with a platform which is eighteen months, or even longer, behind the times.

Further, once in government it may prove expedient to renege on electorally unpopular proposals. The Hawke government quickly abandoned a commitment to uniform land rights. The Whitlam government, on the other hand, was criticised for sticking to its party platform regardless of changing circumstances. Actions which made sense amid prosperity appeared inappropriate during recession. Whitlam later commented:

> The program of domestic reform my Government was elected to carry out was developed during years of economic growth unprecedented for its length and strength in modern history. It fell to us to carry out the program at a time when the conditions in which it was conceived were being rapidly undermined . . . We did not use recession as an alibi against reform (Whitlam 1985: 183).

Parties are not primarily concerned with policy formulation. Their rationale is to gain and retain office. Certainly parties spend considerable time talking about policy, and for some activists policy development is the reason for membership. Such people often become greatly frustrated by the difficulty of pursuing special policy objectives within a party, for parties can rarely satisfy activists who have one priority above all others, whether it is environmental conservation, Aboriginal land rights, or christian morality. Such individuals must pursue these objectives through other means, and may end up joining single issue pressure groups (Warhurst 1983).

Because parties exist to win government, policies which stand in the way of office are jettisoned or reformulated. This may be done in opposition, but will almost certainly occur once in power. As a consequence, party members are often disillusioned with their party, even if it wins elections. The party community may become at odds with the party government.

Party – Government Relations

Australian governments are not the creatures of their party organisations. The Hawke government has retained the public support of the
ALP National Executive and National Conference even on issues such
as uranium, where the government has clearly deviated from party
policy. Indeed for a decade the parliamentary party has moved away
from the strong opposition to the mining and export of uranium adopted
by the party in the 1970s. In 1982 Labor politicians led a push to
modify the platform before forthcoming South Australian State elections. By 1986 the party did not revolt even when the government sold
uranium to France.

There are at least two reasons why the parliamentary party can
ignore a platform commitment. The first is the status and influence of
politicians. Parliamentarians, members of the cabinet, and particularly
the prime minister are numerically important in party gatherings and
influential beyond their numbers. They have access to the media and
to patronage as vehicles for achieving their ends. In combination they
can usually obtain their way within the party.

Perhaps the more important reason, however, reflects the rationale
of party activity—to gain office. Party members tire quickly of being in
opposition. They are reluctant to do anything which might threaten
their government, however much they disagree with its policies. An
official reprimand by the party may destabilise the government. The
media will paint such tensions as disunity, with fatal electoral consequences. The ALP of the 1950s and 1960s may have rated office
holding as secondary to questions of principle, but no party does so
now. There is no point being a loser in politics, and few policies are
worth the price of office.

Pressure Groups

Like political parties, sectional interests hope to influence public policy.
Sometimes such groups actually are part of a party structure and so
have veto power over proposals. The union movement, for example, is
formally affiliated with the ALP. Business organisations are not directly
linked with the Liberal Party, but are clearly influential. Banking
interests within the Liberal Party prevented the Fraser government
deregulating the private banking system as recommended by the Campbell Report. Yet more often than not sectional interests are locked into
parties to their policy disadvantage. They become too closely identified
with a particular party and so have little influence on other governments.
Some rural organisations, for example, argue that the National Party
has failed to advance their interests, but they have nowhere else to go.

So most pressure groups operate outside the party structure. They aim to influence the making or administering of public policy, but do not wish to exercise the full formal powers of government (Matthews 1980). They want to persuade existing parties rather than establish a new party machine.

There are innumerable interests in Australian society. Most will give rise to a voluntary association of some sort or another. Many of these, including sporting, cultural and service organisations, are not overtly political, for they have no apparent direct interest in public policy. As Matthews notes, however, such organisations 'can usefully be regarded as the organisational substructure of the pressure group universe, in that any one of them could easily become a pressure group ... should its members (or leaders) attempt to influence public policy in its name' (Matthews 1980: 449). Sporting groups demand facilities from government, churches lobby for tax exemption, the Australian Opera expects large state subsidies. Pressure groups seek to influence public policy and devote a lesser or greater part of their time and resources to this end. Even as they deplore party politics such groups pursue partisan policies.

Types of Pressure Groups

Interest in politics varies and access to government is unequal. Some groups are so close to government that they can be regarded as 'insiders', though this is at odds with the traditional notion of exerting pressure from outside the system. Insiders include associations which represent economic interests: the trade union movement, from individual unions to trades halls and the Australian Council of Trade Unions; the business community, including major national associations such as the Confederation of Australian Industry and the Business Council of Australia; the National Farmers Federation, plus State farmers' associations organised around individual commodities.

Insider groups have working relations with the departments and agencies of government. Their concerns are an established and continuing part of the agenda. Their members are involved in the implementation of government policies and programs. They cannot be ignored by any government or party. Their significance was recognised by the invitations to the National Economic Summit called by the Hawke government in April 1983. Almost every invited representative came from one of these economic sector organisations.

The insiders also include organisations representing the professions, such as the Australian Medical Association, law societies, bar associations and unions of teachers and nurses with claims to professional status. The Returned Services League was for a long time accorded direct access to cabinet and to the Department of Veterans Affairs. Beyond sectional economic interests and professional groups the list of insiders tails off, though on certain issues it may include the churches and voluntary service organisations.

Many pressure groups are outsiders. A few prefer it this way. They fear losing their independence or, like the Friends of the Earth, stay distant from government as a matter of philosophical commitment. Given the choice, however, most would prefer to be on the inside. They are outsiders because they are not regarded as central to the economic policy concerns of government, because their interest is not highly valued by social elites or because they represent a view on a central issue which is regarded as immoderate. The outsiders claim to speak for the powerless individual or the marginal concern. They include groups representing women, Aborigines, environmental conservationists, the unemployed and consumers.

Power relations and agenda shift, and some outsiders eventually gain recognition. Though representing interests regarded as marginal twenty years ago, organisations such as the Women's Electoral Lobby, the Australian Consumers Association, and the Australian Conservation Foundation now operate, for some purposes, as quasi-insiders. As public opinion has changed—often largely through the efforts of such groups—the interests they represent have received greater recognition within the apparatus of government. There are now departments for the conservation of the environment, Aboriginal affairs and women's policy units (Hughes 1984; Summers 1986; Sawer 1986). Recognition, of course, is not power. At the National Economic Summit these groups could observe, but not participate in debates.

Access to government is one way of classifying pressure groups. An important distinction is also made between sectional and promotional groups. Some organisations claim to speak for a particular section of the community, usually defined by occupation, training or religious denomination. Other groups are open to any person with an interest in a particular opinion or policy. Business councils, unions and farmers are organised on sectional lines. The Royal Society for the Prevention of Cruelty to Animals, the Festival of Light and temperance groups exist to promote particular issues.

The distinction, however, is not entirely clear cut. Sectional groups promote ideas which are only indirectly related to their sectional interest. The RSL, for example, espouses anti-communist policies. Other groups cannot be easily classified. Is a feminist organisation sectional, promotional or both? The Festival of Light and the Right to Life organisations are clearly promotional, yet their membership largely overlaps with that of a sectional group—the churches. Being sectional is no guarantee of greater influence. Some business organisations are important insiders but others, such as those representing small business, are not. So the sectional/promotional typology needs to be handled with care.

Whether an organisation is local, State, national or international is a third possible distinction between pressure groups. There are 'grass roots' organisations, deliberately unstructured, which reject the notion of larger hierarchies. They are solely concerned with local action. Traditionally, however, many local action groups concerned with the regional environment or development will join State-wide or even national networks. Conservation groups, for example, organise at local and national levels. Other groups are solely national or even global. The Australian branches of Amnesty International and Greenpeace are part of international organisations, as is the Catholic Church (Willets 1982).

Most major Australian pressure groups are national organisations. Local affiliates belong to a State branch, and these branches send delegates to a federal council. There are State organisations of dairy farmers, manufacturers and schoolteachers, and these come together in structures such as the Australian Teachers Federation. These national —in truth federal—organisations tend to be based in Canberra (Canberra Development Board 1985). The State branch does business with the State government, leaving the federal branch to deal with Commonwealth politicians and departments. The Canberra office is specifically political in activities, while State branches spend much of their time providing professional or welfare services to their members. In the case of the RSL, for example, State branches care for the non-political interests of members, while the national office lobbies the federal government on issues such as foreign and defence policy (Kristianson 1966; Sekuless 1986).

These federal organisations may themselves join together under the umbrella of a peak structure. The Australian Council of Trade Unions, the Business Council of Australia and the National Farmers Federation are aggregates of sectional interests.

National representation has become the key to participation in tripartite agreements. Employers, manufacturers and other business associations, for example, combined in 1977 to form the Confederation of Australian Industry (Loveday 1982: 54—68). In 1984 the Australian Industries Development Association merged with the Melbourne based Business Round Table to form the Business Council of Australia. The National Farmers Federation, prominent in organising opposition to the Hawke government, was formed in 1979 through an amalgamation of the Australian Farmers Federation, the Australian Woolgrowers and Graziers Council, and the Australian Wool and Meat Producers

Federation (Smith and Harman 1981). The oldest of the peak organ-
isations, the Australian Council of Trade Unions, was formed in 1927
(Hagan 1981). It has recently widened its base through the incorporation
of white collar groups such as the Australian Council of Salaried and
Professional Associations and the Council of Australian Government
Employee Organisations (Rawson 1986: 41–45).

Increased size means more resources. By 1984 the ACTU could
afford to employ nineteen 'specialist staff' (Rawson 1986: 42). Growth,
however, is not without problems. The wider the membership, the
more likely is disagreement over policy matters. Business organisations,
for example, may be sharply divided over tariff policy. Size can also
instill caution. Peak business organisations are usually reluctant to
attack the government, for hostility reduces capacity to bargain over
wages or protection. Smaller and more ideologically inclined groups
such as the Australian Federation of Employers, however, are more
forthright in their opinions. During 1986 and 1987 the AFE was critical
of both the Hawke government and the large business organisations
for not 'taking a stand'.

Policy Communities

Almost by definition, pressure groups are not concerned with the
whole range of government policy. They are interested in particular
policy areas, and become involved in the issues, inquiries and initiatives
within that specialised field. Over time, working relationships build up
between pressure groups and the relevant State and federal government
departments. Pressure group leaders get to know the government
officials. Indeed leaders and officials may serve together on advisory
committees and councils. The circulation of elites sees experienced
pressure group bureaucrats moving into government service, and former
public servants being employed by the pressure groups. In many policy
fields those involved, government and non-government alike, share a
common professional and educational background. Health department
officials, the AMA, general practitioners and specialists may all work
within the values of a medical training. This can be reinforced by a
professional association which holds conferences and regular meetings.

Collectively these officials and leaders form a policy community
(Pross 1986: 96–107; Jordan 1981). They are a group with a common
interest in a particular policy field. As well as pressure group activists
and government officials, the policy community may include ministers,
parliamentarians, independent consultants and journalists. The policy
community shares a commitment to policies, programs and ways of
doing things. Perhaps the best known policy communities in Australia

are in the regulation of employment and wages—the industrial relations club (Henderson 1983a)—and in agriculture, where government departments act for their 'clients', the private sector farmers (Richmond 1980; Warhurst 1982a). Other policy communities include the ex-services policy field and education (see Crisp 1975a).

Henderson has offered a classic description of the highly institutionalised policy community dealing with industrial relations:

> Industrial relations in Australia takes place in a club-like atmosphere.
> The Club's high priests preside on the Conciliation and Arbitration Commission. The majority of members of the IR Club are Melbourne-based; those who are not have reciprocal rights. The key IR institutions are located in Melbourne—the Commission, Industrial Registry, Australian Council of Trade Unions (ACTU), Confederation of Australian Industry (CAI) and (until recently) the Department of Industrial Relations. The National Labour Consultative Council (NLCC) consists of representatives from union and employer peak councils as well as public servants. It provides advice to the government of the day on virtually all matters relating to industrial relations. The Industrial Relations Society (which exists in all States as well as in the ACT and the Northern Territory) acts as a focal point for Club activities. At its many and varied functions can be found members of employer and employee organisations, public servants, academics, journalists and industrial lawyers—all of whom have a vested interest in the perpetuation of the system (Henderson 1983a: 21).

Not all policy communities are so cohesive or conspicuous. Though the community agrees on the survival of existing institutional arrangements, members do not lose sight of their particular interests. Within the framework of the policy community they will fight for favourable policies, oppose rivals, do deals and contest the rules. A policy community does not mark the end of politics in a particular field; rather it provides agreement between competing interests on common values and a framework for negotiation. A policy community can also be, as Adam Smith noted of businessmen who confer, 'a conspiracy against the public'.

Policy communities segment policy making. Departments and groups join together to defend their turf. They wish to preserve existing ways of determining policy and protect current programs and levels of spending. Such policy communities reinforce a lack of co-ordination in government. Departments use pressure groups to reinforce their position in bureaucratic disputes. The weight of pressure group influence and expertise can be thrown behind departmental claims for funds. Indeed some commentators blame pressure groups for the inability of governments to make coherent policy:

Governance requires that a national, coherent view and scale of priorities be achieved. The multiple subdivision of groups and the proliferation of functional and technical specialities has complicated, perhaps overwhelmed, the capacity of the public choice system to perform this task. However cooperative particular groups, or groups of groups may be, their disposal along vertical hierarchies and their horizontal proliferation complicates, perhaps transforms, the task of achieving concerted action toward common national problems (Marsh 1983a: 439).

In Government Service

Governments need pressure groups. If they do not exist it is necessary to invent them, as the Whitlam government did when it funded the creation of the Australian Federation of Consumer Organisations. Pressure groups bridge the gap between interests and governments. They can tell a government what their constituency is thinking about an issue. They can help government assess the consequences of an action—will a proposal be popular or unpopular, practical or impractical? Pressure groups can include a large number of producers such as the Apple and Pear Growers Association, or a large number of welfare recipients such as the RSL; such groups become a valuable source of statistical information, providing evidence which government could only obtain by itself through expensive and time consuming surveys. When the Industry Assistance Commission inquires into a particular type of manufacturing, it contacts the appropriate industry association and convinces its leaders that it is in their members' best interests to appear.

Governments also need the public support of group leaders to influence policy community opinion. To this end governments establish advisory committees. Group leaders can participate, but they can also be gathered and persuaded by governments about the wisdom of planned policy. If government is convincing, group leaders can then spread the word. They may even force acceptance of the government proposal on their membership. The ACTU leadership served an essential function for the Hawke government by insisting that member unions observe the terms of the Accord. Governments prefer to deal with one group rather than several in the same field. This makes communications easier and ensures that a busy ministry is dealing with a group which can 'deliver'. A pressure group's credibility depends on its capacity to reach agreement which members will honour.

Governments delegate responsibility for the implementation of policy to credible groups. Regulation of fields such as medicine and law is largely left to the profession. Through control of courses of study and bodies to judge professional conduct, doctors and lawyers maintain their domain outside the direct control of the state. Fields such as advertising and broadcasting aim at similar self regulation. They argue that their professional body is now strong and honest enough to keep its members honest without the need for government intervention. Governments may also fund groups to help implementation of programs such as job creation schemes and drug awareness campaigns. Just as self regulation is a cost-effective way of dealing with a policy community, so using voluntary organisations as part of the policy implementation is an efficient way of reaching intended beneficiaries. The result, however, may make central co-ordination of policy more difficult. Governments cannot simultaneously delegate and control.

Pressure Groups and Government

Group—Bureaucracy Relations

Pressure groups lobby the bureaucracy because it is central to the policy making process. This creates a relationship with advisory, executive and representative consequences.

The Commonwealth bureaucracy has instituted advisory procedures for dealing with pressure groups, particularly those concerned with economic and industrial portfolios (Matthews 1983; Loveday 1982: 69–90). From the mid-1950s, Menzies invited pressure group representatives onto advisory bodies. The Whitlam government formed a Manufacturing Industries Advisory Council and a number of subsidiary industry advisory panels for specific sectors. The practice of regular consultation between producer groups, government, unions and the relevant departments was continued by the Fraser and Hawke governments.

Such councils and committees generally meet quarterly to discuss policy issues with bureaucrats and the occasional minister. While not direct representatives of pressure groups, members will have been recommended by industry interests. Pressure groups will also play a part in the nomination of individuals to sit on important government advisory bodies such as the Industries Assistance Commission (Warhurst 1982a). Without this concession, governments may not be able to secure the co-operation of interest groups. In return, governments can bestow a form of patronage to reward or admonish individuals and organisations.

In the primary industries, pressure groups contribute directly to the executive function through their participation in marketing boards. While 'grower' representatives are usually elected, there are cases, such as the Australian Wool Corporation and the Australian Wine

Board, where the industry organisations themselves actually select representatives (Matthews 1980: 461). These boards control the marketing of these products locally and overseas, and attempt to protect the interests of producers.

Pressure groups also serve a representative function. They make submissions on behalf of individual members to departments and to public inquiries on behalf of the association. When an inquiry is considering the future of a policy field, these representations can have a significant influence on outcomes. Most of the substantial submissions to IAC inquiries came from associations, which are able to represent those most directly affected by policy decisions.

Making representation, however, is an expensive business. It requires expertise in the field and an understanding of the government's policy options. For those who can afford it, there are two common methods for preparing submissions. An association may choose to concentrate its resources in Canberra with a professionally staffed national headquarters. The National Farmers Federation, for example, has impressive offices only a few blocks from the federal parliament and the Department of Primary Industry. The federation's officers, by dint of accumulated experience and often from a background in the public service, know the policy making processes. When the need arises they can identify the proximate decision makers and the locus of discussions, and lobby accordingly.

An alternative used by many pressure groups is to hire a private lobbyist on a contract basis. Lobbyists can refine submissions, appear before inquiries, arrange introductions or merely maintain a watching brief. Such services do not come cheaply. While some Canberra lobbyists are prepared to tackle almost any topic, others now specialise, mostly in tariff and industry assistance matters (Sekuless 1984; Beauchamp 1986). The Combe–Ivanov Affair in 1983 highlighted the increased importance of lobbying as part of the policy process. It was alleged that the relationship between lobbyist David Combe and Soviet diplomat Valery Ivanov posed a security threat (Marr 1984). The Hawke government subsequently introduced compulsory registration of lobbyists (Department of Special Minister of State 1983).

Patterns of Incorporation

Some pressure groups are much closer to the bureaucracy than others. A study of advisory committees for the Royal Commission on Commonwealth Government Administration (1976) revealed that 'more than four-fifths of all groups represented on advisory groups were producers groups; and of these almost half were business associations' (Matthews 1980: 462). Business, trade unions and farmers associations were massively overrepresented, while consumers, women, Aboriginal people and welfare recipients were virtually invisible. The distribution is little altered a decade later. The lone Australian Council of Social Services delegate at the National Economic Summit was the only person not representative of government, business, unions or the professions. This pattern of representation was confirmed by a study of federal Department of Health advisory committees. A preliminary estimate found 240 committees and working parties within the Health Department. While professional organisations had about 220 representatives on 65 different committees, 'consumer or community organisations only had 30 representatives on 23 different committees' (Australian Consumers Association et al. 1986: 2).

The Institutions of Corporatism

Though pressure groups have long been part of the decision process, only under the Hawke government did their participation become very public. This reflected Hawke's penchant for summits as an approach to policy making. The National Economic Summit of 1983 was followed by the National Tax Summit of 1985, and several lesser peaks. The approach involved gathering together community representatives to discuss a range of solutions, or draft papers, to economic and social problems nominated by the government (McEachern 1985; Kemp 1983). The process of consultation was given an institutional form with the Economic Planning Advisory Council. EPAC provides a permanent source of advice on economic policy issues from selected business, union and pressure group representatives (Singleton 1985).

The Hawke government also signed a formal contract with the trade union movement, represented by the ACTU. The Prices and Incomes Accord was initialled just before the 1983 elections. It committed the government to a wide range of economic and industry policies, though many accord provisions were subsequently renegotiated (Stilwell 1986).

These mechanisms have emphasised the role of pressure groups in governing. In some accounts the Hawke innovations are little more than an extension of the traditional incorporation of a narrow range of interest groups into Commonwealth policy formulation. Other writers perceive the emergence of an Australian corporatism. A limited number of highly centralised, highly disciplined interest groups are said to join with government in a policy making process which further diminishes the significance of parliament (the debate has been extensive—see Loveday 1984; West 1984; Jaensch and Bierbaum 1985; Stewart 1985; Gerritsen 1986).

Pressure Groups and Politics

How can pressure groups without insider access to the decision process make an impact on policy? Traditionally such interests have turned to electoral politics, petitioned the parliament or appealed to public opinion.

Electoral Politics and Policy

Insiders are involved in election campaigns, but usually through the councils of the political parties and via large campaign donations. Their members are likely to be among the candidates of the Labor, Liberal and National parties. Insider groups rarely need to 'go public'.

For outsiders, elections are a rare and important opportunity to address a wider public. Even if most single issue candidates are unsuccessful, elections enable pressure groups to attract publicity for their opinions and policy ideas. Since 1972 notable election campaigns have been mounted by—among many—the Women's Electoral Lobby (1972), the Movement Against Uranium Mining (1980), the Right to Life Association (1980), the National South-West Coalition (1983) and the Nuclear Disarmament Party (1984). These groups employ a similar strategy. They focus on a single issue or set of issues, identify the views of candidates (WEL, RTLA, MAUM) or parties (NSWC) and urge their supporters to vote accordingly, regardless of their normal party allegiance. The NDP went further and fielded its own candidates for the Senate.

Though the NDP secured a Senate quota in Western Australia, the impact of electoral campaigning by single issue groups is arguable; voters' allegiances are not easily changed (Warhurst 1983a). There can be no doubt, however, that WEL's campaign assisted the introduction of a feminist perspective on public policy within government, that the NSWC's campaign, by gaining assurances from the ALP, stopped the building of the Franklin Dam, or that the NDP success alerted the major parties to a significant voter concern. Other organisations appear to have been unsuccessful. Abortion remains legal and uranium is being both mined and exported. Other policies, however, might have evolved in the absence of MAUM and RTLA campaigns. The ALP could have removed its 'conscience vote' on the abortion issue and even greater shipments of uranium may have found their way abroad.

Pressuring the Parliament

If pressure groups cannot put their own representatives into parliament, then they must influence those who are elected. This can be done by appealing directly to the parliamentarians. Beginning with the Aboriginal

Tent Embassy in 1972, a constant stream of pressure groups and individuals have used the steps and lawns of parliament house to gain publicity for their opinions and policy demands. The tactic is not restricted to outsiders with no other avenue of influence. Groups associated with opposition parties, who for the time being cannot achieve their means by inside influence, have protested in Canberra. The farmers' rallies against the Hawke government outside parliament house drew crowds said to number 50 000, from all parts of Australia. During the Fraser years, steelworkers and coalminers went one better by storming the building itself.

There are, of course, other ways to exert pressure within the parliament. Lobbying MPs, organising petitions and making submissions to parliamentary committees are standard techniques for attracting the attention of politicians. Petitions are still remarkably popular and are treated with proper pomp and ceremony by the parliament, though in a world of word processors, mass produced letters and petitions may lack credibility. Politicians themselves seek to influence their peers by forming chapters of pressure groups within the parliament. There is an Amnesty International parliamentary group, for example, and many MPs become patrons of community and interest groups.

Agenda Setting and Public Opinion

There is no direct correlation between public opinion and public policy. Governments may bow to majority opinion if they feel an issue could cost them votes at the next election. Should they suspect that the majority is transitory, or could not be translated into votes, then a government may dismiss the findings of opinion research. Nevertheless polls are becoming an integral part of policy framing; there is the risk that 'today's leaders may be merely spinning like weathervanes with shifts in public opinion, or attending to their televised image rather than to the substance of government' (Mills 1986: 13).

Pressure groups devote considerable energy and resources to demonstrate that public opinion supports their own opinions and ought to influence policy makers. Politicians find it difficult to gauge community thinking on an issue, so they may be unnerved by a well organised campaign. Accordingly, pressure groups concentrate on creating and parading public opinion.

Organising a protest is the traditional technique for demonstrating support. Marching for a cause is the lasting image of the protest movements of the 1960s, and remains a standard form of pressuring politicians. The Vietnam Moratorium Movement probably hastened the withdrawal of Australian troops, though the link between opinion and policy is not straightforward (King 1983). Such a labour-intensive form of action is suited to groups with a large following but few financial resources.

Groups attempt to create public opinion. The National Farmers Federation, for example, began a $10 million advertising campaign during 1986 to promote the contribution made by farmers to the Australian economy. The NFF cited as its inspiration a long running campaign by the Australian Mining Council to promote its industry as 'the backbone of the country'. From organising letters to the editor to carefully targeted direct mailings, pressure groups seek to create a climate of opinion favourable to their cause.

One of the most important of these public relation techniques has become the use of professional polls. If a pressure group feels public opinion is on its side, then it will engage a professional pollster to test the electorate. If favourable, the results will be presented to the government and released to the media. The NSWC commissioned a poll during its anti-dam campaign, as did the Australian Uranium Producers Forum during the uranium controversy (Hills 1986) and the Australian Teachers Federation following cuts to 'English as a second language' courses in the 1986 budget. In the age of machine politics, pressure groups understand the significance of popularity polls in shaping government choices (Mills 1986).

Parties and Pressure Groups

Parties and pressure groups contribute to policy making on behalf of those who organise. Such groups do not speak with equal voices. Their uneven influence is a cause—and a reflection—of the distribution of power within Australian society. Some parts of that society cannot organise at all. This is a factor, though not the most important, in the interests of minorities such as the unemployed, the homeless and the poor being relatively neglected by public policies.

The influence of a party or pressure group reflects the significance of those it represents and the resources available for action. Those without money must use their ingenuity and their numerical strength to act collectively through the ballot box or on the street.

The effect of pressure groups is to make public policy more responsive though less coherent. Pressure groups represent partial views, and political parties are collections of interests with only limited integration as a coherent package. Party factions and policy communities making sectional demands accentuate the problem of policy co-ordination. When those demands are translated into new agencies and departments, policy making is further divided, and the public sector further fragmented.

104   *Public Policy in Australia*

If government actions are unco-ordinated and the interests of policy communities dominate major fields, then inertia may result. Olson argues that the relative economic decline of Australia and New Zealand can be traced to the web of interest groups controlling markets, stifling competition and preventing change (Olson 1982: 132–36). Beer has coined the term 'pluralistic stagnation' to describe problems of policy making caused by special interest groups (Beer 1980, 1982), while local observers have questioned 'whether Australia too, might be suffering from an excess of pluralism' (Marsh 1983a: 433). The problem is finding 'policy making structures that are capable of reconciling interest groups to public purposes' (Marsh 1983b: 53).

Further Reading

Jaensch, Dean (1983) *The Australian Party System* Sydney: Allen & Unwin.
Loveday, Peter (1982) *Promoting Industry* University of Queensland Press.
Marsh, Ian (1983) 'Politics, Policy Making and Pressure Groups: some suggestions for reform of the Australian political system' *Australian Journal of Public Administration* 42, 4, pp. 433–58.
Matthews, Trevor (1980) 'Australian Pressure Groups' in Heny Mayer and Helen Nelson (eds) *Australian Politics: a fifth reader* Melbourne: Longman Cheshire.
Pross, A. Paul (1986) *Group Politics and Public Policy* Toronto: Oxford University Press.
Richardson, J.J. and Jordan, A.G. (1979) *Governing Under Pressure: the policy process in a post-parliamentary democracy* Oxford: Martin Robertson.
Warhurst, John (1983) 'Single-Issue Politics: the impact of conservation and anti-abortion groups' *Current Affairs Bulletin* 60, pp. 19–31.

Part 2

THE POLICY PROCESS

6

Approaches to Decision Making

Part 2

THE POLICY PROCESS

6
Approaches to Decision Making

In political activity, according to the conservative philosopher Michael Oakeshott, we 'sail a boundless and bottomless sea; there is neither harbour for shelter nor floor for anchorage, neither starting-place nor appointed destination. The enterprise is to keep afloat on an even keel' (Oakeshott 1962: 127).

Oakeshott's image captures the contingent nature of political activity, but not the complexity of institutions through which politics operates. Managing a boat is a relatively straightforward business, for vessels are divided neatly into functions and co-ordinated by a clear chain of command. The Australian state is not so simple, for its parts are dispersed and diffuse. It is not a logically ordered set of institutions, but an 'amorphous mass of interlocking organisations attempting to provide for the many public service demands of a modern industrial society' (Burch and Wood 1983: 41). State institutions disagree or overlap, pursue different understandings of policy objectives and obstruct unacceptable choice. As a result, policy making is 'inherently difficult, frustrating and only partly effective' (Burch and Wood 1983: 41).

The fragmentation of the state makes it difficult to identify a single 'decision making process'. Choices are made at a number of levels by different agencies. Theoretically it is cabinet which has the final say, bestowing legitimacy on 'policy'. In practice, government agencies must make administrative decisions about the allocation of resources, and may maintain or expand programs without cabinet review. Policy can be automatic, determined by economic models of cause and effect which operate without ministerial supervision. So government is not always involved in the choices made by its agencies. There is inevitably discretion in the decision process. Departments and statutory authorities negotiate policy. They stay within broad guidelines determined by cabinet, but decide for themselves the details and arrangements of policy implementation.

Problems vary, so general assertions about the policy process can be difficult to sustain. Some choices are predictable and routine. They can be handled through established procedure without reference to cabinet.

A problem such as AIDS, however, may emerge quite suddenly, and require decisions long before adequate information is available. If there is no obvious solution, existing policies for similar problems may be extended to cope with the new difficulty. Should these fail, policy makers must experiment on the run, dreaming up new procedures until they control—or are overwhelmed by—the crisis.

In a system of cabinet government, departments often disagree about the dimensions, jurisdiction and possible solutions to a problem. Recommendations may be challenged at interdepartmental committees, by other agencies, or within the party room. Cabinet government encourages bargaining, compromise and retreat to defensible suggestions. Policy procedures change with the importance of the problem, the haste with which a decision is required and the likely reaction of interested parties.

Theories of Policy

Problems vary. Policy formation is inevitably different across state institutions. Yet there is still a tendency in public policy literature to generalise about—or lament the lack of—a 'policy process'. This perhaps reflects dissatisfaction with the ad hoc nature of many decisions which emerge from government. It is a familiar Australian complaint that the apparent chaos of Parliament House produces rushed and ill-considered choices based on immediate electoral advantage, rather than a long term 'national interest'.

An inchoate suspicion that there should be more method in the madness has inspired government inquiries and academic reviews to investigate ways of improving the policy process. Recommendations accept that ministers, and not bureaucrats, should be the final decision makers, responsible to parliament. They suggest, however, that the introduction of systematic bureaucratic procedures might produce more coherent policy. Solutions advocated range from the establishment of priorities review staff to complete planning of state activity.

Australian governments have experimented with various suggestions for new policy procedures. Some, including central scrutiny of new policy proposals, proved useful management tools. Others, such as forward budget estimates, created additional work to no end. Yet even successful policy techniques are still subject to political judgement. Governments abandon rules which restrict their range of choices. While ministers are happy to listen to priorities review staff assessments of rival departments, they will ignore or oppose advice about their own. Long term financial strategies have been adopted to restrain government spending and to lower the balance of payments. Should electoral pressure become paramount, however, governments spend anyway. Policies are guided by electoral concerns, not 'rational' solutions.

Nonetheless, there remain optimists who believe the policy process can be made more systematic. Decisions go awry, they suggest, because 'meddlesome' politics interferes with the process of carefully considered, skilfully analysed, policy formulation. What Australia needs are more formal policy procedures which use objective techniques to improve choices. Implicit is the assumption that a better *process* will produce better *policy* (see, for example, Frazer 1986).

The debate over policy formulation techniques draws on an international literature about decision making theory. The argument centres on normative models of policy making. Is there a common technique which will aid decision making and enhance public policy? How successful have such procedures been in practice? For these models of the decision process are more than academic constructs; they affect how organisations try to tackle problems. Choice models offer policy process prescriptions. They reject ad hoc decision practice and hold out instead the bright hope of better policy.

Rational Models

The debate about prescriptive decision models precedes the discipline of public policy. Key arguments were first articulated in American public administration journals of the 1930s, when aspirations for 'scientific management' were criticised by those who perceived limits to human rationality.

Herbert Simon, in the second edition of his influential *Administrative Behaviour* (1957), was drawn to those early hopes for a 'rational' approach to decision making. He also recognised the practical constraints on any such procedures. In theory Simon wanted goals to be specified, all alternatives measured and compared, and a choice made which would maximise an organisation's objectives. He acknowledged, however, that administrators have limited ability to compare options, and may not be able to identify with certainty the 'correct' decision. As a compromise, Simon developed a 'behaviour alternative model' premised on 'bounded rationality'. *Satisficing* relaxed the criteria for a successful policy. Because means and ends are not always clear, decision makers should accept the limits of their situation, seek through approximation to identify the consequences of various alternatives, and choose policies which at least satisfy, if not maximise, organisational goals.

Simon's satisficing proposal acknowledged limits in the application of scientific method to organisational choice. Most writers shared his pessimism about the prospects for order and rationality in decision making. Some, however, continued to discuss an ideal procedure for choice. This prescription for a perfect technique of decision making became known as the *rational comprehensive* model—rational because it follows a logical, ordered sequence, and *comprehensive* because it canvasses, assesses and compares all options.

There are six basic steps common to rational–comprehensive models:

1 A problem must be identified.
2 The values, goals and objectives of the decision maker must be determined and ranked in order of priority.
3 All the options for achieving the goals must be identified.
4 The costs and benefits of each option must be determined.
5 Costs and benefits must be compared.
6 On the basis of this comparison, the rational decision maker selects the course of action which maximises the outcome in line with the values, goals and objectives identified in step 2.

Faithfully followed, this process will produce a 'rational' outcome by selecting the most effective means of achieving an end. It breaks down decision making into phases, introduces technical criteria for comparing options, and provides a single answer which is logical and can be defended.

The difficulties with this method are numerous. Problems are not always clearly defined, values and goals may conflict, all options may not be identified, time and resources for analysis may be limited, and the techniques for comparison may be crude and unreliable. Further, there are impediments of co-ordination. The rational comprehensive model is based on the metaphor of an individual making a choice. In practice, complex decisions emerge from an involved process incorporating bureaucrats, interest groups and politicians. The scope for disagreement, differing emphasis or just misunderstanding about values, goals and choice of means is considerable. Extensive co-ordination is required, for unless agreement in stage 2 is absolute, the outcome will not be 'rational' for some participants. The more consultation the process requires, the more difficult becomes the prerequisite of consensus about objectives and values. Indeed Dye notes that 'there are so many barriers to rational decision making that it rarely takes place at all in government. Yet the model remains important for analytic purposes because it helps to identify barriers to rationality. It assists in posing the question: Why is policy making not a more rational process?' (Dye 1978: 31).

The rational comprehensive technique has only limited applicability for public policy. Though there are now statistical models which assign weights to variables and quantify options, complex comparative devices often disguise value judgements; such techniques are 'neither neutral nor necessarily benevolent instruments' (Schaffer 1977: 147). Peter

Self's *The Econocrats* (1975) indicated problems for economic models when policies are not sufficiently specified, nor values made explicit. In particular, he noted the limits of one standard technique, cost benefit analysis (CBA). His exposition and examples indicated how models which look detailed, thorough and objective in fact are based on arbitrary values and guesses. To evaluate the cost and benefit of particular sites for a future third London airport, 'econocrats' had to include in their model figures for a Norman church and the breeding grounds for a flock of brent geese. Such valuations can only be subjective. CBA and similar techniques offer the appearance but not the substance of rationality. Assigning weights to variables may be no more than rule of thumb guesstimates.

Recent Tasmanian experience indicates how elaborate modelling can be polemical rather than analytical. Experts did not agree about the costs and benefits of a proposed dam on the Franklin River. The Hydro-Electricity Commission and the Wilderness Society both constructed 'scientific'—but totally contradictory—costings for the proposed project. Both valuations were based on 'objective' techniques, and were complete to several decimal points. Pressure groups understood that the authority of figures outweighs mere opinion. These models were produced for political consumption. They aimed to legitimate—as much as to help formulate—a particular policy.

Concerns about the impartiality of analytical techniques raise two central problems for the rational comprehensive model. The first is internal: if complex options cannot be compared accurately, then the model loses its virtue of rationality. When valuations are approximate, the final choice is not necessarily the single superior option.

The second limitation reflects the substance of policy problems. Choices are not always about technical criteria. Ethical considerations are often involved. The cost of preserving the Franklin wilderness area cannot be precisely compared to the benefits of more hydroelectric power. The price of electricity and construction may be quantified and to some extent the opportunity costs of not proceeding can be calculated. The worth of a wilderness area, however, or of an archaeological site, is an individual judgement. Techniques for accurate comparison do not, and will not, exist. Intangibles such as aesthetic pleasure or historical significance cannot be reduced to reliable figures. When we list our values at step 2 of the rational comprehensive procedure we have already made our choice.

Despite such major shortcomings, commentators on the rational comprehensive model argue that it remains a goal worth aspiring to, 'an ideal, a target at which to aim' (Burch and Wood 1983: 25). The rational comprehensive model may not describe the reality of most public policy formulation, but it does describe the only 'scientific' approach to making choices.

A second best solution, however, is not always achieved by the same method. In neo-classical economics a perfect market is said to achieve ideal allocation of resources. On the other hand, a market which fails to clear can produce a serious misallocation. Its outcome may be inferior to results achieved through state intervention. So too, there are problems with assuming that a decision process which approximates —but falls short of—perfect rationality will still be superior to other techniques for choice. Bargaining may produce an agreement which is electorally—rather than technically—rational. An informed guess can produce the same result, while saving considerable search and time costs. Either may prevent the unanticipated consequences of a 'nearly rational' choice.

There are important constraints, then, on using the rational comprehensive model as a basis for public policy choices. These are not just abstract methodological flaws. They suggest considerable dangers in proceeding along scientific lines. Decisions may only include variables which can be quantified. Technical rationality may be given precedence over ethical concerns.

There are also limitations within the model itself. The cost of undertaking a comprehensive comparison of all options, for example, may be greater than the savings which result from making the right decision. Sunk costs or previous decisions may preclude the best option. Decision makers can never be certain that *all* values and options have been identified, compared and ranked. Solutions to a problem may be infinite. 'The model seems to commit the decision maker to the endless search for the best possible decision and in that sense it appears a recipe for paralysis' (Emy 1976: 36).

Incrementalism

Economist Charles Lindblom found the rational comprehensive model a poor guide to the reality of most decision making, for it preached what few practised. Seeking a more accurate description of policy formulation, Lindblom returned to Simon's notion of satisficing— decision making through approximation. In his key 1959 article 'The Science of "Muddling Through"', a title suggested by an editor of *Public Administration Review*, Lindblom reworked Simon's concepts to offer an alternative model. Policy, he argued, proceeds by increment. Perhaps appropriately, this model of 'successive limited comparisons' has been modified and refined by Lindblom over two decades, though it is still usually known by the original title of *incrementalism*.

Lindblom noted that in making a decision, means and ends are not always distinct and that there is rarely the time, resources or inclination to conduct a comprehensive search. Further, Lindblom observed that the test of a good policy is not whether it is rational, but whether it is acceptable to participants. From these axioms Lindblom outlined his notion of policy proceeding by increment.

Faced with a problem, the decision maker reaches for the familiar by suggesting some variation on existing practices. If the variation satisfies participants then the problem is solved. If not, the decision maker moves to the next most familiar solution, always proceeding through comparison of existing policy with possible marginal alterations. The process continues until an acceptable answer is agreed—though in practice problems change or are superseded, rather than solved. Incrementalism offers not the definitive, justifiable, single answer of the rational comprehensive technique, but a series of small steps which continually experiment by modifying and improving policy. The incremental process, claimed Lindblom, characterises most public policy formulation. Even when social engineers attempt radical policy departures, such as constructing satellite towns or planning economies, they eventually rely on incrementalism to overcome unforeseen consequences and problems of implementation.

Few observers have difficulty with Lindblom's contention that our normal method of problem solving is to modify existing practice rather than start from scratch with each new difficulty. Less persuasive, however, has been Lindblom's claim that incrementalism is not just a valid description of how governments and bureaucracies make choices, but also a good prescription for policy formulation. Lindblom argued that incrementalism has the advantages of being both simple and practical, since it could cope with uncertainty, and of being flexible since it allows policy changes to be reversed should they prove unsuccessful. Further, Lindblom asserted that incrementalism is essentially democratic since it encourages bargaining, can accommodate change and avoids the 'serious lasting mistakes' which might result from fundamental decisions taken on the basis of rational comprehensive planning. It enables governments to adjust ends to available means. He argued that in the face of multiple pressures, the best test of a policy is the degree of agreement it commands.

By 1965 Lindblom had discovered an additional virtue for incrementalism. In *The Intelligence of Democracy*, he proposed an explanation for apparently coherent outcomes emerging from a diffuse decision making process. *Partisan mutual adjustment* suggested that even in a decentralised state, various autonomous participants still affect one another, and adjust to each other's actions. Acting incrementally, they can react to changes in the environment and modify their own policies accordingly. Like the 'invisible hand' of Adam Smith guiding a market, partisan mutual adjustment 'will achieve a coordination superior to an attempt at central coordination, which is often so complex as to lie beyond any coordinator's competence' (Lindblom 1979: 523).

If some order can arise from apparent chaos, so too progressive outcomes can result from a disjointed, ad hoc decision making process. While attempts at sweeping reform often fail, significant change can be achieved through a succession of small steps. Indeed, advancing reform through trial and modification, while hardly idealistic, may produce more substantive and lasting change. The growth of state welfare services since the second world war, for example, has been incremental rather than the result of a sustained plan.

Lindblom's claims provoked considerable controversy. Dror attacked incrementalism as an 'ideological reinforcement of the pro-inertia and anti-innovation forces prevalent in all human organisations, administrative and policy making' (Dror 1964: 155). Incrementalism, he argued, could only work in a stable, pluralist society with relative consensus about goals and acceptable means. Accepted uncritically, it could be very dangerous 'since it offers a "scientific" rationalisation for inertia and conservatism' (Dror 1968: 145). Goodin conceded that incrementalism characterised most policy making, but labelled the doctrine 'perverse and pervasive' because it disguised the value judgements underlying the incremental choices of decision makers (Goodin 1982: 19).

Other critics suggested that incrementalism favours the already dominant and may only produce circular movement. It assumes not a pluralist society, but the existence of a 'pluralist policy process' in which privileged groups can maintain dominance because major reforms are impeded. For incrementalism to work there must be elites which can test policies and make technical adjustments. As a theory incrementalism lacks explanatory power; it can make sense of marginal changes to existing programs, but it can not account for radical departures from traditional practice—why governments move into new policy areas or abolish entire programs. Though Medibank undoubtedly developed incrementally, this is no explanation for government intervention in health insurance.

Reconciling Rationality and Incrementalism?

A number of theorists sought to overcome objections within the two dominant prescriptions for policy making. While Yehezkel Dror hoped to reformulate the rational comprehensive tradition, Amitai Etzioni offered a *mixed scanning model* combining a comprehensive overview with incrementally determined policy details.

Despite his criticisms of incrementalism, Dror recognised that the rational comprehensive model of decision making was impractical. 'With a few exceptions (some very important)' he conceded, 'pure rationality policymaking is in fact impossible. The exceptions are problems that are susceptible to quantification' (Dror 1968: 133). Dror proposed instead an *optimal model* which could combine rational and 'extra-rational' (intuitive) components (Dror 1968: 154). A decision maker should examine a problem, clarify objectives, survey the major alternative approaches and then decide whether greater benefits would accrue by proceeding incrementally or through a conscious strategy of innovation. If innovation is chosen, then the major options identified from experience, literature and experts should be explored and compared. Over time new decision structures could be established to take advantage of knowledge gained through experiments, so that experts are given more input and change is institutionalised.

Etzioni chose a somewhat different tack in his attempt to reconcile the practicality of incrementalism with the comprehensive advantages of a rational approach. He first distinguished between fundamental decisions establishing the broad framework of goals in a policy area, and incremental choices used to fill in the details. Etzioni evoked the metaphor of a 1960s weather satellite to explain how 'mixed scanning' would work. A wide angle lens covers all parts of the sky, though not in great detail, while a second camera zeroes in on areas identified by the first as requiring more study. If fundamental decisions are made on rational criteria, and then details decided incrementally, the resulting mixed scanning policy making would be 'more realistic and more effective than its components' (Etzioni 1967: 390).

Twenty years later over fifty articles and doctoral theses have been written on mixed scanning. It is being used as the basis of a computer program to simulate decision variables. Empirical research on the practical applications of the technique, however, is still lacking (Etzioni 1986: 13).

In fact neither Dror's nor Etzioni's formulations overcame the substantial objections to the rational comprehensive model originally raised by Lindblom. Each relied on being able to determine rationally at least broad priorities. Both still assumed that problems are clear, objectives can be separated, and that technical expertise will be able to identify— and accurately assess—possible solutions. In practice, Dror could not say how a decision maker should decide whether a problem required an incremental or innovative synoptic approach. Etzioni also failed to clarify a technique for distinguishing between fundamental and incremental decisions, and did not specify how his mixed scanner would react if incremental practice worked against the values embodied in the rationally determined framework. Neither seriously addressed the problem of assigning weights to conflicting variables, though Etzioni asserted that 'an informal scaling of values is not as difficult as incrementalists imagine' (1967: 390). Rather than synthesise, Dror and Etzioni only demonstrated that the two models of decision making cannot be reconciled.

Problems Combining the Rational and the Incremental

The divergence between policy making prescriptions reflects two very different notions about what constitutes a problem. For rationalists a problem can be specified and separated—at least for the purpose of analysis—from its social context. Then, given the application of logic, a single optimal solution can be proposed. The technique is universal, and so valid for all government agencies and policy processes. The world becomes an equation where even multifaceted difficulties can be addressed provided all variables are understood and represented in the correct sequence. This extension of the scientific model assumes that objectivity is possible in comparing options, and that problems are discrete and solvable; implementation will settle the matter, not raise new difficulties.

The incrementalist school expressed doubts about the intellectual validity and practical application of any rational comprehensive technique. Problems do not arise one at a time, but are interconnected so that to ameliorate one may be to aggravate another. Causal links cannot always be established, so a technically rational solution may have disastrous, unanticipated consequences. Much public policy does not deal with puzzles which can be solved, but with intractable social problems. One can never offer an 'answer' to poverty, for definitions alter with material conditions, just as expectations about what constitutes adequate public housing, health care or education have changed over time. The alternative proposed by Lindblom recognised problems as contingent, information as imperfect and analysis as incomplete. Incrementalism was designed for a polity where values are challenged and policies altered to reflect a volatile electorate.

Later Debates

The rational comprehensive and incrementalist models, with their competing prescriptive claims, were well established in the literature by the late 1960s. Since then the controversy has developed little—'debate' between irreconcilable models addressing different types of problems is not very productive.

However useful for investigating discrete and quantifiable problems, rational comprehensive techniques can not overcome the limitation of being only 'partially rational'. Lindblom, meanwhile, accepted the need for a 'synoptic overview' of policy problems outside the normal operation of incrementalism. He proposed a notion of 'strategic analysis' which used formal analytical techniques, though in a manner which 'short cut the conventionally comprehensive "scientific" analysis' (Lindblom 1979: 518).

Lindblom also acknowledged a weakness in his prescriptive claims. Partisan mutual adjustment assumed some form of structured pluralism, with interests which bargain and can adjust to the decisions of others. Yet pluralist processes are biased in favour of particular interests. It means that large business corporations can dictate unwelcome and non-incremental change for less powerful groups. A cartel supplying essential services, for example, can impose price increases on disorganised consumers who have no collective voice; without government intervention pluralism becomes very one sided. In an unequal world, not all change is voluntary or progressing toward a 'better' policy.

Further, not all issues are treated as policy 'problems' which can be subjected to adjustment and incremental change. Society is structured by norms and values, such as the right in a capitalist economy to own property. There is a homogeneity of ideological opinion, a set of prevailing beliefs and values which keep 'grand issues' outside the agenda. Lindblom described this domination by ruling concepts as a 'failure of the competition of ideas'. In *Politics and Markets* (1977) he concluded that such ideologies are not neutral, but favour the interests of key social actors.

Non-decisions

These later arguments over the distribution of power and its impact on the policy process draw on British and American debates about *non-decisions*. Bachrach and Baratz defined the non-decision process as operating 'when the dominant values, the accepted rules of the game, the existing power relations among groups, and the instruments of force, singly or in combination, effectively prevent certain grievances from developing into full-fledged issues which call for decisions' (Bachrach and Baratz 1963: 641). A similar perspective was developed by E.E. Schattschneider in *The Semi-Sovereign People* (1960). He argued that 'all forms of political organisation have a bias in favour of the exploitation of some kinds of conflict and the suppression of others because organization is the mobilization of bias. Some issues are organized into politics while others are organized out' (Schattschneider 1960: 71). For Schattschneider the definition of alternatives is the supreme instrument of power, and those who can determine what debate is about run the country. Non-decision making then is more than declining to choose; it is about keeping issues out of discussion altogether.

It is hardly controversial to suggest that power to influence decisions is not evenly spread, or that public attention favours some topics over others. There are serious problems, however, with non-decision making theories and their assumption that an elite can manipulate the issues of politics. Polsby has pointed to difficulties verifying any mobilisation of bias, to problems identifying how powerful interests shape the agenda, and to the possibility that a 'non-decision' may reflect a genuine consensus rather than a conspiracy of silence (Polsby 1979; see also Lukes 1974 and Bradshaw 1976).

Lindblom on Politics and Markets

The non-decision debate raised questions about power and its social context. These issues were taken up by Lindblom in his later work. Surveying decision making among western capitalist nations, Lindblom maintained that a market economy produces interests whose veto powers make 'even incremental moves difficult and insufficiently frequent' (Lindblom 1979: 520). He sought a modification to incrementalism which could offer potential for radical outcomes. This, however, did not prove easy to find. Lindblom's earlier work had already demonstrated the failure of planning based on rationalist techniques. Aware of flaws in the alternative models of decision making, Lindblom was left to advocate the rather unsatisfactory notion of muddling through more skilfully. Moving close to Etzioni's formulation, Lindblom advocated a *strategic incrementalism* which combined the advantages of disjointed incrementalism with a synoptic overview of the 'grand issues'. He wanted a competition of ideas and reform by experiment. This strategy, he suggested, had been used by liberal thinkers such as J.S. Mill, and by Chairman Mao, who emphasised the achievement of economic growth 'not by a fine-tuning of development from above but by tapping intelligence and incentives broadly through fragmentation of responsibility and the cumulation of fast-moving incremental gains' (Lindblom 1979: 524).

The arguments of *Politics and Markets* suggest a substantial shift in Lindblom's position. Gone is the optimistic tone about incrementalism and partisan mutual adjustment. It has been replaced by scepticism about the community's capacity to agree on big step policies which challenge the established order:

> ... in his early writings Lindblom was content to endorse incrementalism because of his interpretation of the US power structure in pluralistic terms. In contrast, in his later writings, Lindblom, reflecting the changing political conditions of the USA, and the accompanying challenge to pluralism within political science, explicitly acknowledges the limitations of pluralism, and is less sanguine about incrementalism (Ham and Hill 1984: 93–94).

The Limits of Modelling Through

Existing theoretical models do not provide very helpful prescriptions for decision making. The methodological problems of the rational comprehensive model, and its variants, have not been overcome; rationality is not possible if we cannot choose between competing non-quantifiable values, or if the analytical techniques for comparison of options are unreliable and incomplete. Attempts to construct 'partially rational' strategic methods of decision making assume—but cannot prove—that their outcomes are still superior to rule of thumb approximations.

Incrementalists, on the other hand, question whether any decision process could produce 'better' policy solutions. If problems are contingent, and information limited, then approximations are all that is possible. In any case, if participant acceptance is the criteria for policy success, then proceeding incrementally will throw up all options in order, for as each proves inadequate a more radical alternative must be found. 'Muddling through' can be considered a policy technique, albeit an unstructured, ad hoc and sometimes unconscious one. This is why Heclo's notion of 'puzzling' (Heclo 1974) is so persuasive. Policy makers want to do more than provide guesses, but their subjects will not stand still for long enough to allow proper evaluation of values, ends and means. Decision making is about puzzling—trying to understand a problem as much as trying to solve it.

Yet incrementalism cannot overcome systemic biases about the way public policy problems are defined and addressed. Public policy literature acknowledges the pervasiveness of incrementalist practice. Critics, including the later Lindblom, argued that proceeding through successive limited comparisons perpetuates existing distributions of power and resources. It would be a mistake to interpret this as a failure in *process*. If powerful interests structurally control the agenda, then offending policy options will be ignored. Within departments, it is impossible to force bureaucrats to stand outside pervasive social beliefs, judge that a particular interest lacks adequate access, representation or equity, and incorporate them into policy options. We cannot respond until we perceive a problem, and no comprehensive policy technique will generate demands not yet understood. The decision making process cannot correct the biases of politics.

So decision making models do not propose valid general techniques. Any policy formulation procedures based on such theoretical models will reproduce their methodological and practical limitations. Further, policy techniques which seek to impose coherence cannot be expected to prevail over electoral considerations. To the tidy minded 'public

policy appears an unplanned, disjointed and thus wasteful activity'
(Emy 1976: 38). For the political process does not approach politics in
a systematic, rational way. The emergence of a problem is often
unpredictable, issues are not addressed until they acquire political
impact, and they are often not solved, only ameliorated or recast.

The Policy Cycle

The unpredictable emergence of new issues was emphasised by Anthony
Downs in his work on ecology. Downs observed what he characterised
as an *issue attention cycle*. A problem 'suddenly leaps into prominence,
remains there for a short time, and then—though still largely unresolved
—gradually fades from the centre of public attention' (Downs 1972: 38).
The public perception of 'crises', suggested Downs, is repeated with
each issue—heightened awareness followed by boredom, a cycle which
moves through five stages.

In the first, the pre-problem stage, the issue is the concern of experts
and those involved. The problem is usually at its most acute at this
stage, while interest groups lobby for public attention.

Alarmed public discovery becomes the second stage, with sudden
pressure for action. A dramatic series of events, such as a riot, may be
the catalyst for public attention. With discovery comes confidence that
society can tackle this problem, a euphoric enthusiasm that 'things are
happening'; the problem can be resolved without any fundamental
reordering of society itself.

This leads to the third stage, the realisation of the cost of significant
progress. Addressing the problem may in fact require sacrifices by
large groups in the population. People realise that problems have
winners and losers, and that the losers may be themselves as taxpayers.

New issues emerge, and the electorate becomes frustrated, frightened
or just bored with the original problem. So the issue enters stage four,
a gradual decline in public interest. By this stage some other issue may
be entering stage two; its novelty gives it a more powerful claim on
public attention.

Finally there is the post-problem stage, the 'twilight realm of lesser
attention or spasmodic recurrences of interest' (Downs 1972: 40). The
process is not entirely without result, however, for by the final phase
agencies, programs and legislation will be established, and the problem
will be better treated than in early stages (Downs 1972: 39–41).

Not all problems, of course, go through this scenario. Yet as Downs
noted, an issue attention cycle for even some problems has implications
for public policy. It creates a series of 'crises' and so prevents sustained
attention to significant if less newsworthy problems (Downs 1972: 43).
The issue attention cycle makes it imperative for pressure groups to get

policies quickly into place, before public interest in a problem declines. Furthermore, the cycle affects the way policy is made. Problems cannot be addressed 'rationally', for means may only become available when an end is suddenly discovered. Solutions are required immediately. Even with predictable long-standing policy areas, goals will shift as bargaining or regulation highlight different aspects or favour particular interests. Though health care is a constant problem, the particular issue is ever changing. Raising the wages of nurses solves an industrial problem, but it may create budgetary difficulties, as funds are no longer available for other public health facilities.

'Garbage Can' Solutions

The frantic pace imposed by an issue attention cycle may encourage bureaucracies to offer *garbage can solutions* (Cohen, March and Olsen, 1972). Government departments and agencies have policies they would like to try. These may be old rejected cabinet submissions or new proposals dear to the hearts of senior managers. When a problem arises and options are suddenly required, an existing proposal can sometimes be passed off as the solution. It is as though a decision maker reached into a garbage bin, pulled out a problem with one hand, a policy proposal with the other, and joined the two together to proclaim the result a resolution. These are preconceived and available answers looking for questions; the solution manipulates the problem.

When the Menzies government wished to woo the Catholic vote in the 1960s, the Department of Education saw an opportunity to pursue a long-standing objective of improved secondary education. It suggested funding libraries for state and private schools—so matching an electoral need with an unrelated, but satisfactory, pre-existing solution (Hawker et al. 1979: 167). Lateral thinking, not logic, is the genesis of these public policy choices.

A rigorous, rational policy technique would no doubt aim to exclude such opportunism. To assume, however, that policy makers will objectively assess competing options to find optimal solutions is perhaps to overlook the interests and usual behaviour of institutions. Successful policy proposals bring additional resources and responsibilities. Government departments in any case are arenas for differing interpretations of the problem and disputes about answers. Arguments about conflicting values will be fought out in the bureaucracy as well as in cabinet and politicians will recognise that departmental advice may incline to favour the preferences of the departmental secretary, or disguise considerable disagreement among experts. A uniform policy procedure would be no guarantee of public service neutrality nor would it necessarily confer legitimacy on the options advocated by bureaucrats.

Developing Policy

Australian public bureaucracies develop policy options by employing experts to write position papers, by suggesting modifications to existing programs, by adopting the proposals of interest groups, royal commissions or academics, and by developing the suggestions, hints and whimsy of politicians. These options respond to, and help shape, choices. They often incorporate the findings of elaborate models—economic theorems, CBA, or the matrices of environmental impact studies (EIS). Options may also reflect the influence of new technology, particularly financial control systems and the computer analysis of information such as social security payouts.

What Australian bureaucracies have not done is to synthesise these diverse practices, models, approximations and techniques into a single, permanent, structured policy process. The complexities of public problems, and the changing demands of electoral fortunes, mean puzzle solving is tailored to particular problems. As a result, no single procedure for policy making exists. Any 'metapolicy' prescription for improving the policy process is circumscribed by limited analytical methods, difficulties in comparing values, and the problems of implementation and unintended consequences. No policy process can work in all circumstances.

Matching process with problem does not necessarily mean incoherence or an inability to learn from mistakes. As Heclo observed, 'much political interaction has constituted a process of social learning expressed through policy' (Heclo 1974: 306). In developing new policies we experiment with types of institutions, new forms of implementation and alternative techniques for evaluation. Such learning is part of the normal operation of public administration, incorporated by bureaucracies with a collective memory, becoming part of the structure of the state. The process of policy formulation cannot easily be separated from the problem being addressed, nor implementation from the structures created by, and for, the policy. We learn by doing, even if we do not recognise the lesson.

So hopes for a single 'theory' of decision making are misplaced. When the problem is distributing resources according to agreed, unambiguous specifications, then standard operating procedures for decision making are viable. When goals are contested, however, agreement can only be established through bargaining and peer evaluation. As Samuel Huntington noted about one policy field, 'military policy is not the result of deductions from a clear statement of national objectives. It is the product of the competition of purposes within individuals and groups and among individuals and groups. It is the result of politics not logic, more an arena than a unity' (Huntington 1961: 2).

Technique cannot be substituted for politics. Major public policies are the outcome of a complex game of negotiation, of expert opinion weighed against electoral imperative, of competing interests seeking to advance self-interest through a favourable choice. There are no single 'best' options for any player in this game, for the 'best' outcome depends upon what others do. The process will not be improved by insisting upon rational comprehensive or strategic incremental procedures. Rather, politics must be made more explicit in the policy process. As Wildavsky notes, 'there must be more than one alternative; they must come from more than a single source; and there must be sufficient dispersion of power in society so that competing sources of advice have a chance of being heard and acted upon' (Wildavsky 1985a: 29). Let departments, activists and ministers find the flaws in the proposals of their rivals. The best option is the one which persuades, the best policy process the one which encourages argument.

Further Reading

Bachrach, Peter and Baratz, Morton S. (1963) 'Decisions and Nondecisions: an analytical framework' *American Political Science Review* 57, 3, pp. 632–42.

Cohen, Michael D., March, James G. and Olsen, Johan P. (1972) 'A Garbage Can Model of Organisational Choice' *Administrative Science Quarterly* 17, 1, pp. 1–25.

Dror, Yehzekel (1964) 'Muddling Through—"Science" or Inertia?' *Public Administration Review* 24, 3, pp. 154–57.

Etzioni, Amitai (1967) 'Mixed Scanning: a "third" approach to decision making' *Public Administration Review* 27, 5, pp. 385–92.

Ham, Christopher and Hill, Michael (1984) *The Policy Process in the Modern Capitalist State* Sussex: Wheatsheaf Books, chs 4 and 5.

Lindblom, Charles E. (1959) 'The Science of "Muddling Through"' *Public Administration Review* 19, 2, pp. 79–88.

Lindblom, Charles E. (1979) 'Still Muddling, Not Yet Through' *Public Administration Review* 39, 6, pp. 517–26.

Schaffer, Bernard B. (1977) 'On The Politics of Policy' *Australian Journal of Politics and History* 23, 1, pp. 146–55.

Simon, Herbert A. (1957) *Administrative Behaviour: a study of decision-making processes in administrative organisation* New York: Macmillan, 2nd edn.

7

Implementation, Evaluation and Accountability

Tax is a perennial problem for governments. Everyone accepts that taxes must be collected, but there is always disagreement about the mix of levies, their level, and the social and equity functions of the taxation system. In the 1980s tax became an intractable political issue. There is agreement on the need for reform, but all specific suggestions are controversial.

In July 1985 the Labor government held a national summit on taxation reform. The initiative fulfilled a promise made on the run by Prime Minister Hawke during the protracted 1984 election campaign. To set an agenda for the summit, the government devised a series of alternative tax reform proposals. Treasury prepared a White Paper with three major options. Most public attention focused on the two extremes, options A and C. Option A contained a collection of new taxes described by the press as the 'nasties'. These included capital gains and fringe benefits taxes. Option C proposed a massive shift towards indirect taxation. Reductions in personal income tax would be traded for a universal consumption tax.

When the White Paper was released, option C was clearly the preferred proposal of cabinet. Significant community opposition, however, alerted the government to the electoral consequences of new indirect taxes (Mills 1986: 43–59). When it became apparent that the summit would not reach consensus, the prime minister sought to downplay its significance. The summit, said Hawke, was not a deliberative body, but an exercise in consultation; 'these discussions would not be a substitute for the government's decision-making process' (Pemberton and Davis 1986: 60).

Stressing the process rather than the outcome of the summit was a wise move by Hawke, for the government did not prevail. Treasurer Paul Keating described the experience as 'the wheels falling off the tax cart'. Opposition from the ACTU, business and the social service community led the prime minister to repudiate option C. He accepted criticism of rubbery Treasury figures, concern from welfare recipients

124

about indirect taxation, and the problems of implementing new con-sumption levies. Though Keating defended his preferred option, the summit ended without any clear agreement on tax reform. The decisions were left to the government.

In September 1985 the government announced its compromise tax policy. The package included many of the 'nasties' from option A. Included was a fringe benefits tax on the company cars, tax-deductible lunches and the payment of school fees which had become part of many salary packages. These devices for minimising or evading tax had been much criticised by all parties and had been the subject of legislation by the previous Liberal government. With the prospect of bipartisan support, there appeared no objection to the principle of taxing such perks. Yet the new fringe benefits tax was immediately greeted with protest, and opposed by the Liberals in the Senate. Restauranteurs de-clared that an end to tax deductability for entertainment may mean the end of their businesses. 'Australia can't afford to stop working through lunch' they argued. Car firms predicted a decline in the purchase of fleets for use by employees. A national 'axe the tax' campaign was organised, with the inevitable newspaper advertisements and public rallies. Business executives who had criticised the government for not taking 'the hard decisions' now attacked cabinet for unreasonable impositions. Self interest prevailed as people sought to protect their perks; equity in taxation was fair as long as only others were affected.

The treasurer defended the principle of using a fringe benefits tax to reduce the incidence of tax evasion. If wealthier people paid tax on all their income, he argued, then overall levies on the majority of PAYE taxpayers could be reduced. As always, however, it was easier for a specific group with concentrated interests to arouse anger than for a government to sell the advantages of general and dispersed benefits. In particular, critics of the tax pointed to the problems of implementation. Exactly what constitutes a fringe benefit is not easy to define. If graziers are required by industrial award to provide shelter for shearers, is it reasonable to also tax them on that accommodation? Are free parking places a fringe benefit and, if so, at what rate should they be taxed? To address these difficulties, the tax commissioner had to draw up a complex set of rules and exemptions, and an equally complex and lengthy set of forms and guides to the tax. Even so anomalies remained, and the commissioner and treasurer did not always agree on some of the conditions and exceptions.

Political controversy centred around the administration rather than around the principle of a fringe benefits tax. It was the details which offended, and these were used to undermine the proposal. Eventually the prime minister agreed to reassess the administration of the tax to remove any 'unintended effects'. Hawke recognised that however valid the proposal, the effectiveness of a policy is determined by its implementation.

The taxes proposed in option A began operating in the 1986/87 financial year. How can their effectiveness be evaluated? This is not a simple problem, for it depends on an interpretation of intent. The amount of money collected by the fringe benefits tax, for example, would not be a useful guide to its success. The government made the tax payable by the employer, not the recipient of the benefits. This provides an incentive for employers to remove fringe benefits and pay cash in lieu, so catching the income in the normal PAYE tax net. Many businesses quickly restructured their salary packages accordingly. Hence, the more money brought in by the fringe benefit tax, the less successful it may have been. On the other hand, the new imposition may only encourage further tax evasion, as fringe benefits are disguised and tax minimised. Evaluating the policy is not easy, for it is not obvious which criteria should be applied.

Australian academics tend to focus on decisions. Yet the policy process involves much more than making choices. All but purely symbolic policies require further action by government and the agencies of the public sector. It can not be assumed that policies will work; decisions run into unanticipated problems during implementation. Further, there are problems conducting an 'objective' assessment of a policy once it is operating. Should the program falter, decision makers must assess whether the failure resulted from bad policy design or inadequate implementation. Finally, there are difficulties assessing who should take the blame for a program that fails.

Policy implementation, evaluation and accountability are key issues for public policy. They raise important questions about how the decision process does—and should—operate. Assessing why policies run into difficulty raises issues about the authority and power of governments. This chapter will explore implementation, evaluation and accountability in Australia to consider their implications for the making and analysis of policy.

Implementation

Implementation can never be achieved in a vacuum; policies are part of a social environment. Some theorists have constructed an ideal set of circumstances with no impediments to perfect administration. Such an exercise can be no more than a means of identifying all the factors that can go wrong.

Gunn, for example, has identified ten preconditions for perfect policy

implementation: no crippling external constraints, adequate time and
resources, a suitable combination of resources at each stage, a valid
theory of cause and effect, direct links between cause and effect, a
single implementing agency, or at least a dominant one, understanding
and agreement on the objectives to be achieved, a detailed specification
of tasks to be completed, perfect communication and co-ordination,
and perfect obedience (Gunn 1978; for a similar approach see Hood
1976).

To study implementation by positing a set of perfect conditions, and
then illustrating how the real world creates obstacles, may be to assume
away too much. Working from ideal types encourages 'economists'
syndrome'—a tendency to restructure the world to match the model.
These obstacles to implementation are not going to disappear, however
inconvenient they are for abstractions. They are part of the complexity
of policy making, able to serve as both problem and advantage for
various interests. Policies are made through bargaining and coercion,
amid pressures of scarce resources and often entrenched opposition.
Instead of listing the conditions for perfect administration, it may be
more useful to identify some environmental factors which policy makers
must use or overcome to put a policy into effect. For policies interact
with their context. They are altered through the process of delivery.
Principles may not survive reduction to workable details.

These potential constraints on implementation raise questions about
the capacity of governments. Policies may fail if the government has
insufficient power to enforce compliance. This is an important constraint
in a federal system. The initiatives of Canberra can be stalled by unco-
operative States. During 1986 and 1987 the federal and Queensland
governments argued over a rescue package for the ailing sugar industry.
The federal government sought to trade financial aid for deregulation;
the Queensland government was happy to accept the money but not
the conditions attached. Meanwhile cane growers went bankrupt and
mills remained idle. When authority is disputed, levels of government
must compromise. The initial policy proposal is modified, and the
intent perhaps diluted or lost. Governing is a frustrating process.

Technical Knowledge

Policies seldom have the luxury of trial runs; they must be announced
as final and authoritative, not as tentative explorations of difficult
policy fields. Yet the design of big schemes is often uncertain. Information is inexact or inadequate, and there may be few reliable predictors
of likely consequences. Even with a repetitive policy process such as
budget formulation, the government must make estimates on the basis

of forecasts of revenue, inflation rates and expenditure increases, knowing these can be no more than guesstimates. This budget, framed in uncertainty, becomes the foundation upon which all other public spending decisions are based.

When knowledge is uncertain, predictability is a valuable commodity. Policies become technically determined, chosen because expertise can provide an easy and available solution, even if not the best or most applicable. The introduction of an Australia Card was not criticised at the tax summit. It was one of the few proposals attracting apparent consensus. In the revised tax package of September 1985, the Hawke government included a card as part of its strategy to reduce tax fraud. There was no planning before the announcement. Problems of logistics were only considered once the government was committed. Cabinet decided that the card would be introduced by the Health Insurance Commission, simply because a year before the commission had introduced a similar card for Medicare. The Australia Card was meant to save social security costs and reduce tax evasion, both the responsibilities of departments other than Health. It was a technology driven project, with the ends determined by the available means. Current computer capability decided the scale of the proposal. Costs were guessed, for government had only limited experience of large computer-based initiatives (and most of these had failed to come in on budget). The government did not decide important policy details until the principle was announced, such as whether the cards should have a photograph. The Australia Card project was not a logical answer to a pressing difficulty. Rather it was a solution in search of a problem, made attractive by its apparent technical feasibility and by polls indicating the idea was popular (Graham 1986).

Objectives

Governments do not and cannot identify clear policy objectives. Most government programs have multiple purposes, some explicit, others implicit. The Fraser government, for example, had to decide whether to build a railway from Alice Springs to Darwin. The railway could be justified on opportunity cost grounds. All the necessary plant was already at the Alice because a line from Adelaide had just been completed. It would be expensive to regather the plant and workforce at a later date. The railway could also be supported on defence grounds for internal supply routes, on equity grounds so Territorians were not cut off from easy transport to the rest of Australia, and on electoral grounds so that the Territory seat could be retained.

Each objective was important for the government, and the eventual choice reflected these multiple goals and rationales. The Fraser cabinet decided to proceed because it gave great weight to the strategic, developmental and electoral advantages. The Hawke government, on the other hand, cancelled the project. Ministers argued on economic criteria that the railway would absorb scarce resources for little return. They may also have been influenced by the continuing coalition domination of Territorian politics. Deciding which set of technical data will be given priority is a political decision.

In other cases policies may be symbolic, designed primarily for ideological reasons. Consider, for example, the Thatcher program of selling off state enterprises:

> Shortly before the flotation of British Telecom, I talked to a friend who is deeply experienced in the ways of Whitehall. 'Tell me', I asked him, 'what privatisation is really about. Is it about raising revenue, or improving the efficiency of privatised industries, or what?' He thought for a moment, and said 'The mistake in that question is to suppose that privatisation is actually about anything. It is a political imperative, pursued for itself. If any arguments for it can be found, or any benefits from it can be perceived, a grateful government will seize on them as rationalisation; these are not objectives. The policy is the policy because it is the policy. There is fundamentally no more to it than that' (Kay 1985: 1).

Deciding on policy objectives is thus a value judgement, though the detailed and expert technical justifications will later be paraded in reports and parliamentary speeches. Wildavsky makes the point:

> Objectives are not just out there, like ripe fruit waiting to be plucked; they are manmade, artificial, imposed on a recalcitrant world. Inevitably, they do violence to reality by emphasising some activities (hence organizational elements) over others. Thus the very step of defining objectives may be considered a hostile act ... Strategically located participants often refuse to accept definitions of objectives that would put them at a disadvantage or in a straight-jacket should they wish to change their designation of what they do in the future (Wildavsky 1979: 216).

Some policies are required by circumstances. These include the perennial dilemmas posed by troublesome policy fields. They frustrate all governments, regardless of objectives. Such policy difficulties have been characterised as 'wicked problems' (Rittel and Webber 1973), those which defy definition or permanent solution. All governments face a 'wicked problem' with interest rates. These can only be controlled at enormous cost to other government objectives. Should cabinet keep interest rates low as the primary objective of economic policy? Presumably not, when the economic record of governments in the last decade is examined. Low interest rates may not be compatible with reducing inflation and unemployment. Government economic policies are likely to be a mix of conflicting aims; the 'wicked problem' will not be solved, only balanced against other priorities. Objectives are not isolated, final or definite. Solutions cannot be permanent. The multiple goals of economic policy will be contested, and then re-contested as circumstances change.

Vagueness about objectives is not always accidental. Just as it suits oppositions not to be too specific about policy proposals, so governments may benefit from ambiguity. The authors of a policy are often unwilling, or unable, to be precise about their objectives. A vague promise to maintain Medibank can be fulfilled by the retention of the name. Objectives can be redefined to a government's advantage, and policies designed around one vague objective can be hijacked to solve another problem. Overseas aid programs are established as charity operations. An astute foreign minister, however, uses the offer of aid in diplomatic negotiations.

Plans for Implementation

Implementation is rarely, if ever, considered before a policy decision is made. An 'in principle' decision is therefore not a policy, for its viability and impact will be determined by the details of administration. Decisions become policies when they are implemented. The Hawke government's crusade against drugs was announced first, with the details to be worked out later by State and federal ministers and the National Crime Commission.

A failure to plan for implementation enables public servants, pressure groups and politicians to argue over the details once the decision has been announced. A 1984 cabinet decision about an assets test, for example, was the cue for various interests inside and around the bureaucracy to lobby over implementation (Marsh 1985). The details of policy administration can redefine the intent of a decision. Implementation is therefore not simply a technical question, but a matter for continual dialogue, interaction and compromise.

Resources

Programs never have as many resources as they could use. This is a source of aggravation for those involved. People identify with the objectives of a program they implement, and resent any constraints which limit its impact. Social workers, for example, often criticise the restrictions and demands placed on welfare projects by bureaucrats at the centre of government. These are portrayed as unreasonable and detrimental to the good conduct of the policy. To the centre, however, this program is just one of hundreds, each of which is given a very high priority by their participants. Programs must compete for funds, a process which inevitably produces winners and losers. While the middle manager is concerned more with the overall number of cases processed, and the centre with keeping down total costs, the CES counter clerk will place great stress on helping those in poverty and so argue that more staff are needed. 'People who spend tend to believe in what they do. They do not like the idea that for the manager of the economy, an offensive missile, a motorway or ten new hospitals may amount to the same thing' (Heclo and Wildavsky 1981: 78). So resources are always more limited than ambitions. Yet final decisions are seldom taken at any single moment and chances to try again are frequent. Participants have the opportunity at a later date to argue that their program is essential and that their success justifies a greater allocation of funds. The policy process is continuous. Current priorities are always under challenge.

Time for policy implementation is likely to be short. Clients expect immediate action, and the public sector seldom has the luxury of bringing a policy slowly on stream. Policy reactions are in part determined by the pressures of the issue attention cycle, in part by electoral considerations, in part by the likely response of pressure groups, and in part by the dangers of a perceived failure to act. Good politics may lead to poor administration. It is usually technically 'rational' to design a program before the intention is announced, but political imperative does not always allow such contemplation. The government had to announce proposals to combat AIDS before it could really assess possible options and strategies. Professional procedures clashed with the demands of electoral rationality.

Opponents

In the classic study *Implementation* (1973), Pressman and Wildavsky examined an American federal program designed to alleviate poverty in the Californian city of Oakland. The program required co-operation from several levels of government to deliver federal grants to the local community. Pressman and Wildavsky concluded that although the program enjoyed the support of all participants, it still failed to achieve any significant results. This was not the result of direct opposition, but reflected the program premise that action would be based on the consent of numerous actors and agencies. Agreement in principle did not extend to details. 'Given contradictory legislative criteria, inherent administrative antagonisms between federal agencies, and the uncertainty of local action on the part of numerous businesses it is no wonder that the program failed to achieve its ends' (Pressman and

Wildavsky 1973: 87). The observers subtitled their study 'How Great Expectations in Washington are Dashed in Oakland'. They found that as more people became involved, the program ran into difficulty. 'The longer the chain of causality, the more numerous the reciprocal relationships among the links and the more complex implementation becomes' (Pressman and Wildavsky 1973: xvi).

So policies can fail even when everyone agrees that the program is desirable. Implementation becomes even more difficult when those whose co-operation is required are opposed to the policy. Co-operation can be a scarce resource in a federal system, for each level of government wishes to protect its own interests. For example, the Whitlam government wanted to introduce lands commissions. These would minimise the increase in land prices in metropolitan areas and so prevent a housing shortage. The program required State involvement in administration, though it was directed by a federal Department of Urban and Regional Development.

The Whitlam cabinet endorsed the DURD submission in principle, approved funds in the 1974 budget, and reached agreement with the South Australian government. Implementation required the consent of the federal Treasury both in determining the terms and conditions of the agreements, and in deciding what information was required before money could be handed over. A recalcitrant Treasury managed to contest the details of the cabinet proposal until the last moment in the financial year; payment to the South Australian government only occurred following the intervention of the prime minister.

The DURD scheme for lands commissions failed. The federal government could only reach agreement with one State over the program (see Hawker et al. 1979: 136—39; Troy 1978). The process of implementation allowed the federal Treasury to obstruct progress of an approved government program. While DURD saw this as opposition, the Treasury argued that it was only ensuring that government money was spent wisely and properly. As Lloyd and Troy ruefully noted, 'a contemporary Machiavelli would not write about princes but about the knights in the upper echelons of the bureaucracy' (Lloyd and Troy 1981: xv). Resisted by the federal bureaucracy and many of the States, the Department of Urban and Regional Development could not implement government decisions during its brief existence.

In assessing the prospects for implementation, it is therefore necessary to ask not just who is in favour or who is opposed to the policy, but what opportunities these interests have for promoting, delaying or subverting a cabinet choice. Implementation can require skill in mobilising allies. Other departments, State governments and pressure groups may be important, whether their aim is to respect cabinet's intention, or to subtly change the policy during the transition from decision to implementation.

Discretion

Most legislation only spells out its aims in general terms. Cabinet decisions are short, stating the principle and perhaps indicating broad plans for implementation. A policy must be interpreted before it can be put into effect. Discretion to implement may therefore devolve to State governments, to the public servants who deliver the service directly to the public at the counter, or to bodies such as marketing boards and other statutory authorities. Discretion enables bureaucrats to alter the meaning of laws and policies, particularly when the delegation of responsibility determines who will benefit from a government policy.

Discretion has a variety of meanings, from the strictly legal to the organisation of social policy (Ham and Hill 1984: ch. 9). There are, however, two key levels of discretion in policy interpretation. The first relates to the role of experts within the public sector. Those with professional qualifications, such as doctors, teachers and social workers, argue that the requirements of government offend proper professional practice. Government regulations are therefore ignored or circumvented. The Queensland Minister of Education, under the influence of fundamentalist christians, demands that creationism be taught alongside evolution in the science classes of Queensland schools. Most science teachers, however, mention the creationist view very briefly (if under the odd euphemism of flood technology), and then return to teaching orthodox science. The government cannot monitor what occurs in every classroom, and so cannot enforce its regulation. The teachers have complied with the requirement, but not the intent, of the policy.

The second operation of discretion occurs in client oriented departments. The street level bureaucrats, those officials who deal with the public, develop strategies for dealing with the pressures of their job and the endless flow of individual cases. They exercise discretion about the level of assistance provided. Some street level bureaucrats prove helpful, exploring ways within the program guidelines to provide maximum benefits for their clients. Others become blunt and rude, giving only the minimum assistance required by the regulations. Action over a policy may therefore produce results very different from the original intent (Sanders 1984, 1985). Ideally, the policy will be more sensitive, more attuned to local conditions. On occasion the formal rules are eventually changed at the top level to take account of decisions and practices at the workface. As Sanders observes, the pressures of daily life at the counter for social security bureaucrats mean that 'officials often adapt existing rules and procedures to indeterminate cases without reference to more senior decision makers. Only later, when trends in rank and file decision making and resource allocation become evident ... can rules be "officially" interpreted, procedures "officially" changed and resources "officially" redeployed' (Sanders 1985: 46). This is implementation-led policy.

If resources are not available to meet demand, then governments may use queuing as a means of control. The Australian government normally requires a reasonably swift response to requests for visas or immigration papers. To maintain that standard in places like New Delhi, where demand is almost infinite, a massive increase in staff would be required. Instead, pressures are kept under control by limiting staff and letting deadlines slip. Applicants are forced to queue for access because normal bureaucratic procedures have been deliberately relaxed.

Discretion is given to street level bureaucrats because government guidelines cannot anticipate all eventualities. The more discretion in the process, the more difficult it becomes to predict implementation. When expertise and experience resides with the bureaucrats, governments must negotiate—rather than impose—policy.

Power

Federal governments cannot always make the decisions they would like, for in many fields they lack exclusive constitutional authority. Power is frequently shared between two levels of government. In the 1980s, High Court judgments have perhaps strengthened the Commonwealth's position. The Franklin Dam decision, for example, gave the federal government power to override Tasmanian State legislation because it contradicted the obligations of an international treaty.

The Franklin decision, of course, does not signal the end of the federal system. Even where the federal government does have power but is in dispute with a State, it must decide whether the costs of intervention are worth the benefits which might accrue. In the Daintree case, Canberra may have been able to hinder the construction of a road through the rainforest, but decided to avoid a fight with the Queensland government. Disappointed conservationists accused the Hawke government of lacking the political will to act. The term 'political will' is a rather hackneyed, and not very useful, analysis of a situation. Governments are never working in only one area at a time. A decision is likely to have implications for other, often unrelated, policies. The Labor government decided not to intervene over the Daintree because it judged that the costs of a dispute with the Bjelke-Peterson National Party government in Brisbane would be too great. The Hawke administration also withdrew plans for uniform national Aboriginal land rights legislation, for which it has undoubted constitutional power, because it was more important to maintain close working relations with the Burke Labor government in Western Australia.

Every decision is part of a political calculus. Nothing is seen in isolation. Governments do not have 'political wills', they have priorities, and they make their choices accordingly.

Federal programs and policies depend on co-operation from other levels of government. Consultation occurs through a diverse range of advisory boards, from the Loans Council to joint federal—State committees considering topics from legal reform to primary marketing schemes. Links between federal and State public servants are continuous and vital for policies where authority is shared. When organisational power is diffuse, it can often only be exercised through negotiation.

Obstacles to Perfect Implementation

Opportunity, resources, opponents, discretion and shared power are sometimes regarded as obstacles to implementation. They can be characterised as problems which must be 'overcome' to allow more perfect, rational, administration. In fact these factors are integral parts of the context of all policies. Good policy design must take them into account, working around the obstacle if it proves too much to change. Such constraints on implementation, however, help explain why policies rarely achieve the precise results imagined by government. Sometimes the difficulty is due to sectional demands, other times to bureaucratic incompetence or social responses beyond the control of government. The electorate may anticipate policies and so unintentionally subvert their effect. Policy design can be inadequate or outdated, given the tendency of any organisation to fight yesterday's wars. Options may prove to be outside the government's constitutional powers. There are rarely simple, single, explanations for policy failure—or policy success.

Evaluation

How can governments assess whether a policy has achieved its objective? In the USA, administrators and academics have developed sophisticated techniques for evaluating the effect and cost of a program. An evaluation industry has emerged in Washington, offering expertise to report on almost every government activity. It is an industry with standard operating procedures and an extensive literature about the method and practice of judging public policies. The Americans call this process 'systematic evaluation', the attempt to conduct 'systematic, objective evaluation of programs to measure their societal impact and the extent to which they are achieving their stated objectives' (Anderson 1984: 135).

This evaluation industry has made little progress in Australia. While some research is conducted within the bureaucracy and through one-off commissions of inquiry, systematic evaluation of government programs remains rare.

There are at least three important differences between the use of evaluation in the United States and Australia. With no tradition of evaluation in Australia, few public servants or political scientists have the methodological skills to conduct viable evaluations. Academic programs in the field are very recent, so there are as yet few graduates with appropriate multidisciplinary training in public policy, finance, economics and law. While the Americans employ such graduates in the bureaucracy, research institutes and private think tanks, there are relatively few—though expanding—opportunities for professional policy analysts within Australia. Without demand, there is no supply. Without supply, there is no lobby of professional analysts demanding policy evaluation.

Economies of scale may also limit the development of a local evaluation industry. American federal bureaucracies are huge by Australian standards. The US Department of Health, Education and Welfare, for example, has a staff of 145 000—equivalent to almost the entire Commonwealth public service. The potential cost savings from economies within HEW programs identified by external evaluations are likely to be very great, whereas in Australia the potential savings are likely to be considerably less. With multi-billion dollar programs, the Americans can afford to invest in expensive, full scale program evaluations. The costs of evaluation would be much the same in Australia, but the returns in program savings would be less significant.

Yet the main obstacle to local evaluation remains institutional. Australia has a Westminster system, with the executive drawn directly from the parliament. The prime minister has to answer to the House of Representatives, and relies on the support of that chamber for continued office. Party dominance ensures that the executive controls the legislature. This enables government to avoid sustained scrutiny. Expenditure analysis is largely left to the bureaucracy, and does not become public.

The United States constitution, in contrast, separates the executive from the legislature, and so creates a consistent need for programs to be explained and justified. Congress writes evaluation requirements into presidential legislation. Studies of particular programs are commissioned by Senate committees, which also conduct regular reviews of government department spending. Only through the findings of evaluative studies can the federal administration and bureaucracy defend their programs and professional integrity. Because program assessment has become important in ensuring executive accountability, the evaluation industry remains viable in the United States; it now also operates in a Westminster system such as Canada, where external evaluations are aids to parliamentary scrutiny (see Dobell and Zussman 1981; Hartle 1976).

Australian Efficiency Audits

The limited Australian evaluations have primarily been conducted by public auditors. In the mid-1970s, the office of the Commonwealth auditor-general extended its role to include efficiency studies. This followed the example of the American General Accounting Office, which is directed not just to check compliance with financial regulation, but to 'review and analyse the results of government programs and activities carried on under existing law, including the making of cost-benefit studies'. Such efficiency audits are conducted by the Office of Program Review and Evaluation within the GAO (Anderson 1984: 145).

James Cutt (1978) has identified three notions of 'efficiency'. Efficiency I refers to normal legal accountability: was the money spent within the letter of the law? Efficiency II asks whether, within the terms of the stated policy, the money had been spent in the most suitable way: was the program run efficiently? Efficiency III questions whether the program was the best way of tackling the problem: is the policy effective or should it be changed?

In 1974 the secretariat of the Royal Commission into Australian Government Administration began studies of value-for-money auditing of public functions (Parker 1986: 25). Though the eventual RCAGA report did not recommend independent efficiency audits, the Fraser government gave the federal auditor general authority to extend evaluations from the traditional notion of legal accountability to efficiency II inquiries about the use of funds. These efficiency reviews were never a great success; they took too long to do and, apart from some telling criticisms of the tax office, had little impact. The division within the office of the auditor general was eventually disbanded.

Significant difficulties arise when government agencies are made responsible for program evaluation. It has been argued that adequate technological tools for measuring performance are not available (Walker 1977). Perhaps more significant are the constitutional problems which result from any expanded auditing role:

> The Auditor-General is an agent of parliament, and it is argued that he cannot fulfil this role—with Parliament as his client—and at the same time oversee the pursuit of Efficiency III which would involve criticising the implementation or indeed intrinsic nature of government policy, which has received legislative authority in Parliament. The respect accorded the observations of the Auditor-General is, it is argued, very much a function of his independence from what is at least in substantial part, a political debate on policy (Cutt 1987: 229).

Other writers are more optimistic about reconciling parliamentary prerogative and efficiency audits. Dillon argues that the ascendancy of the executive has transformed parliament from a law-maker into an executive watchman. An expanded role for performance auditing would now complement parliamentary scrutiny of the executive. Provided the criteria were agreed, objective and independent, then the office of the auditor general would be 'the appropriate body to undertake the comprehensive audit of the public sector in Australia' (Dillon 1985: 266).

Dillon acknowledges that such audits will only happen if 'policy makers see it as in their interests' (Dillon 1985: 269). So far they have not. There has been a 'mutual reluctance on the part of some Governments and Auditors General to undertake "political judgements" or to invite political criticism through the audit of public policy' (Parker 1986: 28).

Australian Legislation and Evaluation

Only one major federal program, the Australian Assistance Plan (AAP), has been based on legislation which included demands for evaluation. Once the program was running, the Social Welfare Commission was to evaluate its progress and improve priorities (Chapman 1975; Graycar 1974, 1979a). The evaluation was never completed, so it is difficult to assess this experiment. The evaluation began even as the AAP itself was being established, and the program was abolished with the evaluation still in progress. Amid this rush, it is not surprising that the evaluation process suffered conceptual, methodological and operational problems. Graycar argues that conceptually the evaluators failed to identify the program's problems or define its objectives. Methodologically the evaluators did not determine what research approaches were appropriate, and operationally their role within the organisation as external evaluators was never defined. Perhaps most worrying was the failure to calculate the effects of government decisions in the evaluation (Graycar 1974: 257–60). The AAP evaluation was not a striking success or a promising precedent.

More recently, the Department of Social Security has employed a team of outsiders to evaluate its programs. The researchers, headed by Dr Bettina Cass submitted their first report in June 1986. The review assesses a number of major programs operated by the department, with performance reviews and suggestions on alternative options for achieving departmental goals.

Elsewhere moves towards a more formal process of policy evaluation have been slow. A Senate committee report entitled *Through a Glass Darkly: Evaluation in Australian Health and Welfare Services* (1979) espoused evaluative principles drawn primarily from USA experience. The recommendations were never implemented. In South Australia the Public Service Board hoped a new system of Planning Programming Budgeting (PPB) would introduce more systematic assessment processes, though results are still ambiguous (Strickland 1982; see also McCallum 1984). Other States are experimenting with agency performance indicators, administrative objectives and variants of PPB. Yet all these are essentially internal bureaucratic checks. They are concerned with better management, rather than with policy evaluation for its own sake.

Why have Australian federal and State governments been so reluctant to introduce evaluative procedures? In part because they recognise the multiple, sometimes inconsistent, objectives of policies. A compromise policy constructed around electoral, economic and legal impediments may not show up well on purely technical criteria. The evaluation will reflect only those objectives defined in the legislation or administrative order, and not the other aims of maintaining party support, avoiding brawls with a State, or trading concessions with interest groups.

In any evaluation, the initial contest is to decide whose definition of policy goals will prevail. Once completed, evaluations are not and cannot be objective. Findings depend on where the author looks and what questions are asked. Stretton comments:

> In my own experience most conventional policy analysis and programme evaluation is one or another kind of political or bureaucratic warfare. Contenders select for 'rational analysis' the benefits of programmes they support, and the costs of programmes they want to dismantle ... Any public policy of any importance has diverse support, from people and interests expecting different things of it. It has a range of immediate, secondary, and continuing effects, some intended and some not, some measurable and some not; and some of those effects may well be defined as costs by some interests and as benefits by others. It is good to trace and measure as many of the effects as possible, as carefully as possible ... But all such analyses are selective. Necessarily and unavoidably they are shaped by the values that guide the analyst's selections and by the values built into prevailing 'world views', 'frameworks of analysis', and institutional rules and routines (Stretton 1984: 33−34).

All evaluations can be contested. As losers will point out, analysis can never be neutral or objective.

A completed evaluation is judged not only in terms of the quality of analysis, but also in the light of its possible impact. Governments may choose to publish or keep secret, to ignore or to implement, to accept partially or to return an evaluation for further study. The Vernon

report on economic management was shelved in 1965, while the Campbell report on the Australian financial system in 1981 eventually became
the blueprint for substantial change. The fate of an evaluation is
determined by the electoral significance of its recommendations.

Alternative Evaluations in Australia

Australian parliaments have not adopted the formal evaluations of US
experience. Instead a range of diverse, non-systematic, quasi-evaluative
procedures have been developed to provide some assessment of programs. There are departmental policy units, such as the Social Welfare
Policy Secretariat, which examine policy from within the public service.
Parliamentary committees often examine, and find wanting, the administration of departments. Royal commissions and committees of inquiry
also make recommendations, often about the more 'wicked' policy
problems of government.

The federal bureaucracy includes research bodies such as the Bureaux
of Transport and Agricultural Economics. These departmental units
monitor, comment on and evaluate policy fields and government programs. This research is often published, and the bureaucrats provide
some feedback by participating in conferences and seminars. Leading
policy advisers such as former IAC chairman Alf Rattigan may use
their expert position to dispute vigorously with ministers (Rattigan
1986; see also Warhurst 1982a). Yet not all the findings of advisory
bodies are published, and research generally stays within the parameters
of government policy. Departmental policy units provide a series of
informative and useful papers. As part of the government machine,
however, their more critical comments are likely to be kept private.

Parliamentary committees can also provide some evaluation. The
individual and joint committees of the House of Representatives and
the Senate can examine the administration of departments and criticise
the structure and implementation of programs. They may also assess
particular actions and agencies. There have been notable reports in the
last decades: on the securities and exchange industry, on freedom of
information legislation and on statutory authorities, such as the very
embarrassing investigations into illegal Asia Dairy dealings in the
Pacific.

Yet there are limits on the scope and effectiveness of such parliamentary examinations. As bi-partisan ventures, parliamentary committees are not meant to challenge policy assumptions which are the
basis of programs. Public servants who appear before hearings refuse
to answer questions relating to government policy. The parliamentarians
on the committees often have little specific knowledge of the field
under review, and extensive commitments elsewhere. Consequently,

they rely on parliamentary bureaucrats to do much of the research and drafting. Committee reports are tabled in parliament and may appear on the cabinet agenda, but they can also be ignored by an indifferent or antagonistic government. Committee reports are more a way of educating parliamentarians than of systematically monitoring the operations of the public sector.

Sometimes governments appoint committees of inquiry to investigate a particular policy problem. Such independent full time review committees may be established for a range of reasons: to establish facts and make recommendations about subjects of limited compass, to undertake general investigations where something is vaguely wrong (a process that may require a redefining of the terms of the inquiry as it proceeds), to conciliate conflicting interests, to educate the public and mobilise support for action which governments do not want to take entirely on their own responsibility, to show concern without actually doing anything and thus to postpone action, to allow an expression of grievances, or to follow up another inquiry (Smith and Weller 1978: 3). Inquiries offer outside opinion on intractable problems, allow the articulation and evaluation of dissent, and help forge consensus about government action. Inquiries may also be devices for avoiding decisions; as Harold Wilson quipped, a royal commission can 'take minutes and waste years'.

The style of public inquiries has changed little in a century. Commissioners or committees of inquiry still act as semi-judicial figures. Solemn behind their bench, they sift through submissions, listen to evidence, cross-examine witnesses, take advice from their secretariat, and retire to weigh the evidence and reach a verdict. A good report will survey the evidence, evaluate current practice and provide recommendations about possible changes.

Yet governments must be wary about establishing an inquiry, for cabinet has no control over what will be discovered. The Costigan Royal Commission of 1981 was created by Liberal governments in Canberra and Melbourne to investigate the Painters and Dockers union. The diligent Costigan uncovered the operation of 'bottom-of-the-harbour' tax rorts. Using union members as fronts, people close to the Liberal Party were involved in massive tax evasion. The interim reports and scandalous revelations were a severe embarrassment to the State and federal governments. Once the first interim report was delivered, it became impossible to stop Costigan without appearing to suppress important evidence. An attempt to embarrass the union movement had been badly misjudged.

By contrast, the Ranger report provided a convenient justification for government action. This inquiry into the export of uranium was established by the Whitlam Labor government but eventually reported to the Fraser Liberal government in 1977. The report by Mr Justice Fox proposed guidelines about international safeguards for uranium sales. The Liberal cabinet accepted the recommendations and cited the report as an independent evaluation of its decisions. The Ranger inquiry thus provided legitimation for government policy.

Yet public reports are still documents which can be shelved or ignored. Commissions deliver their findings and then disband. Implementation may be left to the agencies which have been reviewed. The Royal Commission on Australian Government Administration (1976) lamented a lack of planning in the public sector; RCAGA proposals for forward estimates were then analysed by the Treasury, the very body which had been criticised. Nothing happened (Smith and Weller 1978).

Accountability

If independent evaluation has yet to make a substantial impact in Australia, what are the processes for holding politicians and officials accountable for policy choices? The traditional answer has been that ministers are accountable to the parliament. The executive must explain the actions of its officials, and through such parliamentary scrutiny the effectiveness of the public sector is assured. This ideal ignores the growth of party discipline and the limits on parliamentary monitoring of a complex and diffuse state. In ascending order of importance, ministers are now more effectively answerable to their party, the cabinet, and the prime minister or premier. Electoral imperative, not constitutional doctrine, determines the level and effectiveness of ministerial responsibility.

The difficulties of enforcing accountability can be exacerbated by the pressures of federalism. Many programs are the joint responsibility of State and federal governments. The system of tied Commonwealth grants for roads, hospitals, schools and welfare functions requires that federal funds be administered by State departments. Both governments may compete for the credit, and neither will take the blame. With vacation childcare programs, for example, the money comes from Canberra. Yet messages to local parents groups announcing the success of a grant application appear on State government letterhead. Indeed in one case, the Queensland minister of welfare services informed a local childcare group that a cheque would be presented to them by the National Party State member. When the seat was later won by a Liberal member, the cheque arrived in the mail. The Commonwealth Bicentennial Roads program legislation requires signs indicating clearly that federal money is funding construction. At openings of bridges and freeways, State and federal transport ministers juggle for the kudos. Yet accountability is avoided whenever there is bad news. Spending cuts in State education are always blamed on reduced funding from the federal ministry. Each level of government blames the other for administrative delays. In a federal system with shared accountability, it is difficult to force a single minister to take responsibility for a specific program. Ambiguity is a useful disguise and potential excuse.

Alternatives to Parliamentary Accountability

If responsibility to parliament is limited and often confused by the structures of federalism, are there alternative means available to enforce executive accountability for policy decisions? In 1976 the RCAGA argued for a system of accountable management. The report recommended that governments assign a block of resources for a specific policy and then hold senior public servants responsible for its efficient implementation.

The RCAGA proposal ran counter to traditional notions of ministerial responsibility. It also seemed unfair, for if a policy is badly thought out then no management can make it appear efficient. Moreover, the recommendation was predicated on a clear distinction between the policy role of the politician and the management function of the public servant (RCAGA 1976: ch. 4). Yet many of the sensitivities of a program arise in the detail of administration. Policies are altered in action, and so ministers must be involved in implementation. The management function in the public sector is therefore not distinct and discrete, but may be shared between the elected politicians and the permanent official. The proposal for accountable management was never adopted.

A more influential form of accountability has been the gradual extension of administrative law. If the introduction of accountable management was intended to solve problems of accountability in the broader scene, then administrative law is designed to ensure external review and checks on the individual decisions of officials. The new administrative law includes four components: the Ombudsman, the Freedom of Information Act, the Administrative Review Council and the Adminstrative Appeals Tribunal (Griffiths 1985; see also Jinks 1981; Senate Report on Freedom of Information Bill 1979).

The Ombudsman is empowered to investigate complaints from citizens and to inquire whether their case was properly dealt with by the bureaucracy. The Ombudsman cannot criticise the content of a policy, only its implementation. If he finds the complaint justified, the Ombudsman recommends remedial action. He cannot require redress, only request that a department review its decision. Should the department refuse to co-operate, the Ombudsman must register a complaint in his annual report to parliament. Senior public service officials have criticised the right of the Ombudsman to scrutinise their departments. For example, John Stone, as Secretary of the Treasury, sent acerbic letters to the Ombudsman about scrutiny of Treasury decisions. The then Chair of the ABC, Professor Leonie Kramer, also argued that the Ombudsman had no right to question editorial matters within the ABC. A long dispute, including a complaint from the Ombudsman to the prime minister, failed to resolve this issue of jurisdiction. The exact authority of the Ombudsman is still being worked out (see the special edition of the *Canberra Bulletin of Public Administration* 22, 4, 1985).

The Freedom of Information Act allows citizens to question the bureaucracy about their files and about government decisions. A large amount of detail, however, is exempt. Some internal public service working papers and all cabinet papers need not be released for thirty years. The main clients for freedom of information legislation have been journalists, opposition politicians and citizens requesting their personal files from welfare departments. The problem for potential users is knowing what to request, for only specific existing documents can be nominated for search. When a Senate committee was investigating potential freedom of information legislation, senior public servants argued against its introduction. The bureaucrats suggested that FOI would involve the public service in an increased amount of work; some massively exaggerated figures were cited as evidence. Further, public servants asserted that FOI would break the confidential relationship between ministers and their advisers. Yet there is little evidence of these problems after nearly a decade of operative FOI legislation. Rather, freedom of information has allowed individuals to discover and challenge bureaucratic decisions. It has also extended access to those internal public service manuals which state the guidelines and rules of areas such as social security. FOI has probably reinforced observance of official rules by street level bureaucrats, and ensured that public servants provide written justification for administrative decisions (McMillan 1981).

The Administrative Review Council and the Administrative Appeals Tribunal are both judicial bodies. The ARC maintains a watching brief on the process of administrative law. It conducts research into the effects of changed administrative procedures, and so provides a basis for continued reform. The AAT reviews specific decisions. Individuals can appeal to the tribunal about the decision of a minister, and the AAT is allowed to demand the relevant files within a prescribed time. The AAT then proclaims judgement on the merits of the case. Authority to assess the reasonableness of a decision allows the AAT to overrule a decision of the minister. The AAT does not just determine that the

decision was improperly made; it can rule that the decision could on its
merits have been decided differently. For instance, the AAT has over-
turned decisions of a minister to deport convicted illegal migrants. This
can imply criticism of the minister, though often by the time the AAT
hears the case circumstances have changed or facts have been discovered
which were not available to the minister. The establishment of the
AAT gives the judiciary an important veto over the right of ministers
to make administrative decisions. Like the rest of the court system, the
AAT provides a forum for interests to delay, harass or circumvent. It
does, however, also mean that remedies are available to the citizen
where formerly there were none.

The use of administrative law has perhaps gone further in Australia
than in any similar parliamentary system. The changes have introduced
new forms of accountability for individual cases. These come at the
cost of increased rights of judicial intervention. The powers of the
AAT enable judges not just to assess whether a decision is within the
legislation, but to reformulate public policy. Reid (1978) regrets that
Australian judges are becoming heavily involved in decisions of value
rather than of law. He suggests that lawyers have moved beyond their
area of competence. The legal fraternity are now divided on questions
of overall jurisdiction. The Victorian judiciary, for instance, always
declines to head royal commissions and committees of inquiry, while in
New South Wales judges regularly participate. Debate centres on
whether lawyers have the necessary special skills and expertise to rule
on issues such as the export of uranium. What gives those with legal
training a greater capacity for value judgements than other citizens?
And how can judges, who are not elected, be included in the already
tenuous chain of accountability? Administrative law allows policy to be
assessed on legal rather than electoral grounds. It raises important
questions about the desirability of judicial constraints on the power of
ministers in areas where all decisions must be matters of values and
discretion.

Implications

There are no decision making models which could make all policy
choices 'better'. There are also no prescriptions for implementation,
evaluation or accountability which could correct all problems in the
formulation of public policy. Finding 'better' policy is not simply a
question of more skilful use of the social sciences, or more precise
quantification. Ambiguity of objectives and the need to satisfy several
constituencies at once is part of political life. There are significant
economic and social constraints on implementation, and a risk that

more formal policy review processes simply increase the influence of sectional interests, judges or policy analysts. While particular policies may be improved by better planning, the totality of governmental action cannot. Political judgement should not be overruled by technical or judicial criteria as though these are uncontested and unbiased. The seductive jargon of technical objectivity should not be allowed to disguise its ideological basis.

The problems of implementation often reflect the relative powerlessness of government. The economy is beyond direct ministerial control, there are diffuse centres of authority, pressure groups make endless, contradictory demands, the public sector is complex and fragmented, and agencies can try to subvert unacceptable instructions. These impede the process of turning decisions into policy. Evaluation techniques may provide valuable insights to government about more effective action. Accountability is important for asserting executive control over the actions of officials. The major issues raised by debates over implementation, evaluation and accountability, however, centre on what is decided and who should decide.

Further Reading

Griffiths, John (1985) 'Australian Adminstrative Law: institutions, reforms and impact' *Public Administration* London 63, pp. 445–63.

Hood, Christopher (1976) *The Limits of Administration* London: Wiley.

Lloyd, C.J. and Troy, P.N. (1981) *Innovation and Reaction: the life and death of the Department of Urban and Regional Development* Sydney: Allen & Unwin.

Marsh, Ian (1985) 'The Assets Test: a case study in the politics of expenditure control', *Australian Journal of Public Administration* 44, 3, pp. 197–223.

Pressman, Jeffrey L. and Wildavsky Aaron (1973) *Implementation: how great expectations in Washington are dashed in Oakland* University of California Press.

Reid, G.S. (1978) 'The Changing Political Framework', in Theo van Dugteren (ed.) *The Political Process: can it cope?* Sydney: AIPS/Hodder & Stoughton.

8
Policy Making: Economic

The economy hangs like the Sword of Damocles over governments of all persuasions. A government considered incapable of managing the economy is invariably condemned as unsuitable to hold office, whatever the impact of its other policies. Indeed, before attempting any broader policy innovations, governments must first 'get the economy right'. Yet what is considered 'right' depends on the criteria invoked. For an economist, profit maximisation and anti-inflation strategies may be crucial. A politician, however, may be more concerned to appease interest groups and create employment. There are different tests of policy effectiveness.

A central concern with the economy has not always been the accepted role for the state. Liberal thinkers often claimed that the economy performed according to invisible market forces. Government intervention only interfered with the equilibrium of the natural market (Friedman and Friedman 1980). Yet it can also be claimed that modern capitalist economies are not inherently self-regulating. Unfettered markets cause problems. They are prone to recession, crises, market failures and an unequal distribution of economic resources. This places governments in a difficult position (Wilson 1985).

Some business leaders and economists still argue for a classic liberal state. Governments, however, generally find it impossible to desist from economic policy intervention. The impact of such policies may be positive or negative, broad or selective (Driscoll and Behrman 1984). Even 'de-regulation' and 'privatisation' strategies still involve regulatory requirements, restrictions and patterns of intervention (Wettenhall 1983a). Deregulation becomes reregulation. Existing rules are replaced by alternative forms of regulatory control. The 'deregulation' of the banking sector by the Hawke government provides a case in point. The government eased some restrictions to enable a further sixteen licence holders to operate in Australia, and to allow other financial institutions to perform some trading bank activities. The exercise relaxed some government regulations over the banking sector but maintained others, and the significant regulations imposed by private banks themselves were not eroded. While the degrees and methods of economic policy change, governments maintain policies of intervention (Clark and Dear 1984; Head 1984).

Governments place fundamental importance on economic policy, and take credit or skirt blame for movements in economic indicators. Yet, governments have limited influence on the economy. Certainly governments regulate economic activity and have a number of important levers or policy tools at their disposal. Much government economic policy, however, is necessarily indirect, and facilitative rather than coercive. Its impact may be marginal. The state exercises virtually no control over key areas of the economy such as the stock market, many banking practices, international currency movements, investment decisions, multinational intra-corporate operations, profit levels and the 'black' economy.

Economic Policy: Points of Departure

Much economic policy literature works from particular causal assumptions when discussing the relationship between the economy and state activity. Government options are seen as constrained by the primary importance of structural features such as the market, capital or power relations. It is common to read accounts that either depart from the premises of a laissez faire economic system or conversely insist that the economy should be under 'responsible' control (Stretton 1987).

Traditional political science accounts start from a notion of government as sovereign. Accordingly, government either intervenes through economic policy as a representation of electoral concerns, or chooses to eschew directive or coercive policies so that social forces or a 'liberal market' can operate. Government regulation is variously considered a result of democratic will, electoral pressure or a response to market failure. For example, trade practices legislation governing acceptable codes of business behaviour can be viewed as a government response to consumer and business concerns over 'fair' market practices. It can also be seen as a set of interventionist policies designed to prevent market failures caused by systematic abuses, price fixing or discrimination, takeover improprieties, monopolistic tendencies, or outlawed 'inside' dealings. In this account, government establishes democratically endorsed 'rules of the game' within which economic interaction takes place.

Other society-based interpretations begin by examining power relations within the economy. The economic system gives rise to significant interests which determine the broad parameters of policy outcomes.

Pluralist and most Marxist accounts analyse economic policies as the translation of societal economic power into political power and public policy (cf. Dahl 1961; Manley 1983; Cawson 1982). Macroeconomic policies, finance and currency controls, wage policies, state arbitration and trade union regulations are public policy interventions largely in response to the structural needs of the economic system, or manipulated by organised dominant interests with economic power. There are important debates within each of these theoretical frameworks over the centrality of the economy, the cohesiveness of economic power and the influence of other competing or counteracting social forces (Lindblom 1977; Shonfield 1965; Abbey 1986).

Increasingly, however, explanations of the state—economy relationship suggest more complex forms of interaction (Lehner and Keman 1984). From this departure point, attention is directed to the intermeshing of the economy and state, with economic policy reflecting cross-currents of interests. The economy has important consequences for public policy. It establishes much of the actual policy agenda, but its requirements do not invariably appear as policy outcomes (Evans et al. 1985; Therborn 1986; Carnoy 1984).

On the contrary, policy demands from the economy are sectional, conflicting, and conditional on diverse factors. Some of these influences include the size and level of economic units (across firms, corporations, institutions, unions, consumers), the characteristics of organisational groups, and the leadership of key policy-formulators. Changes to retail shopping hours or the imposition of indirect taxes may advantage big business but undermine the position of the small business sector. Alternatively, tight monetary controls and high interest policies from government may be approved by the finance sector yet constrain the manufacturing and construction industries. With such policy issues it is not the reconciliation of capital and labour which is the problem for business organisations and trade unions; rather, they are frustrated by the lack of unanimous agreement over policy directions within their own sectoral groupings (McEachern 1986). Capital and labour are loose aggregations with diverging and sometimes inconsistent internal interests.

Yet economic policy making is not a matter of rudderless sailing across uncharted waters. It is about adapting policy processes to the structures of economic power, so that scope exists for political initiatives (Coombs 1982). Economic policy is about engineering economic growth, the allocation and transfer of resources, preference, regulation, discrimination and choices, and about shaping the material existence of the economically active and those reliant on economic redistribution. Given uncertainty, economic policy is also about governments responding to the unanticipated.

Political Variables

There are many models of decision making. Most are inadequate because they concentrate on the technical dimensions of decision making, without sufficiently acknowledging the role of politics in policy formulation. The same criticism might be applied to the economic field. Despite the hopes of some 'econocrats', economic policy is not primarily a science or technical process (Self 1975; Shonfield 1965; Galbraith 1967). Rather, economic policy making by government in Australia can be characterised as a combination of three political elements—underlying assumptions, objectives and means (cf. Grant and Nath 1984).

Underlying Assumptions

Dominant values and priorities are established by political means. They provide durable principles across society about the objectives of policy. These longer-term values may support a desired 'good society', a type of social order, legitimate practices, and preferred levels of equality or distribution. The social values attributed to profit, private property or entrepreneurial activity rely on a particular set of assumptions derived from the economic order. Capitalist societies attribute greater priority to profit than, for example, corporate responsibility. Similarly, the promotion of individualism in contrast to collectivism is not a question of expediency but involves the implementation of specific values.

When conservatives and liberals praise the virtues of a property-owning capitalist democracy based on self-reliance, they assume the capacity of individuals to cope in society (Birch 1984; Rose 1981; Withers 1983; Henderson 1983a; James 1986). Conversely, social democratic values tend to emphasise provision for the social being as a fundamental principle of social improvement (Wilenski 1983; Castles 1985). They stress priorities toward education, social services, sponsored culture, planning and protection. Whether social democratic governments actually provide better funding for these areas than conservative governments is not so certain (Wildavsky 1985a; Castles 1982; Hawker et al. 1979).

Objectives

Objectives are embodied in particular policy choices, or in thematic 'packages' of policy intentions. Such objectives are usually medium-term in application and concerned with broad goals rather than single programs. Examples include an 'inflation-first' strategy, attempts to generate growth through balance of trade surpluses, and restraint on the size of government. The second Hawke government proclaimed a 'trilogy' as its economic objective. Hawke gave commitments not to increase government borrowing, taxes or the deficit as proportions of gross domestic product. These overall strategies may guide the specific programs of government action, but contain the flexibility for change in emphasis or direction.

Means

The tools available to governments and the state are extensive but not predetermined. They combine institutions and processes within the limits of the economic system. Available means include legislative and regulatory activity, policy intervention by state and semi-state agencies, public sector assistance measures, strategic or indicative planning, persuasion, and allowing firms to opt out of arbitration awards.

Government and state means are limited by the international economy, the capitalist arrangement of society, the historical structure of institutions, the import of the constitution, and the effect of judicial interpretations. Though the tools used by the state depend on information, reliable and up to date data on the economy are difficult to obtain. Hence economic policy must be based on forecasts, estimates and trends.

Major Agencies of Economic Policy

Key economic policies are formulated and implemented by central organisations working with a number of specialist economic agencies. A shared concern with economic objectives, however, does not necessarily produce coherent policy advice. The central economic agencies begin with much the same paradigm. Yet bureaucratic interests, opposing interpretations and fragmented responsibilities can produce a policy process which is disjointed and capable of incompatible decisions.

The Commonwealth Treasury is largely an input—output manager drawing together federal and much State-level financing. It is also a major source of economic policy advice on macro-level developments in the private sector as well as overseas. Treasury therefore is mainly responsible for formulating the budget, regularly monitoring economic trends and recommending levels or types of government intervention. With the Department of Finance, it scrutinises departmental submissions and offers advice on revenue, expenditure and programmes. Treasury 'experts' have often adopted an internal 'line' on policy

issues, and this factor has led elected governments into conflict with
this powerful department (Whitwell 1986; Weller and Cutt 1976).

Treasury policy formulation responds to two 'publics'. One is internal—
government departments and programs seeking money. The other is
an external public—the markets which respond to business confidence
at home and abroad, and seek the 'right' mix of economic policies.
Federal and State Treasuries liaise regularly, often informally. The
degree of policy co-operation between Treasuries appears to rest on
shared values, the conservative professionalism of Treasury staff, esti-
mations of their non-partisan advice, and intergovernment relations
between federal and State treasurers.

Treasury's role in financial management is supplemented by the
semi-independent state-owned Reserve Bank. This central bank, separated from the older Commonwealth Bank in 1959, administers government monetary and banking policies. The Reserve Bank operates in
liaison with the treasurer, but retains its own board of directors. In
conjunction with other government trading and savings banks, the
Reserve Bank retains an important policy influence through interest
rate modifications, exchange rate levels, and the availability of capital
in Australia (Johns 1984).

Other federal government agencies with an economic policy role
include the departments of Finance, Employment and Industrial Relations, Trade, Industry Technology and Commerce, Primary Industry,
and Immigration and Ethnic Affairs. Other important non-departmental
economic agencies include the Taxation Office, Commonwealth Employment Service and the Commonwealth Public Service Board.

Three further agencies play a fundamental role in domestic economic
policy making. The Conciliation and Arbitration Commission sets wage
patterns, adjudicates on disputes over the costs of labour and attempts
to ensure continuous production. The Trade Practices Commission
regulates and enforces legitimate business practices in the areas of
market abuses, merger controls, price fixing, contracts and patents
(Caves et al. 1981). Finally, the Industries Assistance Commission,
superseding the Tariff Board, is responsible for recommending levels
of tariff protection. More recently, the IAC has established policy
guidelines toward structural adjustment and tariff erosion (Warhurst
1982a; Ewer and Higgins 1985).

A number of development agencies, often matched by State-level
counterparts, have specialised spheres of responsibility. These organisations are charged explicitly with economic policy matters relating to
particular problems or issues. Such agencies include the Australian
Trade Commission, the Development Assistance Bureau, the Dairy Corporation, the Australian Agricultural Council, the Export Development
Grants Board and the Australian Industrial Development Corporation.

The Australian Loan Council supervises the total borrowings of general capital funds by the federal and State governments. Established in 1927, the Loan Council imposes limits and co-ordinates the allocation of government borrowing from private sector sources and overseas lending institutions. Since the early 1980s the Loan Council has worked from a 'global approach' policy, which restricts public enterprises from borrowing development funds outside Loan Council aggregates.

The premiers' conference meets annually as a forum of government leaders to decide the amount and nature of federal payments to the States. The central concern of premiers' conferences is to negotiate with the federal government over the allocation of specific purpose and capital grants to States. It also discusses the formula arrangements for revenue sharing. Because federal grants are 'tied' in terms of where and how the funds can be spent, Canberra has some leverage over spending by States.

All of these institutions involved in economic policy are dominated by specialists. Each agency retains a coterie of 'expert' policy advisors who argue the line of their own department (Crisp 1975a). Moreover, virtually all these agencies are non-elected, and in many cases only tangentially accountable. The process of economic policy making does not involve wide participation nor is it markedly democratic. Elections may select leadership, but on economic policy matters the main agencies largely function outside direct cabinet control. They have established their own policy precedents from which to operate. Shared and sometimes competitive responsibility makes policy formation disjointed, specialist and partial.

Figure 8.1 indicates the institutional structure of Australian economic agencies.

Economic Policy Concerns

Governments use a series of broad policy instruments in economic management. These can be classified into five main areas of policy concern: financial regulation, fiscal matters, incomes policies, employment and productivity policies, along with a range of economic services (for a survey of these policy concerns see INDECS 1986; Nevile 1983).

There are other important economic areas to which governments pay relatively little attention. There is little direct government intervention on prices or investment levels and directions. This may reflect uncertain constitutional authority, but it also suggests that governments remain in those policy areas which are familiar and comfortable. Within a capitalist economy, governments have access to a limited range of policies. Despite evident failure to bring monetary and budgetary

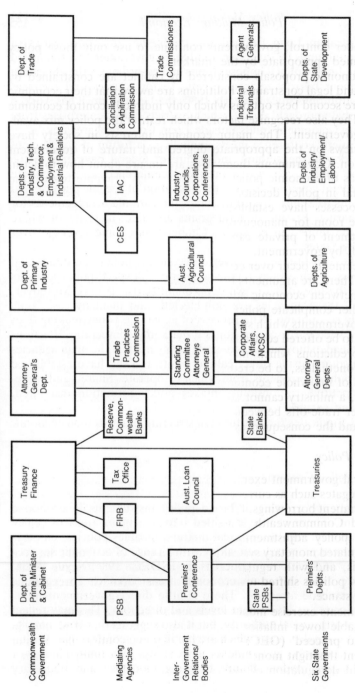

Figure 8.1 Institutional structure of Australian economic agencies

This is not meant as a complete institutional schema, but a representative sample of the significant agencies.

KEY: CES - Commonwealth Employment Service
FIRB - Foreign Investment Review Board
IAC - Industries Assistance Commission
NCSC - National Companies and Securities Commission
PSB - Public Service Board

Commonwealth Government

Dept. of Prime Minister & Cabinet
PSB

Treasury Finance
FIRB
Tax Office
Reserve, Commonwealth Banks

Attorney General's Dept.
Trade Practices Commission

Dept. of Primary Industry

Depts. of Industry, Tech. & Commerce, Employment & Industrial Relations
CES
IAC

Dept. of Trade
Trade Commissioners
Conciliation & Arbitration Commission

Mediating Agencies

Inter-Government Relations/Bodies

Premiers' Conference
Aust. Loan Council
Standing Committee Attorneys General
Aust. Agricultural Council
Industry Councils, Corporations, Conferences
Industrial Tribunals
Agent Generals

Six State Governments

Premiers' Depts.
State PSBs
Treasuries
State Banks
Corporate Affairs, NCSC
Attorney General Depts.
Depts. of Agriculture
Depts. of Industry/Employment/Labour
Depts. of State Development

trends under control, governments continue to use only those policy tools deemed appropriate by the 'market'.

The economic proposals considered by cabinet are constrained by electoral and legal constraints. Politicians are aware that their economic policies are second best options which only indirectly control economic activity. They also recognise factors which restrict the policy mix available to government. The major economic interests in society have definite views on the appropriate degree and nature of government intervention. Governments themselves are unsure about how to act in many areas of economic policy, and accordingly gravitate toward the incremental in policy decisions. Institutional structures and previous policy processes have established traditional policy concerns which leave little room for manoeuvre. Important economic decisions about the investment of private capital can be influenced, but not easily controlled, by government.

Disagreements occur over economic strategies, outcomes and consequences. There are arguments between different institutions. Technical disputes between economic advisors over the use of particular policy tools further complicate policy formulation. Economists rarely agree, so even governments which surround themselves with 'their' economists are likely to be offered contradictory advice. Policy option prescriptions rest on predictions which may be based on doubtful and rubbery figures. Nonetheless, to be credible, governments must appear to be in command of the whole economic policy field. On these issues, above all others, a ministry cannot appear divided. Governments may need to consider trade-offs between the 'rational' advice of their economic advisers and the consequences of state action.

Monetary Policy

The federal government exercises monetary policies designed to influence aggregates such as currency, institutional deposits, credit, private and government borrowings. Along with cabinet, the Treasury, Reserve Bank and Commonwealth Bank have been mainly responsible for monetary policy adjustments. Traditionally, Australia has operated with a regulated monetary system involving a fixed dollar, tight financial regulations, and with regular intervention from the Reserve Bank. Since 1984 policies shifted toward a more 'open door' and deregulated monetary stance.

Governments exercise monetary policy 'to promote an environment of sustainable lower inflation while allowing the expected pick-up in demand to proceed' (OECD 1985: 8). However, under the Hawke government this tight monetary policy occurred in conjunction with a fairly rapid deregulation of the financial sector. The policy assumed that with regulation lifted, market forces would restructure financial markets. The government relied on overseas confidence and speculation as policy instruments, in preference to continued regulatory controls.

Fiscal Policy

Fiscal policy involves government revenue, expenditure and borrowing from federal, State and local governments. It must also include the incomings and outgoings of public enterprises and statutory authorities. While fiscal policy generally refers to the total budgetary impact of government, all departments and programs contribute to aggregate outlays. Elections appear to expand greatly budgetary outlays, so the process of generating votes is also a consideration in fiscal policies (Gruen 1985).

The total public sector is by far the largest economic unit in Australia, currently with access to around 43 per cent of gross domestic product (*Budget Statements* 1986–87 paper 1: 368). Where the public sector spends its money and how it raises finance, have a major impact on the economy. For instance, the relative proportions of taxation levied on individuals directly or indirectly, or on companies, shapes patterns of spending, investment and savings.

Alternatively, the weighting allocated through the budgetary process to items of government expenditure according to recurrent spending, capital works or transfer payments, provides a major tool of economic policy. Governments can stimulate selective sectors of the economy through major capital works allocations, such as funding a major construction project, or by numerous smaller contracts to private sector suppliers.

In the 1980s, most government fiscal policy has been mildly expansionary. While Canberra has been responsible for a series of short bursts in GDP growth, State governments have adopted a more consistently expansionist fiscal approach. The deficit created by this net government expansion has been funded by public sector borrowing. The deficit as a percentage of gross domestic product has oscillated from 5 per cent under Whitlam in 1975, to 3 per cent and then 7 per cent under Fraser between 1980 and 1983, and under Hawke to 6 per cent by 1986 (OECD 1985: 27–9). Other factors besides government spending influence the deficit size, such as the international value of the Australian dollar and the rate of interest for existing borrowings.

Wages Policy

Australian federal governments can only apply a wages policy through indirect means; they lack the constitutional authority, and the real power, to set and hold all wage (or price) levels. The principal mechanism for implementing incomes policies is through compulsory arbitration. Here state influence on the institutional framework and processes is marked, though governments cannot control all outcomes. Rather, arbitration serves as a policy tool to make wage adjustments predictable and reasonably uniform.

Government economic policy has traditionally focused on wage regulation, often with an explicit support for wage restraint (Hancock 1981). Governments of different persuasions have argued that Australian real wage levels have become comparatively high, and so require some erosion. It is often claimed, for instance, that the crisis of the seventies and eighties in the Australian economy was due to inflationary wage pressures. Economists argued that government must bring down wages to maintain international competitiveness. Yet there is no clear proof that high real wages can be blamed for unemployment, nor evidence for the policy prescription that a fall in real wages would produce a systematic decline in unemployment (Hughes 1979; Nevile 1983). Indeed, by international standards, it is doubtful whether Australia can still claim to provide 'high real wages' in the 1980s.

In 1981 the Fraser government decided to experiment with a partly deregulated labour market. The cabinet abandoned a wages policy of partial indexation to allow collective bargaining (cf. Plowman 1981). The predictable result was a significant round of real wage increases—so significant, in fact, that the government was panicked in December 1982 to negotiate with the States an ad hoc public sector wages freeze. The subsequent Hawke government replaced the 'freeze' with the Accord, a voluntary incomes policy agreed between the government and the ACTU. In return for promises of broad social and industry policies, the union movement accepted wage restraint. Any increases would again be determined by a centralised wage fixing system. After four years of the Accord, the advent of a two-tier wages system attempted to introduce greater flexibility, while retaining a formal system of wage fixation. Under the two-tier policy a first tier of arbitrated adjustments was supplemented for some unions and occupational groups with a second tier of payments above the award and agreed to through private negotiation.

Employment and Productivity Policies

Governments need productivity growth to sustain levels of economic activity and to increase employment. Following Okun's law, economies require around 3 per cent increase in economic growth per year to avoid recession and to reabsorb portions of the unemployed back into the workforce. In recent years, Australia has achieved such growth rates only between 1963 and 1965, 1968 and 1973 and in 1979 (INDECS 1986: 72−4). Since the mid−1970s there has been insufficient economic growth to employ fully the available labour force. Faced with the prospect of permanent unemployment for a significant portion of the electorate, governments have sought to induce growth through granting productivity inducements to producers, taxation subsidies, depreciation and investment allowances, government grants to assist enterprise expansion, and managerial, trade and product advice. At a general level, under the broad ambit of industry policy, governments have responded with a series of specific industry 'plans'. They have also offered inducements to expand high technology industries and enable applied technology transfer.

Other policies aimed at avoiding bottlenecks in the area of employment have included manpower and training policies, education and curricula development, and specialised migrant intakes. Through various employment services such as the CES, the state seeks to find vacancies in the private sector for the available stock of unemployed labour.

Economic Services

Australian governments traditionally have provided economic services as stimulants to economic development. Infrastructure has been built and maintained by governments, including publicly funded railways, ports and roads. Subsequently, economic services expanded to include banking facilities, transportation, telecommunications, and a range of public utilities such as electricity, water, sewerage and gas. Governments have also provided industry assistance through tariffs, subsidies, packages such as the passenger motor vehicle plan of 1983, and trade assistance to expand overseas markets.

Economic Management: the Problem of Co-ordination

Monetary, fiscal, wages, employment and economic services policies do not necessarily fit together as an economic package. Policies can be contradictory or work against each other. With different policy makers and agencies responsible for each, policies tend to be discrete rather than integrated. Departments bid for additional resources, even as governments work toward a non-expansionary overall fiscal strategy. With rival bureaucracies, indirect policy tools and competing problems and solutions, the economic policy process becomes a fight about priorities.

Total government budget outlays as a percentage of Australia's gross domestic product increased from 15 per cent in 1939, to 27.4 per cent in 1945, to 38.2 per cent in 1975–76, and to around 43 per cent by 1987. Yet such post-war public sector expansion did not produce for Australia the 'mixed economy' of many European nations. The large gaps in state intervention restrict the scope for public influence over the private sector. Australians claim to participate in an advanced mixed economy. Yet government policy toward the banking sector, for instance, has remained largely at the level of mutually agreed but informal arrangements. There are no directive controls from a central nationalised bank.

Much economic policy advice from the 1940s onwards, perhaps most evident in the 1965 Vernon Report, argued that Australian economic policy was erratic, ad hoc, and unco-ordinated (see also RCAGA Task Force on Economic Policy 1975). Advisors urged a greater emphasis on economic planning. Australia had developed a substantial public sector which supported private capital. Yet the state did not assume an overhead role of planning and co-ordinating economic development (cf. McEachern 1980). The result was a partial mixed economy. A large public sector works within a corporate capitalist economy.

This Australian state operates within an international economy. It is subject to external economic forces and cycles. Control of the local economy through co-ordination is an objective governments have rarely entertained, let alone attempted. Menzies, for example, rebutted recommendations in the 1960s for economic planning. He claimed that Australia was still a pioneer economy that did not require government guidance (McFarlane 1968; Arndt 1968). Economic development was based on entrepreneurial risks rather than planning decisions. This tended to give Australia a pattern of stop—go and unco-ordinated economic activity.

Some writers argue that co-ordination is difficult because the Australian economy has been dominated by transnational corporations (Crough and Wheelwright 1982). Such companies make their investment and employment decisions based on international rather than local considerations. With Australia dependent on a world economy, any government inspired proposal for national co-ordination and planning is likely to be counter to external interests. Overseas producers, traders and investors are keen to exploit domestic resources. They are unlikely, however, to be enthusiastic about making commitments to a co-ordinated long-term economic strategy.

The relative lack of co-ordination is not due only to external factors. Some commentators suggest that co-ordination was institutionally bypassed within the agencies of government. Treasury, for example, was much more concerned with control over government financial management and regulation than with co-ordinated planning (Weller and Cutt

1976). This does not mean that Australia has been marked by an absence of economic policy. Rather, the particular economic policies adopted were fragmented, partial, conflicting and without a single direction.

Not surprisingly, external pressure and restricted internal controls limit the effectiveness and viability of many economic policies. Some critics have argued that much of Australia's economic policy has been transient, inappropriate and swiftly redundant. Spokespersons from the 'new right', for example, assert that the business sector is forced into the business of managing government, rather than left to worry about the business of business (Porter 1978; Swan 1979; Sawer 1982). Entrepreneurs have not only to calculate business factors in their decisions, but also to guess likely government actions. This is not to imply that government is in control of the economy, for the new right also blame inept regulation of otherwise functioning markets for Australia's economic problems. Rather, it is being argued that government policies disproportionately, and the new right would argue unreasonably, occupy the time of otherwise productive entrepreneurs.

Government as 'Crisis Manager'

During and immediately after the second world war, the main policy concern of the Labor federal government was to establish a 'Keynesian state'. Governments sought to avoid economic crisis and set the climate for economic activity. Keynesian economic theory was adopted as a solution to the severe economic crises produced by capitalism. Following the massive unemployment of the Great Depression, Keynesian economics insisted that the state was the only large organised body, sufficiently powerful and above individual private interests, to sustain patterns of economic activity. Governments had to accept responsibility for the entire national economy. It followed that the state should intervene to modify internal and external economic forces, and so manage the economy.

As most forms of intervention required government spending either through assistance or costs associated with regulation, governments were committed to deficit spending. Previous maxims of balanced budgeting and relatively low public expenditure were regarded as contractionist and likely to worsen economic downturns. Instead, government spending during recessions would supplement low private investment and provide public works to achieve higher levels of economic growth. These policies continued under a succession of federal Liberal governments during the 1950s and 1960s (Simms 1982). Thus crude party ideology is not a useful guide to understanding the development of Australian economic policy.

The two main post-war techniques used to sustain and stabilise economic activity were demand management and policies designed to realise full employment. Demand management relied on government to stimulate consumption through welfare spending, progressive taxation and credit access. Full employment policies also served to lift effective demand. Employment policies worked through fiscal injections such as public works expenditure, job creation programs, industry assistance and protection, and public service growth. The major strength of the post-war Keynesian state was its capacity to sustain higher and more stable levels of economic growth through a combination of public expenditure and central government regulation over macroeconomic trends.

The Keynesian state had two major weaknesses. Its policies were restricted to the nation state. As a result, Keynesianism was reliant upon favourable responses from international economic forces, in particular finance capital. The nation state was often unable to influence or counteract the impact of overseas capital interests. At home the Keynesian state could not direct investment; it could only encourage investment from private interests while awaiting sufficient levels of 'confidence' or speculative opportunities to arise.

The second problem for Keynesian governments was the electoral consequences of reducing expenditure once a recession was over. Governments found it acceptable to stimulate through spending, but more difficult to contract an economy that was 'overheated' and developing inflation. This reluctance to contract reflected a number of factors. Full employment carried with it economic consequences that tended to disrupt the finely tuned economy through higher wages, worker militancy, 'excessive' expectations and declining profitability. Moreover, popular pressure through the ballot box, together with the activities of interest groups, generated increasing and costly demands from society. Within government, bureaucratic leverage and empire building helped create a large public sector. An incremental budget system created a tendency for yearly increases in government programs.

Amid the stagflationary economic recession of the 1970s, with its rising inflation and high unemployment, the Keynesian state was discredited. Keynesian management principles were replaced by two types of macroeconomic policies (Withers 1978). Some administrations, notably the last year of the Whitlam government and most of the period of the Fraser governments, experimented with monetarist solutions. These policies sought to reduce inflation through quantitative monetary restrictions, higher levels of unemployment, lower deficits and reduced government spending. This scenario saw government not as crisis-resolving, but as an integral part of the crisis itself (Jones 1983).

The second common post-Keynesian approach has been characterised as the 'new interventionism'. This policy prescription did not assume that state-induced deficit levels and high interest rates were the only cause of inflation and unemployment. New interventionist governments responded to the recessions of the 1980s with a policy mix. They provided some level of economic stimulation within an overall direction of economic management. Some commentators in Australia have questioned whether such policies constitute 'corporatist' trends in economic policy making (Loveday 1984; Stewart 1985). During its first term, for example, the Hawke government used public sector spending to boost the building industry while restricting wage rises through the accord.

Not all the Keynesian contribution to government economic policy has been eroded. The lasting legacy of the Keynesian state has been its emphasis on central government influence over economic activity. However, two features clearly emerge from the recent attempts to resolve economic crises. First, governments do not possess the economic controls sufficient to avert crises. Following from this, and given the limitations of available policy tools, governments are forced into endless short term adjustments. Such stabs in the dark at best only ameliorate; today's policy adjustments become part of tomorrow's crisis.

Taxation and Expenditure

Government revenue raising and spending is shaped by electoral priorities. It involves the allocation of resources according to 'political needs': which groups need to be placated, which existing arrangements will be continued or expanded, what programs demand resources, and which concerns generate most noise. The budget, then, is explicitly a political document, outlining government intentions not through policy speeches but through actual resource transfers (Emy 1978: ch 9).

The budget process relies on estimates. In theory these figures are objective technical data accurately expressing the importance attributed by government to particular programs. Such data, however, provide only the illusion of precision. Budgets are structured for public consumption, based on estimates which are partial, uncertain and frequently already out of date before the budget bills reach parliament. Those who budget for government must rely on guesstimates of revenue and expenditure levels. These figures are 'soft', for they are based on forecasts of anticipated behaviour and trends. The treasurer must estimate the effect of a policy decision and build a conjecture about its financial implications into the annual budget.

When, for example, the level of unemployment rose dramatically in the mid–1970s, government had to increase cash transfers to meet new entitlements (Stanford 1978). Similarly, estimates for single-parent support programs have depended partly on the electoral significance of the 'problem', on changing clientele numbers and on comparative welfare policy estimates (cf. Wilenski 1983). When introducing such programs, governments cannot know the precise allocation of resources needed.

Since the late 1970s, the key figure for the federal budget deficit has been formulated with business confidence in mind. Cabinet and Treasury gauge the deficit according to political perceptions. Budget expenditure 'figures' are calculated to fall within a prescribed and electorally acceptable range.

Despite these difficulties, governments persist with budget estimates. There are three principal reasons for continuing to invest faith in uncertain budget statistics. Governments need figures as the basis of forecasts. Some figures are better then none. Further, power over the figures is an important resource in debate and in asserting authority over the public sector. The responsibility to draw up figures, along with the capacity to 'use' figures, is a major instrument of control within government. Without 'their' figures, cabinet and departments would hand the initiative to others. Further, budget estimates persist because they represent an exercise in accountability. Declared budgetary figures provide governments with legitimacy.

In a period of sustained recession, the cost of maintaining many state services has been financed through a current account deficit. Australian governments have always been major borrowers, usually from overseas sources. By 1987 the gross external debt representing public and private borrowing had topped $100 billion, or about one third of gross domestic product. Though business groups often criticise high government overseas borrowing, most of this deficit was created by loans to the private sector. Business spokespersons nevertheless equate government borrowing with overspending. They recognise that a collective decision to provide public goods eventually requires collective repayment through higher taxes. Conversely, private borrowing is regarded, somewhat myopically, as involving only private, self-regarding decisions, paid for out of profits, and with little 'flow on' costs to others. Business defines its own borrowing as inherently 'productive', despite the fact that much of it is speculative or passed on through higher prices to consumers. Both types of borrowing involve costs to those unable to transfer the burden of repayment to others, notably PAYE taxpayers and consumers.

Private and public borrowing at a high level can potentially erode future living standards in Australia, particularly if funds are not used for long term productive ventures, but for takeovers, speculation or direct consumption. EPAC has argued that Australia will stabilise its external debt only if borrowing is kept within 40 per cent of gross domestic product by 1991. However, the combination of this outstanding debt with a weakened Australian dollar, may mean that one quarter of Australia's total export receipts would be required simply to service the loans (BCA 1987). Excessive government expenditure is not the main culprit here, but it is often singled out as a convenient explanation and target for blame.

Continuing fiscal problems mean taxation policies have asssumed a new electoral importance. For some time there has been discontent with inequities in taxation schedules and with the increased burden which has fallen on PAYE middle income earners. Because both major parties advocate some taxation relief, the difficulty of matching revenue to expenditure has become an acute problem for state managers. As a consequence, the principles of taxation policy have occupied much political debate. This issue is made more complex by federalism. Taxation powers are shared, with the central government responsible for income revenue, and the States collecting from other taxes and charges. Just as representatives failed to agree on taxation reform at the July 1985 national taxation summit, so each level of government advocates tax relief but seeks to protect its own income base (Sharman 1980).

Theoretical explanations for the increases in government expenditure have identified a range of possible causes. 'Wagner's Law' claims that government expenditure rises as a function of increased disposable income throughout society (Rose 1984). Peacock and Wiseman (1961) developed the notion of private sector 'displacement' caused by expansion of the public sector during crisis or 'abnormal' periods. Public tolerance of higher taxation, for example, increases in wartime; with the cessation of hostilities the state does not return to its pre-war levels of expenditure.

Other explanations point to the logic of incremental growth. Governments make regular but small additions to programmes. Such increments continually augment the size and activity of the public sector (Wildavsky 1975; Lindblom 1959). Wildavsky has since argued that the pattern of expanding government is too pervasive to satisfy monocausal explanations. Instead he argues that the growth of government is tied to cultural factors and especially to a bias that generates 'solutions looking for problems' (Wildavsky 1985a). In this view, sectarian divisions, religious based parties, strong social hierarchies, and the pursuit of equality of results, each contribute to increased state spending. While these factors are significant, Wildavsky's hypothesis does not adequately distinguish whether cultural bias correlates with the growth of government expenditure or is the major cause (cf. Olson 1982; Offe 1984).

State Governments as Economic Policy Makers

State governments have fewer macroeconomic policy tools at their disposal than do national governments. State government budget expenditure is largely consumed in salaries, running costs, goods and services. Even so, States play an important role in stimulating local industry and influencing their regional economies. State purchasing and tendering policies, acting as informal State preferences, provide a valuable stimulus to local business. State industry policies serve to attract investment, sponsor location, assist in establishment costs, provide support facilities and subsidise production costs. Each of these government measures contributes to a pervasive network of State-level economic support to business. In the past State economic assistance was traditionally directed toward the rural industries, but increasingly States have induced, supported and expanded their manufacturing, high technology and tertiary sectors.

An emphasis on development has emerged as the enduring principle of State government economic policy (Horne 1976). In less populated States such as Western Australia and Queensland, the 'developmentalist ideology' comprises a shared set of beliefs centred on government promoting entrepreneurial ventures. This developmentalism has been marketed as a 'pioneer spirit' shown by 'big capitalists' in the form of property developers and tourist entrepreneurs (Head 1986).

The Fraser government policy of 'new federalism' gave the States greater authority over public sector expenditure (Groenewegen 1976; Saunders and Wiltshire 1980). The result has been an expansion of State borrowing as a percentage of gross domestic product from under 1 per cent to 3 per cent (ABS 1985). Increases in State expenditure have been designed to offset cutbacks in federal funding. This shift in government borrowing indicates how State governments as regional governmental institutions will defend their local economies (Head 1986; Galligan 1986a). State governments occupy a strategic political level. They mediate between the macroeconomic concerns of central governments and the demands of local industries. State governments have expanded borrowing to cushion their own economies from external forces.

State economic policies are also involved in cross-subsidising industries. Historically, States such as Victoria and South Australia diverted economic resources mainly from their rural base to assist manufacturing.

More recently, States have consciously subsidised 'sunrise' industries in the high technology area as a means of broadening the employment base within their State. The rural industry also enjoys cross-subsidisation from State policies. In the case of Queensland, rail freight charges extracted from coal producers provide a subsidy toward the rail costs of rural producers (Galligan 1986b). State governments use 'surplus' resources from one industry sector to sustain the economic development of another.

Economic Decision Making

Economic policies emerge through a negotiated process involving various networks of interests. Governments at the macro level are unsure which directions to follow. Policy 'succeeds' if it is not overtly resisted by influential sectors of the economy. In the regions, governments act to protect those interests with access to, and influence on, the local State.

This structure, in which responsibility is shared and authority fragmented, does not encourage agreement between governments on economic policy. Through expanding the public sector and the use of monetary, fiscal, wages, employment and economic services policies, governments have demonstrated some capacity to shape the level and nature of economic activity. The main problem for economic decision makers, however, remains the difficulty of matching changing economic conditions with short term policy adjustments. Though governments must accept responsibility for the economy, it is difficult for any single federal or State cabinet to formulate coherent policies or to impose controls over the direction of economic life.

Economic policy, then, is a demonstration of hope rather than certainty. The possible is restricted, if not shaped, by international forces. The tools of policy are unsure, and influence indirect. Effects must be built into budgets before they can be measured, and policies must make heroic assumptions about causal relations within the economy. Yet all these constraints have not impeded the 'making' of economic policies. Indeed, whenever unsure, Australian governments resort to policy. Any economic policy represents some control. To be caught without a policy would be to surrender even the illusion of power.

Further Reading

Butlin, N.G., Barnard, A. and Pincus, J.J. (1982) *Government and Capitalism* Sydney: Allen & Unwin.

Catley, Bob and McFarlane, Bruce (1983) *Australian Capitalism In Boom and Depression* Sydney: APCOL 2nd edn.

Galbraith, J.K. (1975) *Economics and the Public Purpose* Ringwood: Penguin.

Grant, W. and Nath, S. (1984) *The Politics of Economic Policy making*, Oxford: Basil Blackwell.

Hall, Peter (1984) 'Patterns of Economic Policy; an organisational analysis' in S. Bornstein, S. et al. (eds) *The State in Capitalist Europe* London: Allen & Unwin.

Hughes, B. (1980) *Exit Full Employment* Sydney: Angus & Robertson.

9
Policy Making : Industrial

State intervention is often about protecting business, farmers, unions or consumers. Governments design measures which will advantage or preserve the position of these sectional groups. Many interests are safeguarded by a broad set of actions known as industrial policies. While the label is fairly new, Australian governments have long implemented sectional policies for industries, and so have always had industrial policies of sorts.

The difficulty for politicians has been satisfying endless sectional demands for protection and support. Any industry policy benefits one sectional group over others, so creating problems of co-ordination and equity. Further, governments need to link industrial measures with broader economic policies, such as those on interest rates. The formulation of policy, therefore, is often piecemeal and incremental. Governments must pursue macroeconomic objectives, yet not disturb the micro environment of industries. Only through cautious experiment, and by remaining within the traditions and expectations of Australian state intervention, can governments hope to balance industry policy with other priorities. For these are not just technical economic decisions. Through parties and pressure groups, sectional groups can oppose unacceptable industry policy proposals. Industrial choices have electoral consequences.

Industrial policies are directed almost exclusively toward the private sector. Governments depend upon business to invest, to provide employment and to pursue social ends for private gain. Politicians entice business growth through indirect economic policy, and through the specific, targeted interventions of industrial policy. Australian governments, however, lack the constitutional authority or political incentive to force private sector compliance with state objectives. Industry policies must encourage, rather than order.

Limited direct power forces government to rely on a combination of incentives and restrictions. Government can only intervene using the carrot and the stick. Excluding state enterprises such as Qantas, it is generally privately owned firms which invest in production and new technologies, which build factories, explore for oil and minerals, and export commodities. Only rarely do Australian governments enter industrial production directly, and then only through ownership of defence related aircraft, shipping and military clothing factories. The limited influence of government is demonstrated repeatedly when companies announce factory closures. Despite pleas, threats and inducements, there is very little government can do to prevent the job losses.

The Australian constitution divides responsibility for industry between the Commonwealth and State governments. Commonwealth powers are limited to the import and export of industrial products; only since the second world war has Canberra established independent departments for primary and secondary industries. Changing financial resources were the impetus for increased Commonwealth participation. Canberra became responsible for income taxes in 1942. Through tied grants or direct funding, the Commonwealth became involved in a wider range of industry policies than envisaged by the constitution. Nevertheless, State governments have a long history in industrial development, and are increasingly involved in industrial promotion (Head 1986; Sheridan 1986).

With two levels of governments responding to different sectional demands, there is a danger of contradictory Commonwealth and State policies. In the late 1960s and 1970s, for example, the Commonwealth government sought to lower rates of protection against imports for the domestic textiles, clothing and footwear industries. At the same time, decentralisation policies of the Victorian government encouraged those same industries to establish in country towns.

Another consequence of competition between State development policies can be the proliferation of uneconomically small or fragmented industries. The Industries Assistance Commission reported in 1980 that both the South Australian and Western Australian governments had required BHP to build steel plants in their States. These foundries at Whyalla and Kwinana were a condition of BHP access to deposits of iron ore. As the commission argued, 'both plants are now far smaller than that at which most economies of scale are realised and could be expected to suffer substantial cost disadvantages compared to plants with an optimal scale of production' (IAC 1973–74: 39).

The fragmented policy formulation evident in other policy arenas also affects industrial choices. Federalism muddles national strategies, as different levels of government compete for the prosperity they hope will follow the establishment of industries within their jurisdiction. The skilled industrialist learns to bargain between governments for maximum sectional advantage.

The Range of Industry Policy

State intervention in industry has multiple objectives. Governments have been concerned primarily to ensure that industries grow, for with expansion comes employment and general economic well-being, so State and Commonwealth governments have introduced policies for industry promotion, industrial development and industrial assistance. Since the early 1940s such policies have been far more extensive and detailed, and the relationship between government and industrialists far closer (Loveday 1982: 3).

Governments have promoted the development of particular manufacturing industries, partly to provide jobs and partly to reduce reliance on imports. Increasingly, governments have also sought to influence the location of industry. National and State governments have adopted decentralisation policies. These aim to induce industrial settlement in other than New South Wales and Victoria, or to encourage industry to move outside the metropolitan centres within individual States. So keen are State governments to develop industries within their boundaries that they compete for attention. In the case of aluminium smelting, States tried to out-bid each other for investment by providing a range of subsidies and incentives.

Governments also regulate the relationship between industries and the wider society. Such policies include competition measures which define trade practices to ensure that market conditions prevail and that competitive benefits are passed to the consumer. Consumer protection policies specify trading responsibilities and include product standards, while environmental protection policies prescribe factory pollution levels, methods of toxic waste disposal and standards for the exploitation of natural resources. These policies can be characterised as controls, and are often criticised by business as government interference. They can also be interpreted as policies which produce socially desirable behaviour from industry. Regulatory policies mediate the relationship between producers, consumers and the environment.

Though Australian industries are part of a world market, successive governments have sought to insulate them from international competition. Traditional tariff policies have protected locally based industries by imposing high costs on overseas products. More recently, foreign investment policies aim to guard Australian-owned firms against takeover by international companies and to prevent the exploitation of natural resources by overseas interests. While foreign investment regulation can restrict international investment, in practice these controls are rarely activated. The primacy of economic growth as a goal makes governments more concerned with higher investment levels than with the origins of investment funds.

Industrial relations policies are the measures used by governments to regulate the wages and conditions of the workforce. While industrial policies generally are concerned with the development and provision of employment, industrial relations policies aim to contain wage levels while ensuring appropriate wages and working conditions within industries. Moreover, industrial relations policies seek to prevent industrial disputes. Again, governments must use a combination of carrot and stick measures. Unions are given recognition within the system so that the state can establish agreed procedures for dispute resolution. As the public sector is the largest single employer, governments also have a direct interest in industrial relations policies which affect their own workforce.

Recognition for unions within the system is not the same as union influence over the range of industrial policies. Traditionally, industrial development policies have been designed to induce investment by industrialists; it is assumed that unionists will benefit through increased employment opportunities. In making choices about industrial policy, governments face employers and employees with largely divergent interests. Only in instances where both groups benefit from state intervention and tariff protection, such as in the vehicle industry, will the interests of capital and labour coincide. The Hawke government's car industry plan was based on support from car companies and vehicle unions; if the policy had been unfavourable, these groups would combine to lobby against the decision.

A divided jurisdiction produces multiple agencies involved in promoting, developing and assisting industry. While the constitution leaves industrial relations as a residual power for the States, High Court judgments have subsequently given the Commonwealth a larger role. The development of a federal trade union movement led to a High Court interpretation that the Commonwealth can intervene if a dispute crosses State boundaries or when similar claims or disputes occur in two or more States. Federal and State awards have segregated the workforce, allowing different levels of government to mediate in industrial relations policy. Yet the federal government is not automatically the most influential, particularly when disputes are confined to a single State. When the Queensland government imposed new restrictions on disputes within the electricity industry (Gardner and McQueen 1986), or when the Tasmanian government removed the holiday pay loading for workers under the State award, the Commonwealth found it difficult or impossible to intervene. As the Hancock Report argued in 1985, such examples emphasise the fragmentation of policy formulation in this field.

Industrial policy making commonly involves the devolution of responsibility from government and departments to statutory authorities.

Two of the most prominent statutory authorities in Commonwealth administration are involved: the Industries Assistance Commission which tenders advisory reports on levels of tariffs, subsidies and government support for particular industries, and the Conciliation and Arbitration Commission which is pivotal to the system of wage fixing. State development policies are also commonly implemented through statutory authorities and, at both levels of government, financial assistance to industries is often allocated by statutory development banks.

The Tools of Industrial Policy

The development of industry relates to wider economic issues. There are trade implications, with consequences for defence and foreign relations. An industrial workforce requires policies about immigration and ethnic affairs, while industry promotion and decentralisation affects the distribution of population and so requires urban and regional policies.

The tools used by government to promote industry are remarkably varied, though all involve subsidising the private sector. The range of assistance to manufacturing industries alone serves as an example. Of greatest moment are import protection policies, supported by a wide range of grants and subsidies, a number of schemes for tax exemptions and various forms of indirect assistance.

Types of industry policy include export incentive grants, subsidies and bounties on items as diverse as books and tractors. Governments can also assist through investment and depreciation allowances, training of industrial workers, the scientific research of the CSIRO, purchasing policies, and the cost of departmental export and trade promotion machinery. At the State and local level, governments may also supply industrial land, support the building or leasing of factories, and the provision of employee housing, and subsidise the cost of transport.

Because the tools of industrial policies are so diverse and the impact of policies so extensive, industrial policy formulation and implementation involves numerous federal and State departments and agencies (Loveday 1982: ch 4; Warhurst 1986). Co-ordination of policies within the state apparatus is time consuming and difficult. It requires numerous taskforces, interdepartmental committees, and meetings to seek agreement between officials, ministers, industries and unions. The interdepartmental committee which considers the reports of the IAC, for example, never has less than half a dozen departments represented. For a particularly contentious report, with implications across multiple portfolios, up to ten departments may participate in discussions. This occurred in 1980, when the public service considered IAC recommendations on the textile, clothing and footwear industries.

To formulate options and operate these tools of policy, the industrial field relies on professional advice from economists. Policy discussions commence with the submissions of economists which estimate the costs of industry assistance and the implications for a proposal on other interests, such as producers or consumers. Economists generally bring to their reports an ideological and professional preference for a free market over state intervention. Because claims must be justified in the technical language of costs and benefits, industry policy community debates centre on rival economic analyses. Each sectional group hires economists to produce reports favouring its position. Those advocating privatisation or reduced government support are attacked by interests which benefit from state intervention. Should economic arguments fail, an industry can put forward 'public good' arguments for continued support, such as the need to maintain production for defence purposes. Despite rhetoric about the place of the free market, the industrial development and industrial relations policies of all major parties remain strongly interventionist.

Most government choices are made amid uncertainty, but the industrial field includes many of the information problems which plague economic policy. Those deciding industrial policies must estimate the costs of assistance and predict the consequences of particular government interventions. As with budget formulation, consequences can be unpredictable, however superficially elaborate the technical model of calculation. Only in the last twenty years, for example, have coherent estimates of the costs of tariff protection been available to those who make industrial policy. Even these figures are not universally accepted, but are criticised for including only limited, quantifiable factors. Furthermore, the consequences of many courses of action are reliant on the actions of others; governments are easily swayed by predictions—or thinly veiled threats—that a particular policy choice will produce substantial increases in unemployment.

Competing sectional pressures, backed by well documented but contradictory economic reports, create difficulties for governments which hope to make 'rational' decisions in the contentious industrial field. One extensively discussed example of a cabinet caught between economic prescription and electoral imperative was the decision of the Whitlam government to abandon planned reform of assistance to the motor vehicle industry and opt instead for protectionist policies (Robertson 1979; Glezer 1982: 159–67; Warhurst 1982a: 182–208; Rattigan 1986: 213–31). Early in its first term, the Whitlam government announced plans to rationalise the local car industry. The appropriate report from the IAC arrived in 1974. It advised cabinet to discontinue local content plans and to slowly reduce tariff protection. The IAC calculated the result as a decline of uneconomic sections of the industry, costing 15 000 jobs over ten years. Benefits would include cheaper cars and a more efficient car industry creating 13 000 new jobs over the same period.

Employers and employees both felt threatened by this potential new policy. They lobbied the Commonwealth government to ignore the IAC recommendations. The industry argued that the net loss in employment, should government assistance be lowered, would not be 2000 as the IAC predicted, but closer to 50 000 jobs (Ford Motor Co.). At a time of rising unemployment, the government could not accept this possibility. The IAC recommendation was shelved.

The range and diversity of policies and policy tools makes it difficult to speak of a single 'industrial policy'. Different levels of government and multiple state agencies are pursuing measures with industrial consequences. There are many industry policies, often competing and inconsistent. It is a policy arena which emphasises the limited power of government, and the reliance of state measures on business agreement.

Commonwealth Industry Assistance Policies

The Australian manufacturing sector is a creation of the assistance provided by successive governments. From the 1940s until the 1970s, 27–28 per cent of the workforce was employed in manufacturing. As a share of GDP and as a proportion of exports, the manufacturing sector more then doubled over the same thirty years (IAC 1974: 42). Government policies, especially tariff protection, underpinned the development of most major industries in this sector. Forms of government assistance remain vital to many manufacturing firms. Despite the economic crisis of the mid 1970s, the sector still employs 20 per cent of the Australian workforce. These employees are concentrated in the industrial States of New South Wales, Victoria and South Australia—not only in the capital cities, but in depressed regional centres such as Wollongong, Geelong and Whyalla. Employers and trade unions, as well as State and local governments, have a direct interest in how policies affect employment prospects. Some local manufacturing industries are also protected for defence reasons or because they offer potential employment for particular categories of workers such as migrants, women or unskilled men.

Critics of government assistance for manufacturing industry include importers who make their living from importing and selling overseas made products, foreign firms and their governments. Other vocal opponents are industrial consumers such as farmers. Rural production costs are increased if farmers rely on imported machinery, or if countries retaliate against local tariffs by protecting their own farming sectors from Australian competition. Over the past twenty years, the pressure groups representing these interests have supported the economic orthodoxy which opposes government intervention in markets. The case for reduced state industry policies have been put primarily by the economists within government, teaching in universities, and writing for the media.

The Policies

The consensus about appropriate policies for industry has changed dramatically over time. For sixty years general agreement prevailed on a policy of 'protection all round' (Butlin et al. 1982). Politicians were concerned to reach arrangements and balances between industries and sectional claims. Economic rationalism, which came to prevail in the 1980s, was previously unpersuasive because policy was shaped by national development and welfare goals.

Policy changes emerged from the mid−1960s, hastened by international economic circumstances, the growing influence of the modern economics profession, the infusion of those ideas into the Tariff Board through its chairman, Alf Rattigan, and the decline of the local manufacturing sector. The last twenty years have witnessed a slow rolling back of import protection for manufacturing industries. Average protection for manufacturing fell from 35 to 25 per cent between 1973 and 1983. Any general consensus about policy now appears to favour a more internationally competitive industry structure (IAC 1986).

The reduction of protection has not directly translated into less Commonwealth government intervention. Rather, intervention and assistance have taken different forms. The Hawke cabinet, continuing a trend established by the Fraser government, isolated industries such as steel, automobiles, and textiles, clothing and footwear, for special 'sectoral' treatment with higher but temporary levels of protection to enable restructuring. Following the Accord between the ACTU and the ALP, the government expanded consultative processes between manufacturers, unions and the public sector. These instances of 'new intervention' have been linked with employer commitments to exports and the introduction of new technologies, and to union concessions on matters such as inefficient work practices (Forsyth 1985; Ewer and Higgins 1986).

Policy Making Institutions

When making industrial policy, Commonwealth governments have always sought a statutory buffer between themselves and the private sector. In the industry protection area, the Tariff Board played this role from 1921 to 1973; since 1974 the Industries Assistance Commission has performed a similar function. The IAC is a statutory advisory body. It conducts public inquiries and undertakes research, generally at the initiative of the government, asking questions decided by cabinet. The IAC then reports on individual terms of reference to the responsible ministerial department. The bureaucracy in turn convenes an interdepartmental committee which forwards the report and its own recommendation to cabinet for a final decision. Government choices— to alter or retain a set of tariffs and associated assistance—are then implemented by the customs service and relevant departments.

The use of statutory authorities adds links in the policy making chain; it allows governments to distance themselves from some recommendations while retaining the opportunity to intervene whenever necessary. There is a complex relationship between the government and its statutory authorities in the industrial field. In formal terms, the IAC is governed by legislative rules (the IAC Act 1973 and amendments). Informally, governments establish operating procedures for various investigations. These rules and conventions govern the boundaries of subjects to be investigated and the timetable for submission of reports. The government also determines the level and number of IAC staff. Each constraint affects the policy recommendations which emerge.

Both the government and the IAC seek to manipulate these rules and regulations to their own strategic advantage. In his autobiography, Alf Rattigan acknowledges that he and his ministers, particularly McEwen, realised they were locked in conflict over policy. Outcomes were largely determined by the form and mandate of institutions such as the Tariff Board and later the IAC. Reports were influenced by the relationships between the minister and statutory advisors, and by cabinet decisions about which industries to examine (Rattigan 1986).

The significance of the organisational form of policy advice involves the nature of the statutory authority itself. When John Crawford recommended the creation of the IAC, he argued that the new body could 'because of its independence, provide disinterested advice in an area of government activity which will always be subjected to conflicting pressures from special interest groups within the community' (Crawford 1973: 3–4). The IAC, however, is not disinterested, but politically active. Its own procedures are integral to the policy making process.

The IAC comprises commissioners appointed for terms of five years. These are supported by public service staff. At present there are six commissioners, including a chairman, and the equivalent of 298 staff (IAC 1986). Though in its heyday the IAC has been twice this size, it remains a large and powerful body. Almost without exception, IAC staff are orthodox economists imbued with a preference for market-based policies. They offer solutions to policy problems which often depend on long term restructuring of industries and subsequent loss of jobs. This advice, publicly reported and praised by the wider economics profession, the press and other sectors such as the farming community, has brought the IAC into conflict with successive governments. IAC reports cause embarrassment, for they ask government to take unpopular decisions at times of relatively high unemployment. During a review of the IAC undertaken by businessman John Uhrig in 1983, submissions from manufacturing associations and even government departments such as Industry and Commerce urged the radical restructuring or dismantling of the commission. Other submissions, from allies such as the farmers, defended the work and findings of the IAC.

Politicians cannot easily ignore the IAC, but they may wish to tone down its advice. Recognising that the commission is now an established part of policy making machinery, governments have employed numerous means to constrain IAC influence. The Fraser ministry, for example, appointed commissioners who were more sympathetic to protectionist policies of a kind favoured by the manufacturing lobby (Warhurst 1982a: 91–92). These changes appeared to have little impact on the prevailing ethos of the commission. More importantly, governments kept the IAC from reporting on troubled industries such as textiles, clothing and footwear, automobiles and steel. The Hawke government put much greater emphasis on distinctive policies for particular sectors, and so established separate authorities to advise on the automotive and steel industries (Ewer and Higgins 1986).

The IAC functions to keep government separate from recommendations about industry policy. IAC reports are a way of testing sectional response to a proposal. Once received, a report is examined by an interdepartmental committee. Until recently, interdepartmental advice to cabinet came from a standing committee on industry assistance. This committee was the focus of endless argument, as bureaucrats jockeyed for structures and positions which would advantage their departmental view. Cabinet decisions altered departmental responsibility for the IAC, the chairmanship of the interdepartmental committee, its size and membership, and even aspects of its procedures (Warhurst 1982a: 71–88). Even so, there were occasions when differences of opinion between departments were so great that no report to cabinet could be agreed on. On other occasions, such as consideration of the 1974 IAC report on the motor vehicle industry, the interdepartmental committee virtually conducted its own inquiry before rejecting the IAC report.

Though policy prescriptions may be debated within the IAC and the bureaucracy, it is cabinet which must finally decide. Yet even cabinet will refer industrial policy to a sub-committee before making a decision. Though the subcommittee reports to cabinet, many ministers still find the issues and the IAC reports too technical and difficult. Final decisions are left to those ministers with portfolio responsibility for industry (Weller and Grattan 1981: 110). Months might elapse before cabinet makes and announces it choice. In 1980, cabinet delayed even considering an IAC report on textiles, clothing and footwear, for ministers were divided on the recommendations, and an election was looming (Warhurst 1982a: 66).

Industry Policy Debates

Numerous interests, organisations and individuals participate in an elongated set of public and private procedures before any new industry policy is created. The process has become more complicated over the last twenty years, particularly at the Commonwealth level. More people understand and are affected by the consequences of industry policy, and the connections between industry measures and other economic and social policies are now more frequently elaborated (Tsokhas 1984). More importantly, the breakdown of consensus on 'protection all round' has produced a hotly contested process, with more scope for public and sectional participation.

The IAC has contributed a common language and paradigm to discussions about industry policy. An understanding of orthodox neo-classical economic principles, and submissions structured around economically 'rational' propositions, are now essential for any group hoping to influence policy. As a consequence

... a spread of economic expertise took place. The IAC created a situation in which the discourse largely occurred between professional economists. The other actors geared up to maintain a place in the process. To have not done so would have meant being left behind. The recruitment of professional economists for this purpose occurred most obviously among interest groups and state governments, but also among some federal government departments. Part of the spread in fact took place through the transfer of IAC officers to positions as lobbyists or to state government departments or to the secretariats of interest groups or federal departments (Warhurst 1982a: 229).

In no field was the spread of IAC staff, closely followed by the commission 'ethos', more prevalent than in primary industry. In the reports of government departments, and in the policy submissions of the National Farmers Federation, rural debate has of necessity become more economically literate. Farmers have learned to criticise tariff barriers—and to defend their own subsidies and bounties—in the jargon of economic rationalism.

State Development Policies

State governments are major actors in industrial policy. They have a long history of direct intervention in those fields for which the States have constitutional authority (Head 1986: 36–41). As Loveday comments:

> Denied the use of the tariff since Federation, the states have had to fall back on other methods of promoting industry. Although they did much, directly through such things as freight concessions or indirectly through public works programmes, they seldom had sustained and systematic policies for industrial growth before the Second World War. Since then, all of them have discovered—some sooner than others—the advantages of providing their own inducements to industry in addition to those provided generally by the tariff system (Loveday 1982: 174).

Though denied the power to impose tariffs, State governments seek to intervene in federal decisions about protection. They make submissions to bodies such as the IAC, and apply direct pressures on Canberra should a Commonwealth policy appear to disadvantage a local industry.

The range of direct assistance schemes offered by State governments is enormous. The IAC has identified at least thirty-eight different types of industry assistance measures offered by State governments. These can be grouped in seven separate categories: financial, infrastructure, transport, marketing, technology, employment and special services (IAC 1981: 213–214; see also Warhurst 1986: 65–66). Many are offered on a routine administrative basis to all types of firms. Often a State government puts together a package which it hopes will attract a particular firm or contract.

The States competed, for example, to be chosen as the location for the construction of diesel—electric submarines by private contractors for the Department of Defence at a cost of $2.6 billion (Cooksey 1986). The Queensland government offered a choice of two free sites as well as 'all buildings necessary for the construction and maintenance of submarines'. Both the New South Wales and South Australian governments offered subsidy packages worth about $30 million, including a site and essential services. The chairman of the New South Wales Submarine Task Force was quoted as saying that 'NSW has a deeper pocket than South Australia'. Such competitive expenditure appears wasteful and inefficient from a national perspective, although the winning State will see the investment as necessary and beneficial.

State Pressure on the Commonwealth

For States to benefit from the promotion of industrial development, they must not cut across measures introduced by the Commonwealth.

In particular, States must consider federal control of imports and exports when deciding whether to fund an industry. In the 1960s State governments realised that the Commonwealth had more powerful policy tools and more money at its disposal. In many circumstances, the best a State could do for a firm or industry was to lobby the Commonwealth government. State representatives began to appear before the public inquiries of the Tariff Board. The South Australian government, for example, sought to defend local whitegoods manufacturers, and later made major submissions to the passenger motor vehicle and shipbuilding industry inquiries. Other governments followed suit, both with professional submissions and with lobbying by premiers and senior ministers.

From 1974, officials and ministers met in Commonwealth—State conferences. Yet by the end of the decade, the Crawford Study Group could still criticise the absence of 'standing machinery for co-ordinating Commonwealth and State policies (for example, industry, manpower, regional and housing policies) relevant to adjustment problems at the level of States, cities or regions' (Crawford 1979: Vol 1: ch 14: 14). Though States sought a voice, they could not always overcome a structural bias in the organisation of policy advice. The IAC was generally disinterested in regional variations of national policies, whatever the difficulties this produced for particular State objectives and measures. Because the constitution declared that national policies such as tariffs should be uniform, even an IAC sensitive to regional concerns could not have recommended local exemptions. States were caught in the unpleasant position of arguing for unacceptable regional policies to a national body without constitutional authority to comply.

State Policy Making Institutions

State governments must create specialist institutions and devote resources to industrial policy making if they are to make an impact. Between 1945 and 1974 each State developed an agency with specific responsibility for State development (Hughes 1984: 267). With the exception of the Tasmanian Development Authority, these industry agencies have been upgraded to the status of a full department. They are currently known as the Department of Industry Development (Qld), Department of State Development (SA), Department of Industry and Small Business (NT), Department of Industrial Development and Decentralisation (NSW), Department of Industry, Technology and Resources (Vic), and the Department of Industrial Development and Commerce (WA).

While these departments have primary responsibility for industrial policies, State premiers and their departments are often involved in the negotiation to attract federal support and private investment. State promotion may rely on the 'strong premier type':

They sell themselves and their states with skill and fervour. State development has been a primary policy objective for all, and they have competed with one another in seeking to attract investment. They have been super-salesmen for their States, undertaking diplomatic missions and bargaining by offering attractive concessions to prospective investors (Chaples, Nelson and Turner 1985: 246).

Other State bodies involved in industry promotion, development and assistance include housing trusts, development authorities and transport and energy agencies. Each State, except Tasmania, also maintains international offices in London, Tokyo and in some cases elsewhere (Warhurst and O'Loghlin 1985). With so many agencies competing to control a section of industrial policy, administrative co-ordination within a State can be complicated and uncertain. Authority is fragmented between State departments, which must then negotiate with an equally fragmented array of Commonwealth agencies.

Industrial Relations

Industrial relations involves the interaction between employers, managers and employees in industries, particularly regarding workplace conditions and the determination of wages. Industrial relations 'fundamentally concerns the many ways people behave in the context of work, both as individuals and as members of groups' (Dabscheck and Niland 1981: 13). Just as governments adjudicate sectional claims between industries, so they have also assumed a role adjudicating the terms of employment between capital and labour.

Within the industrial relations institutions, different interests are represented by unions of wage workers, and by associations speaking for major producer groups such as business and farmers. Traditionally, government intervention supported an 'historic compromise' which included protection for manufacturers, assistance for primary producers and a minimum wage for workers (Shann 1948; Butlin et al. 1982). This compromise has been institutionalised, through the creation of 'the Australian system of diffusion' in which 'three quasi-legislative subsystems ... have served to equalise the distribution of resources among the producer groups' (Emy 1974: 500). These subsystems are the arbitration system, marketing boards and the IAC.

Industrial relations issues are intrinsically involved in any industrial policy. An industrial relations policy is also bound up with a government's overall economic strategy. Government control over wages, however, is indirect. Governments must seek compromises, for they cannot always legislate outcomes. This creates major dilemmas for industrial relations policy making.

Institutions

Constitutional responsibility for industrial relations policy making is shared between State and Commonwealth governments (Isaac and Ford 1966: Part iv). Section 51(xxxv) of the constitution, often known as the 'industrial power', enables the Commonwealth government to make laws with respect to 'conciliation and arbitration for the prevention and settlement of industrial disputes extending beyond the limits of any one State'. While on a strict reading this section is relatively restrictive, in recent judgments the High Court has interpreted the powers of the Commonwealth more broadly (Creighton, Ford and Mitchell 1983: 177–185).

Industrial tribunals, operating as either 'courts' or 'wages boards', operate at both federal and State levels (Isaac and Ford 1966: 271). Of these tribunals, the most significant is the Commonwealth Conciliation and Arbitration Commission, created in 1904 as the Commonwealth Court of Conciliation and Arbitration, and given its current title and form in 1956. The original body has been transformed from a tribunal dealing with interstate disputes into a national wage fixing body. Around 90 per cent of the workforce is covered by awards ratified by a federal or State tribunal. Though employees are divided fairly evenly between the two levels of jurisdiction, federal awards tend to dictate the pace of substantive and legal change. The traffic, however, is not all one way. An important 1984 Commonwealth Arbitration Commission judgment on technological change and redundancy drew heavily on existing New South Wales employment protection legislation.

The different levels of jurisdiction and the uncertain division or overlap of powers create institutional fragmentation and make coordination a major problem for industrial relations policy. There are around 100 tribunals in Australia with industrial relations responsibility.

Over time wage fixing, rather than dispute settling, has become the most important function of the Commonwealth Arbitration Commission (Dabscheck and Niland 1981: 305–40). This development can be traced to the 1907 ruling of Justice Higgins in the Harvester case. Higgins established a benchmark 'living' wage, which took the form of a 'basic' wage. From 1921, the tribunal became responsible for 'translating the concept into an actual wage rate', through automatic quarterly adjustments to the basic wage in line with variations in the retail price index (Emy 1974: 502). From 1964 the Arbitration Commission began annual general reviews of the ability of the economy to pay higher wage rates. Deliberations for these national wage cases included submissions from governments, employers and unions. Between 1975 to 1980 the Arbitration Commission supervised a system of wage indexation, in which wage increases were tied to rises in the cost of living measured by the consumer price index. This system was abandoned in 1981, only to be partially restored by the Hawke government under the terms of the Accord.

The constitutional division of responsibility, and the institutional machinery of industrial tribunals which resulted, has influenced the development and strategies of Australian trade unions. Arbitration gives unions recognition, while regulating their structures and activities. In turn, the arbitral model relies on unions to represent workers and implement decisions:

> The arbitration systems of the Commonwealth and the states have not simply encouraged the growth of trade unions in Australia but have made unionism an integral part of their operation. The unions submit or oppose claims, argue their merits or demerits, and initiate or suffer prosecutions for breaches of awards. Clearly, the arbitration procedure would break down in practice if tribunals had to deal with individual workers (Isaac and Ford 1966: 277).

Arbitration provides both costs and benefits for trade unions. The benefit of guaranteed access to the policy process has been balanced by the costs of compromise and organisational conservatism which results from being part of the system:

> Unions everywhere are greatly influenced by the laws under which they operate and this is most obviously true in Australia, where, in every respect, they have been shaped by the systems of compulsory conciliation and arbitration under which they have operated throughout this century. During recent years these systems have increasingly been challenged, principally because they are said to protect the entrenched interests of trade unions. There is no doubt that in the past these State and Federal arbitration systems have had a very conservative influence of trade unionism (Rawson 1986: 5).

Employers, by contrast, have participated in the system both as individuals and through their associations.

An Industrial Relations Club?

The existing system of wage determination was for a long time the subject of a bipartisan consensus; 'for over fifty years, the non-Labor parties accepted that conciliation and arbitration systems would be the arenas within which important industrial relations decisions were made' (Rawson 1986: 111).

Though the Hancock committee on industrial relations law and systems broadly supported the status quo in its 1985 report, this consensus no longer prevails (Rawson 1986: 110–13). The Liberal Party has moved toward industrial relations policies which oppose the institutionalised system of wage fixing. The abolition of the Arbitration Commission is also urged by the National Party, by extra-parliamentary forces generally known as the 'new right', and by militant 'macho-management' groups (see for example Hyde and Nurick 1985; Henderson 1986).

Criticisms focus on what is perceived as a cosy industrial relations club, centred on the Arbitration Commission (Dabscheck 1986: 465). Opponents believe that Commission policies have damaged the Australian economy by regulating wage fixing and preventing the growth of decentralised collective bargaining (McGuinness 1985; for a critique see Whitfield 1987: 181–85). Though it is now possible that a future Commonwealth government will dismantle centralised wage fixation, it is unlikely that any government would abolish entirely arbitration as a system of dispute settlement.

Government through Co-operation?

As with most industrial policy, the industrial relations field is marked by limited government control, fragmentation of the formal machinery and the involvement of powerful private interests. The policy arena is a forum for argument between the three major producer groups of business, particularly local manufacturers, farmers and trade unions. Their structural power and organisational strength, and the electoral significance of the production process, cautions Commonwealth and State governments to tread warily in deciding industrial policy.

Such sensitivities ensure that governments seek to develop and test industrial policy proposals at arms length. Statutory authorities, such as the Arbitration Commission, the IAC and the marketing boards, have policy goals which governments do not share. Governments may influence the formulation of policy by those authorities, and in cases act on advice received. The ability of statutory bodies to dictate policy, however, is strictly limited. Too many departments with conflicting interests are involved in policy formulation to enable any one agency to dominate the process. Federal bureaucrats argue with their State counterparts, just as State governments seek to regain the responsibility for industrial power assigned to them by the constitution.

Industrial policy making is fragmented. It inevitably lacks co-ordination—within the public sector, between governments, and between the state and a powerful private sector. All governments are keen to intervene in industry, yet because employment and growth are largely in the hands of business, politicians must rely on public—private sector co-operation. Industrial choices, like economic policy, severely test the influence and authority of government.

Further Reading

Butlin, N.G., Barnard, A. and Pincus, J.J. (1982) *Government and Capitalism* Sydney: Allen & Unwin.

Dabscheck, B. and Niland, J. (1981) *Industrial Relations in Australia* Sydney: Allen & Unwin.

Head, Brian (ed.) (1986) *The Politics of Development in Australia* Sydney: Allen & Unwin.

Loveday, Peter (1982) *Promoting Industry: recent Australian experience* University of Queensland Press.

Rattigan, G.A. (1986) *Industry Assistance: the inside story* Melbourne University Press.

Rawson, D.W. (1986) *Unions and Unionists in Australia* Sydney: Allen & Unwin, 2nd edn.

Warhurst, John (1982) *Jobs or Dogma?* University of Queensland Press.

10

Policy Making : Social Welfare

During its second term, the Hawke Labor government established a task force to examine the Australian social welfare system. The first report arrived in June 1986. The task force recommended an increase in and indexing of family allowances, the improvement of programs for the handicapped, and special assistance to large families.

The task force identified four major objectives for family support policies: fair benefits for those with dependent children, adequate support for low income families, help with child care, and no impediment to parents entering the workforce. Task force members opposed any restriction on eligibility for family allowances, pensions or other social welfare entitlements. Such means tests, argued their report, could lead to poverty traps.

At first glance, such policy proposals appear reasoned and non-contentious. Yet behind the task force recommendations are a series of controversial and bitterly contested assumptions. These underlie most discussions of social welfare policy. How much should beneficiaries receive, who should be eligible, and who should deliver those benefits?

Economic and industrial policy involve large and organised forces working through state and private institutions. Such policies are influenced by those in society with wealth, power and position: by governments, business and the unions. Social policy only partly follows the same pattern. Certainly the educational policies of State and federal governments are supported, criticised and influenced by highly organised lobbies from the public and private sectors. Medical practitioners, State departments and health funds lobby over health policy. These are policy areas with important professional interests seeking to protect their position, a plethora of experts to argue for particular outcomes, and new technology changing the parameters of the possible. In education and health, large amounts of money are delivered to a concentrated and vociferous group with a high sense of their own value. These professionals know how to use the system and are a key part of the policy community; the resultant policy process resembles that of economic and industrial decision making.

Not all beneficiaries of government largesse, however, are represented by professional lobbyists sharing a long term understanding
with the relevant government department. For many individuals, the
state is a remote and confusing set of institutions which appear to
make and deliver policy without consultation or reference to the citizen.
The state may become tangible only when a tax form has to be lodged,
a licence sought or a rates bill paid. Direct contact with the government
may be limited to facing an official to request a service or a pension, to
register for unemployment benefits, to seek admission to a hospital or
entry to a university. In these one-to-one encounters, the least influential
members of the public meet the least important members of the public
service. Client—official interaction, the basis of much social welfare
delivery, is the politics of daily life (Sanders 1985). It works within the
structures, programs and concerns of the 'welfare state'. Daily life
involves pensions, unemployment and supporting benefits, individually
based and crucial to beneficiaries.

The basis of social welfare policy is highly contentious. There are
ideological disputes about the 'proper' role of the state in the provision
of social services, about the effects of providing welfare and about
criteria for eligibility. There are institutional disputes over responsibility
for the creation and implementation of social welfare policy. Departments and governments claim overlapping jurisdiction or blame inadequate services on others. There are problems of delivery. Will the
implementation of a policy through a particular state agency satisfy the
aims and demands of the decision makers?

Arguments about social welfare policies are disputes over values.
Reformers envisage welfare policy as a form of social engineering.
State action can create opportunities for those disadvantaged by the
social structures they have inherited; affirmative action programs,
Aboriginal land rights and scholarships for education are all based on
public policy as redress, on legislation as a response to the inequities of
a market society.

Such values impinge when the need for social welfare measures is
evaluated. There are few reliable quantitative models to assist policy
formulation. The Henderson poverty line may be cited in the media as
a scientific figure, but it is no more than an informed guess. Poverty is
a contingent concept, shaped by community expectations. Policy makers
might share the principle that everyone should have basic food, clothing,
shelter and opportunities to escape poverty, but they will not agree in
practice on what is basic and what a luxury. The Henderson formula
suggests one definition, but cabinet may prefer another calculation,
perhaps one more acceptable to overall budget strategy. There will be
no single, universally accepted figure, below which poverty is unde-
niable; defining and alleviating hardship are 'wicked' problems.

Since poverty is relative and cannot be abolished, how much of a society's resources should be allocated to welfare? What is an acceptable standard of living—in the 1930s, and in the 1980s? How much should a government promote equity of income? These are ideological questions. Argument is endless, for social welfare is a policy field with few 'once and for all' solutions. The fortunes of agencies, programs and clients shift; compromises shape outcomes as social welfare demands compete with other parts of the state for resources.

An important academic method for assessing arguments about social policies has been through the subdiscipline of 'welfare economics'. This school starts with the notion that a maximising principle can enhance the provision and delivery of welfare. Research uses forms of cost-benefit analysis and addresses welfare on a macroeconomic basis (see Parish 1976; Self 1975). This is welfare defined as the good of the society rather than the security of the individual. In this view, the imperatives of sound welfare may dictate policies of high technology investment to provide jobs, rather than continued expenditure on unemployment benefits.

One key debate within welfare economics centres on which institution should deliver welfare—the state, the economy or community units such as the family. Recent trends emphasise non-organisational forms of welfare support. Though delivery through large state agencies may be functional in economic terms, control of benefits by government departments can have unfortunate Orwellian overtones.

Ideological Disputes in Social Welfare

There are two basic and opposing theories about the role of social welfare. One proposes that services must be available universally, the other that social welfare benefits should be distributed only selectively. The debate can be recast as an argument between an institutional and a residual approach to social welfare.

The universalist approach argues that every citizen has a claim to pensions, schools, medical services and other social provisions on the same terms. Social welfare is a right for all, regardless of income or position. A universalist approach maintains the incentive to work, because recipients do not lose all their benefits when they become self-supporting. Since the system is financed from progressive taxation, it improves the level of equality in the society (Stretton 1980: 23).

The selectivist approach points to the inevitable shortage of resources for social welfare services. Pensions should be given to those in real need; limited funds must not be spread too thinly. The effect of universal provision, it is often argued, is to transfer resources from the poor to the rich. The middle class are the major beneficiaries of welfare services. Childcare centres have developed mainly in wealthy areas, for professionals understand the system; they know how to apply for government funds. Means testing of eligibility for benefits is crucial, assert selectivists. Only then can governments be certain that scarce resources go to the deserving (Jamrozik 1983: 177—78).

A similar line can be drawn between institutionalists and residualists. The institutional approach understands welfare as a normal function of the state. Social policy helps bind the community together. A Scandinavian academic observing Australia commented that:

> To you welfare is something handed out to people who are under pressure. It's not a kind of underlying ideology about where the country is going as it is in Scandinavia. You don't see that welfare can be used as a glue to make the nation work, to integrate people and give them a national identity (quoted in Mendelsohn 1982: 7).

Welfare becomes more than a safety net; it is a set of institutions and a form of social policy concerned with broader goals.

Residualists perceive welfare as insurance. Support such as pensions should only become available when traditional institutions of society fail to operate. Welfare payments are the last resort for the unfortunate. Government should not be involved except when there is no other means of protecting the individual.

This ideological division about social welfare is mirrored to some extent by the views of major Australian parties. With its social democratic tradition, Labor has tended to support the collectivist notions of the universalists. The coalition parties are more inclined to accept selectivist or residual arguments. Gray (1984) notes the differing approaches to health insurance. The Whitlam government proposed a national and universal health insurance scheme. State action would ensure that every citizen was adequately covered. The non-Labor parties opposed the introduction of Medibank. They argued that people should make their own insurance arrangements; the state should only intervene to assist those otherwise unable to meet the costs dictated by the market place.

Ideology, however, can be blurred by electoral expediency. Because Medibank proved popular, Malcolm Fraser went into the 1975 election campaign promising to maintain the universal health insurance scheme. Once in power he kept the form—but not the substance—of Medibank. In a 1984 dispute over a new assets test, the Liberals proposed to abolish selectivist criteria introduced by a Labor government (Castles 1985).

The distinction between the two approaches to social welfare policy is not always clear and simple (Stretton 1980: 24—25). Access to some benefits is determined by a combination of tests. Pensions are paid universally to all people who satisfy a selective criterion by reaching the age of seventy. Whichever principle prevails, other policy questions arise in providing social welfare. Definitions of eligibility are frequently difficult to specify or enforce. Policy makers must determine who should get benefits, whether they should pay for them, and whether benefits should be taxed.

The universalist approach is frequently condemned because it is costly, provides benefits primarily to the middle class and may be regressive. Yet there are important reservations about the efficacy of the means test so central to any notion of selectivity. Means testing may reduce incentive. For someone unskilled and unemployed, taking a job can actually reduce their standard of living. A new income may eliminate eligibility for other social benefits by a greater amount than arrives in the pay packet. The sensible welfare recipient therefore avoids any low paying job—often the only sort available—to stay within the limits of the means test. This poverty trap removes all incentive to work (Stretton 1980: 25). The means test can also be a method of social control. The recipient is placed—and kept—in a subordinate position. Residual welfare services may maintain a status quo of social division. 'The outcome of residualism is legitimation of disadvantage, legitimation of inequality, legitimation of exclusion of the industrial human residue from the mainstream of social life' (Jamrozik 1983: 180).

In this view of welfare provision, the stigma of the poverty trap is a possible consequence of defining some citizens as suitable recipients and others as not. Implicit is a tendency to regard only some sections of society as welfare cases. Yet those supported by pensions or unemployment benefits are hardly the only people receiving public money. Any consumption of government resources, whether a free school place or an export subsidy, is a form of hidden welfare.

The debate on taxation is often treated as totally separate from welfare issues. Yet the tax system includes social provisions. Federal income tax includes, for example, a spouse rebate allowance. Families benefit at the expense of single taxpayers. Concessions in the tax system redirect public resources to individuals and groups through grants and bounties—rather than through payment as pensions or unemployment benefits (Jamrozik 1983: 182–86). Government is a seamless web. To isolate one section of government activities from another is to create artificial boundaries. Social welfare policies take many forms; not all are directed at the needy.

Arenas for Policy

There are numerous methods for delivering social welfare benefits. Some arrive as cheques in the mail, others are annual tax deductions. Multiple state agencies are involved in the design of social welfare decisions, and the right to administer benefits can itself be a source of conflict. Scotton opens a book on social policy under the Fraser government with the comment:

> In its approach to social policy the Fraser government has taken a position strongly opposed to the style and substance of the Whitlam administration which preceded it. The differences are not confined to the philosophy of social policy itself but also flow from a radically different view of the roles of the public sector in the economic system, and of the Commonwealth Government in Australian federalism (Scotton 1980: 1).

Scotton emphasises the arena in which social policy is made. Some governments centralise control at a national level using federal departments; others administer policies through the States or even through voluntary agencies. The choice is significant, for the mode of policy formulation and delivery affects its content and effect.

The use of different arenas often reflects the multiple objectives of government. The Fraser ministry made three separate attempts to restructure the health insurance system inherited from the Whitlam government. Each revised policy was a response to macroeconomic, bureaucratic, electoral or ideological pressures. The Fraser solutions were never exclusively concerned with the social objectives of health insurance. Indeed the second round of changes to Medibank were designed outside the Department of Health; they were concerned primarily to limit the impact of health costs on the CPI (Gray 1984: 6).

Several key departments influence government thinking about social policy. The federal Treasury is interested in the implications of social policy for public expenditure. The Department of Social Security, by contrast, is client-oriented. Its task is to pay benefits efficiently and effectively to those who fit particular criteria. While the Treasury is mainly based in Canberra, Social Security staff work in small offices throughout the country. Daily contact with the poor on the other side of the counter can make Social Security officials impatient with Treasury's central macroeconomic arguments. Economists living in the prosperous ACT, they complain, do not understand the real problems.

This tension between departmental perspectives can be replicated in cabinet. In 1986 the minister for finance demanded reductions in government expenditure. Welfare ministers in portfolios such as Social

Security, Health, Veterans Affairs and Housing argued that cuts would have a severe impact on the poorer sections of the Australian community. The economic and welfare ministers were presenting arguments based on different, incompatible, criteria. Social Security feared the impact of welfare cuts on recipients in a time of recession. Treasury and Finance, on the other hand, sought macroeconomic gains through a reduction in public expenditure. The dispute became a contest between competing priorities—a fight over government values and philosophy. Like most ministerial disagreements, the outcome was determined by the influence and seniority of the participants rather than the validity of the arguments. The advantage lay clearly with the Treasurer and Minister of Finance. They could marshall a quantified economic case against the vague and inevitably imprecise estimates of damage from welfare cuts. A rearguard action by welfare portfolios, however, meant that eventual cuts were nowhere near the reductions sought by Finance.

Social policy departments often act as the voice of client interests. Speaking through their ministers, organising support and lobbying other officials and agencies, these departments are the only government voice for welfare. They look to the social welfare community to back up their case; key lobby groups such as the Australian Council of Social Service are represented on EPAC and seek the status of insiders. Others organisations, such as those representing families with disabled children, are skilled at promoting their cause and bringing pressure to bear on government.

Within the federal bureaucracy, the struggle for social welfare funds is a dispute over two fundamental, yet contradictory government objectives: economic management and social equity. For example, in 1976 the Fraser ministry introduced a system of family allowances to replace the child endowment program and the use of tax rebates for children. The new family allowance system was universal in application, revenue neutral, and paid directly to the mother, rather than to the father through a tax rebate. Treasury opposed the new scheme. It argued that shifting this social welfare support from the tax system to direct payment would appear to blow out the deficit at a time when government fiscal policy called for its reduction.

Prevailing over Treasury, however, was only the first of numerous difficulties for the new scheme. Its objectives were disputed. Payments were not indexed; as a consequence the real value of the family allowance declined with inflation, prompting demands for increases to restore its initial value. Since payment was universal, opponents argued that the allowance should either be taxed or means tested, so that in a time of financial stringency it would go to those who needed it most. The 1976 introduction of family allowances had been linked with temporary tax indexation. This was designed so that the government could argue for a reduced flow-on of the CPI in a national wage case. When economic circumstances changed, the family allowance scheme was no longer required for this purpose; departments within the federal bureaucracy demanded its reduction or abolition.

How ministers viewed family allowances depended on the problem they hoped to solve. For social welfare departments, the scheme rested on assumptions of social equity. Treasury held a contradictory opinion. The allowance was a cost to government, part of a package which should be manipulated for macroeconomic ends. Which view prevailed depended on electoral pressures and priorities (see Cass et al. 1981). The question of family allowances was reopened by the 1986 federal task force report into social welfare; in this field policy outcomes are contingent and can be recontested.

The Delivery of Social Services

Since a 1946 referendum gave it power to make payments to individuals, the federal government has held jurisdiction for the delivery of major social services. Commonwealth departments are now responsible for the delivery of welfare such as single parents pensions. In other areas of social policy, power is either shared with the States or disputed.

Each State has a welfare department concerned with providing services to children and families: for the mentally handicapped, orphans and delinquents. These State departments are largely confined to a residual role, filling in behind the major operations of Commonwealth social security (Mendelsohn 1982: 186; Graycar 1979a: 106–07).

At times the two levels of government overlap, and there may be disputes over authority. Several of the Whitlam government social welfare schemes were designed to bypass State portfolios. The Australian Assistance Plan (AAP), for example, sought to encourage social welfare groups organised at a regional level; the AAP envisaged new structures larger than the local areas but smaller than the States (for details see Graycar 1979a; 1983). The Whitlam cabinet also funded community health centres aimed at the prevention, rather than cure, of illness (Milio 1984). The Whitlam approach has been termed 'organic federalism', with the federal government determining principles and priorities and then leaving the details of administration to State and local governments (Graycar 1979a: 105). Not all States were impressed by these schemes, however, and working arrangements for the AAP had not been resolved when the Whitlam government was dismissed in November 1975.

The incoming Fraser government immediately abolished the AAP and reduced local grants for welfare provision. The Bailey Taskforce on Coordination in Welfare and Health was established to examine the different functions of State and and federal governments. The 1977 Bailey Report noted that income security programs were unambiguously a federal responsibility. In other fields constitutional power was less certain. The task force recommended that federal government grants be consolidated to four programs, the community health and care program (CHACC), the sheltered accommodation program (SHACC), the community assistance and recreation program (CARP) and welfare and health services planning grants. Using federal money, these services would be delivered by the States.

Following the Bailey task force, the Fraser government gradually moved away from the Whitlam practice of tied grants offered under section 96 of the constitution. Instead, the States were given block grants for their welfare services. Separate funding for community health centres, for instance, became incorporated in larger grants (Milio 1984). Whitlam, to little effect, attacked the return of power to State governments as an exercise in buck-passing. The Fraser government defended the move as a proper exercise in federalism which would allow States to develop their own welfare policies. The distinction was ideological, and the arguments often double-edged. Centralisation could be justified as an aid to efficiency, but so too could local State control. The Whitlam government might assert that devolution of responsibility to regions encouraged experiment and diversity, but their successors could claim the same for State rather than national authority over programs. This was not really a debate about the delivery of social welfare services, but a disagreement about the use and form of federalism.

The Hawke government maintained the status quo—federal control of individual payments, with residual services funded from Canberra but delivered by the States. To reduce overall expenditure, the Commonwealth cut funding for programs such as 'English as a second language' and temporary work creation schemes. The prime minister even discussed 'work for dole' proposals, though his ministers were less than enthusiastic. They acknowledged privately that the administrative costs of organising compulsory tasks were likely to outweigh the reduction of voluntary unemployment and the savings in labour for public works.

From welfare economics emerges a debate about whether government agencies need be involved in the implementation of social policy. Many programs are funded by government but delivered through voluntary organisations such as the Salvation Army and Meals on Wheels. It is sometimes argued that voluntary bodies are more caring and flexible. Certainly the professional leadership of the 'voluntary' sector has influenced the policy demands made of governments. With large grants and extensive operations, voluntary agencies can hire articulate staff, including social workers. Often tertiary trained and looking to a career in non-government welfare agencies, these full time workers learn the skills of submission preparation. They provide their organisations with cases for increased state support by acting as spokespersons for their clients. Voluntary welfare agencies are among the beneficiaries of social policy.

Access: Delivering Government Services

Policies must be delivered through organisations. For most social welfare spending, these organisations are Commonwealth government departments. This creates what Bernard Schaffer has called 'the irony of equity'. To operate effectively, institutions delivering equity must themselves create rules and inequities (Schaffer and Lamb 1981:60). Solving one problem creates new difficulties. The equity problems which result from social institutions can only be addressed through the creation and operation of other institutions.

A department with responsibility for delivering a particular benefit will develop its own internal operating procedures. Street level bureaucrats find shortcuts to make difficult jobs manageable or tolerable. Procedures replace objectives. As Schaffer observes:

> Substantive justice demands procedural justice. Unfortunately the procedural justice of institutional action demands in turn the setting up of the procedures, the gates, lines and counters of queues ... in the end, it is those procedures which come to dominate, and so determine outcomes, which are to be evaluated by initial standards of substantive justice. The procedures then are seen to produce highly inequitable outcomes (Schaffer and Lamb 1981: 63).

The policy as implemented is inevitably different from the original program objectives. Social welfare must be delivered through bodies which develop an organisational life of their own. Access to benefits is mediated through a bureaucracy, with implications for policy effectiveness and evaluation.

The problems can be viewed from the different perspectives of the public servant delivering the services and of the recipient. Welfare services involving direct client—department relations are delivered by street level bureaucrats. The public servants who deal with welfare recipients are usually junior. They are powerless to make policy, at least formally. Serving behind counters, they must face people who are poor, desperate and needy, and deal with them expeditiously. During economic recession, the pressures can be considerable as the bureaucrat seeks to fulfil contradictory demands: provide equitable service yet economise. Officials must deal with angry clients who feel they are being refused benefits they deserve.

On at least two occasions during the Fraser years junior public servants rebelled against the rising and contrary demands made of them. As unemployment grew, and so counter work increased, bureaucrats in the Department of Social Security went on strike to demand more staff. Officers of the Commonwealth Employment Service imposed bans. They refused to apply stringent work tests proposed by the government, citing the likely acrimony directed against them by clients.

Other reactions to pressure are more subtle. Street level bureaucrats redefine their own jobs or reinterpret regulations to minimise antagonism. Sanders records how officials solved the problem of whether to insist on a guarantee of maintenance from relatives for some migrants entering Australia under family reunion programs. The rules required the classification of applicants for special benefits into two categories: those who were covered by guarantees and those ineligible for normal benefits because of insufficient residence. If the applicant was placed in the first category, the department was required to means test the income of both the applicant and the guarantor, and to recover the debt. As a result of practice and a later decision of the AAT, officials found it easier to classify almost everyone in the second category. Eventually government regulations were adapted to mirror practice. The officials effectively created policy by interpreting rules and using the discretion available to them (Sanders 1985: 41–4).

Officials also face problems when the rules of the system are contradictory. Migrants are generally eligible for the same rights as other citizens. Yet how can non-English speakers hear about their entitlements? The commitment to universality in many of the social welfare programs makes special treatment unacceptable. Yet in practice, some migrants may not know about their shared right to benefits. Departments respond by defining the problem as one of access, rather than eligibility. Once policy objectives are recast, the government can introduce a range of ancillary services to allow migrants effective equality of treatment. In this way a social welfare delivery department 'combines a commitment to addressing the special needs of disadvantaged groups through ancillary programs and departmental sub-structures with strong confirmation of the commitment to universality in the mainstream of administration' (Sanders 1984: 286).

Access depends on understanding how the system works. In a complex social welfare structure without highly organised client groups, discovering appropriate benefits and eligibility may be difficult. Organisations from migrant community groups and unions of the unemployed to voluntary bodies such as Lifeline all see an important part of their task as providing access through information about the system. The need is clear. Sanders (1985: 40) notes the case of a migrant woman whose unemployed husband had returned to his original country to visit a sick relative. Without his dole cheque she had no source of income. At first she was told to wait until her qualifying period for unemployment benefits was complete. This would have imposed extreme hardship, and it required a sympathetic social worker to speed her progress through the system.

In the economic and industrial policy fields, major interests are well organised, vocal and able to use the system. Welfare beneficiaries lack similar structures for collective action. Yet the less organised they are, the more difficult it is for potential clients to understand the system. Organisation of welfare consumers is not easy when individuals have little in common but their poverty.

Access and bureaucratic discretion are therefore central to the delivery of welfare services. The limits of access indicate the difficulties for policy implementation. Social welfare problems are not solved just by establishing a new agency. Providing a benefit to those who come forward may ignore the legitimate claims of the ignorant and the timid. Yet there is a danger in extending the concept of access too far. As Spann wryly comments, the notion has diminishing value when it is expanded to act as a critique of most administration; 'indeed the problems of getting to Heaven may all be characterized as ones of access' (Spann 1981: 15).

A growing demand that welfare officials become responsive to the public is reflected in the emergence of new administrative law. The AAT has been involved heavily in reviewing social security cases. The Department of Social Security receives one of the highest number of demands for personal files under FOI legislation. Clients are using legal remedy to ensure access.

The debate around universality and access indicates major difficulties for social policy design. Welfare problems rarely stem from a single cause, but the problems of administration require simple, universal categories under which to award benefits. It is difficult to predict the necessary level of discretion required for implementation. Further, many social services can only be delivered through an organisation, with all the attendant risks that objectives will be altered for bureaucratic convenience. As categories are modified or ignored by street level bureaucrats, the effect of policy becomes more difficult to evaluate. Yet without reliable evaluation of experiments, policy makers find it difficult to improve social welfare measures. Incremental change at the counter may eventually produce better official rules, but it may also go unrecognised.

Implications

In some policy fields there is a clear articulation of interests. A policy community assembles around the department and minister. Associations carefully evaluate the likely effect of policy proposals and offer opposition or support according to their particular interests. Policy involves endless bargaining, as a reflection of the political process.

Social welfare measures are often aimed at the disadvantaged and, frequently, the unorganised. There may be no lobbies to complain if policy is ineffective. Clients do not always have a voice in the decision process. Recipients may, at best, be represented by professionals with their own organisational interests. Access presupposes knowledge; not even the voluntary agencies and community self-help groups can be certain that all needy cases are receiving entitlements. The effectiveness of policy delivery can only be evaluated for those who register. Hence the need for regular assessment of overall policy design, such as that undertaken by the federal social welfare system taskforce.

Social policy choices are complicated by multiple objectives. A universal approach may be more equitable, but a selective benefit more economically viable. With limited resources, governments must determine who will be helped, and who left to fend for themselves. In practice, these decisions are made by the organisations which implement social policy. Agencies construct their own norms and rules, within constraints of judicial scrutiny. Departments modify government intentions at the point where it matters, the service counter. To be effective, organisations must have discretion. Yet once they can make their own choices, they become part of the policy process. Their interpretation may not entirely reflect the minister's objective. Policy is as much about procedures as it is about intentions. In the social policy field, politicians, bureaucrats and welfare professionals compete over implementation; clients await outcomes.

Further Reading

Gray, Gwen (1984) 'The Termination of Medibank' *Politics* 19, 2 pp. 1–17.

Graycar, Adam (1979) *Welfare Politics in Australia: a study in policy analysis* Melbourne: Macmillan.

Lipsky, Michael (1980) *Street-Level Bureaucracy: dilemmas of the individual in public services* New York: Sage.

Schaffer, Bernard and Lamb, Geoff (1981) *Can Equity be Organized? equity development analysis and planning* Farnborough: Gower.

Stretton, Hugh (1980) 'Social Policy: has the welfare state all been a terrible mistake?' *Labor Essays 1980* Melbourne: Drummond.

Sanders, Will (1985) 'The Politics of Daily Life in Australian Income Security Administration' *Politics* 20, 1, pp. 36–47.

Part 3

LESSONS

11

Public Policy: Limits and Prospects

The growth of many western states during the 1960s and early 1970s was quite dramatic. In a time of burgeoning revenues and near full employment, politicians and academics argued that state intervention could improve equality of opportunity. Nowhere was this belief more spectacularly acted upon than in the United States. European states had been experimenting with the residual welfare state for some time, but the American government suddenly moved into housing, health, literacy and employment programs on a scale unimaginable in smaller, less prosperous nations. Lyndon Johnson's plan for the 'Great Society' saw Washington involved in extensive new legislative programs designed to address long term problems from poverty to civil rights to urban renewal.

The Johnson presidency was eventually engulfed by the debacle in Vietnam. The domestic programs he initiated, however, provided an impetus—and subject matter—for the developing field of public policy. In America, as in other expanding states, analysts could evaluate the development, implementation and effect of new public policies. Their findings, suggested the more optimistic, might help governments improve decision making and more accurately predict outcomes.

In Australia this enthusiasm was most evident during the years of the Whitlam government. Whitlam believed public policies could improve the lot of the individual through collective programs of social welfare, urban development and health care. Though guided by a coherent philosophy, the Whitlam approach was piecemeal and remedial. Cabinet acted without adequate evaluation procedures and often underestimated the problems of implementation. Inevitably some projects floundered, while others became untenable with the onset of an international recession. The failure of much of the Whitlam program lowered expectations about state intervention. Following Labor's electoral defeat, federal governments backed away from the embryonic Australian welfare state.

Because the academic field is largely defined by its subject matter, the approaches and preoccupations of public policy have shifted as the

201

state has changed. An early concern with implementation reflected new, large scale state initiatives. In the more austere late 1980s, policy analysts study the effects of cuts in existing programs. With the halt of state growth, the public policy literature emphasises questions of government legitimacy and accountability, choice amid hard times, and efficient management of scarce public resources.

Yet though the subject has changed, research suggests important continuities in the process of policy choice. Within the structures, agencies and procedures of decision making, power remains contingent because politics is a key factor in policy outcomes. Choices are not simply a function of structural forces, nor can explanations be reduced to the behaviour of institutions, organisations or individuals. Public policy is the intersection of these elements within a context of politics that both mediates between, and fashions, the very elements themselves.

Hence public policy analysis involves observing politics in action, tracing how economic and social forces, institutions, people, events and chance interact. It requires arguments about cause and effect. How much was state intervention in the steel industry determined by economic considerations, by the stratagem of business, and by angry workers storming Parliament House?

It is the prevalence of disagreement in public policy choices which disappoints the prescriptive hopes of some practitioners. President Johnson's advisors sought administrative techniques which would simplify the setting of priorities, specify program goals, and remove the bureaucratic disputes which can subvert expensive public interventions. From the academic literature, Washington policy makers were able to draw on concepts such as zero and program planning budgeting— prescriptions offering apparently rational technical solutions to the problems of governing. 'Better' policy processes would produce better policy.

When put into operation, such techniques proved disappointing. The introduction of three year forward estimates as part of the Commonwealth budget process in Australia did little to improve long range planning. The administrative experience of the 1970s suggested that while management models can provide more systematic consideration of policy choices, they do not take politics out of the system. It is a lesson apparently lost on those State and federal bureaucracies busy instituting 'new' techniques, such as performance indicator standards and strategic planning processes, in the 1980s.

Certainly there are gains in appearing to be 'rational', and in employing 'neutral' management tools to address contentious public problems. Yet viable substantive changes to the practice of decision making are hard to identify. Governments must balance rival priorities, respond to external demands, and choose between guns and butter. Ministers operate according to contradictory imperatives, and value survival over the consistency sought by a management technique. Electoral considerations do not always accord with economic rationality. Decisions are too complex, priorities too changeable and circumstances too uncertain. Budgeting and choice techniques based on rational comprehensive premises provide no more than the comforting illusion of 'objective' precision in political choices.

So an understanding of the public policy processes requires grappling with the diverse and intangible. Politics makes many choices temporary, contested or ineffectual; explanations and prescriptions tend therefore to be frustratingly vague. Given its subject matter, public policy can never be an exact science. It is the study of relationships, explaining one outcome only by relating it to others. We can describe the rules of the game and discuss its operation, but not predict every outcome. For not all players understand the consequences of their actions, and not all are playing for the same end.

Public policy, however, is not entirely a random process, producing esoteric outcomes in the face of chance occurrence. Policies can be undermined by unanticipated side effects or by changing definitions of the problem. Yet policy making does produce patterns, often incremental, for addressing problems. Important policy levers do exist and can be exercised to maintain some control over events. Politics plays a central role in this process, throwing up problems and limiting possible solutions. It becomes the arena in which participants, groups, organisations, social movements and classes seek to redefine the feasible given the inheritance of the past.

The Capacity of Governments

Despair often followed when analysts evaluated the 'Great Society' in America or, to a lesser extent, the Whitlam experiments in Australia. Many of the programs failed by their own criteria. Rather than solve perennial poverty, policies often did little more than transfer resources to bureaucrats and social workers, break up longstanding local communities, or incite tension when some felt that others were unreasonably favoured by government largesse. Many studies reproduced the favourite finding of economists, that the effect of state intervention had been to aggravate the problem policy makers sought to redress.

Much of the later public policy literature concludes that governments have little power to shape social change. Various explanations are proposed for this apparent stasis within the policy process. Structural impositions may constrain the scope for successful government action. Incremental policy development may confine a government to existing patterns of policy activity and thought. Advocates of technical solutions criticise governments as limited because they seek expedient solutions, or because they give the planners too little power to ensure compliance. Alternatively, planning itself may never work, leaving governments to wallow in ad hoc reflexes without direction or co-ordination. There seems little point in government pursuing new policy directions, for influence is too constrained, knowledge too incomplete, inertia within the system too strong, and outside forces too dominant. There is either insufficient scope for political intervention, or political intervention is the root cause of the problems.

This book has observed limits on the capacity of Australian governments to pursue centralised policies. The economy is subject to international pressures. Interest groups, distributional coalitions, classes and interests are well organised and able to oppose unacceptable policy choices. There are rival if unequal centres of power, disagreements between levels of government, and a division of responsibility which fragments decision making. The public sector includes important semi-autonomous organisations which can pursue their own interests and so affect the prospects for central policies. Bureaucracies wield important influence over the formation and implementation of policy.

In such a diffuse system, it is difficult to predict or control public policy outcomes. Yet power can still be exercised by coalitions, such as parties or policy communities, which learn to operate the system. Fragmented institutions and competing interests require complex bargaining to achieve consent; where coercion is not possible, successful intervention results from negotiated policy—proposals which attract support can be translated into specific actions and will be implemented by the bureaucracy. Given contesting centres of power, negotiated policies must be forged through politics.

Hence governments have a greater capacity to control—or at least negotiate—policy outcomes than might be inferred from the prevalent pessimism of the field. Several overseas national governments in recent years have demonstrated their ability to alter substantially longstanding public policies. The Lange government in New Zealand and the Thatcher government in the United Kingdom both have made radical shifts toward economic restructuring. Each has been characterised by a reorientation of traditional social policy, and by a persistent—indeed unbending—pursuit of particular policy concerns. These are governments which much public policy analysis said could never exist.

The governments of Lange and Thatcher have the advantage of working within a unitary system and of operating during a perceived crisis requiring dramatic action. They do not seek to increase state intervention but to roll back existing programs and institutions. Even so, Lange and Thatcher are working against the pattern of much recent history within their societies, and inevitably at the expense of interests which benefit from state intervention.

Such single minded central direction is less easily obtained in the federal systems of Australia, Canada and the United States. Governments can establish policy themes, such as the expenditure reductions of the Fraser years, or the Accord of the Hawke years. Macro objectives provide a central organising concept for policy choice, and allow ministries to relate proposals to some overall objective. Yet Fraser frequently deviated from his proclaimed goal of constraint, and the Hawke ministry renegotiated the Accord as economic circumstances changed. Australian federal governments can influence the policy agenda, but they must work hard to obtain co-operation, however grudging, from conflicting levels of government, from a divided public sector, and from policy coalitions and private interests with influence over the outcome of state decisions. The rhetoric of easy technical solutions is no substitute for negotiations. A government's capacity to control outcomes is not simply the result of 'political will' or the voluntarism of leaders. It is testament to the central agency of politics in public policy.

Bibliography

Abbey, Brian (1986) 'Business, Power and Politics' Paper to APSA Annual Conference, Brisbane, August.

Aitken, Hugh G.J. (ed.) (1959) *Conference on the State and Economic Growth, New York 1956* New York: Social Science Research Council.

Aitkin, Don (1983a) 'Where Does Australia Stand?' in Withers (1983), pp. 13–31.

———— (1983b) 'Big Government: the Australian experience' *Australian Quarterly* 55, 2, pp. 168–183.

Albon, R.P. (1985) *Private correspondence: competition or monopoly in Australia's postal services?* Sydney: Centre for Independent Studies.

ALP (1984) *Platform, Constitution and Rules as approved by the 36th National Conference Canberra* Barton, ACT: National Secretariat, ALP.

Aldred, Jennifer and Wilkes, John (eds) (1983) *A Fractured Federation? Australia in the 1980s* Sydney: Allen & Unwin.

Allison, Graham T. (1971) *Essence of Decision: explaining the Cuban missile crisis* Boston: Little, Brown.

Anderson, James E. (1984) *Public Policy-Making* 3rd edn, New York: Holt Rinehart & Winston.

Arndt, H.W. (1968) *A Small Rich Industrial Country: studies in Australian development, aid and trade* Melbourne: Cheshire.

Australian Bureau of Statistics (1985) *Year Book Australia 1985, No 69* Canberra: Bureau of Statistics.

———— (1986) *Year Book Australia 1986, No 70* Canberra: Bureau of Statistics.

Australian Consumers' Association et al (1986) Press Release: Review Recommends Strong Consumer Voice in Health, 6 February 1986.

Bachrach, Peter and Baratz, Morton S. (1963) 'Decisions and Nondecisions: an analytical framework' *American Political Science Review* 57, 3, pp. 632–42.

Bagehot, Walter (1966 [1867]) *The English Constitution* with an introduction by R.H.S. Crossman, Ithaca New York: Cornell University Press.

Bailey Report (1977) Task Force on Coordination in Welfare and Health. Proposals for change in the administration and delivery of programs and services. Chairman, Peter Bailey, Canberra: AGPS.

Beauchamp, Katherine (1986) *Fixing the Government: everybody's guide to lobbying in Australia* Ringwood: Penguin.

Beer, Samuel H. (1980) 'British Pressure Groups Revisited: pluralistic stagnation from the fifties to the seventies' *Public Administration Bulletin* 32, pp. 5—16.

———— (1982) *Britain Against Itself: the political contradictions of collectivism* New York: Norton.

Beetham, David (1974) *Max Weber and the Theory of Modern Politics* London: Allen & Unwin.

Beilharz, Peter and Watts, Rob (1983) 'The Discovery of Corporatism' *Australian Society* 2, 10, pp. 27—30.

Beresford, Melanie and Kerr, Prue (1980) 'A Turning Point for Australian Capitalism 1942—52' in Wheelwright and Buckley (1980), pp. 148—71.

Berger, Suzanne D. (ed.) (1981) *Organising Interests in Western Europe: pluralism, corporatism and the transformation of politics* Cambridge: Cambridge University Press.

Berrill, Sir Kenneth (1980) *Strength at the Centre: The case for a prime minister's department* London: University of London.

Bilney, Gordon (1986) 'The Whitlam Government: Some Personal Reflections' in Fabian Papers (1986), pp. 16—40.

Birch, Anthony H. (1984) 'Overload, Ungovernability and Delegitimation: the theories and the British case' *British Journal of Political Science* 14, pp. 135—60.

Blondel, Jean (1982) *The Organisation of Governments: a comparative analysis of governmental structures* London: Sage.

Boyle, Lord (1980) 'Ministers and the Administrative Process' *Public Administration* 58, pp. 1—12.

Bornstein, Stephen, Held, David and Krieger, Joel (eds) (1984) *The State in Capitalist Europe: a casebook* London: Allen & Unwin.

Boston, Jonathan (1980) 'High Level Advisory Groups: The Case of the Priorities Review Staff' in Weller and Jaensch (1980), pp. 186—95.

Bradshaw, Alan (1976) 'A critique of Steven Luke's "Power: a radical view"' *Sociology* 10, 1, pp. 121—32.

Brennan, Deborah and O'Donnell, Carol (1986) *Caring for Australia's Children* Sydney: Allen & Unwin.

Brugger, W. and Jaensch, Dean (1985) *Australian Politics: theory and practice* Sydney: Allen & Unwin.

Budget Statements (1986—87) *1986—87 Budget Paper No 1* Canberra: AGPS.

Burch, Martin and Wood, Bruce (1983) *Public Policy in Britain* Oxford: Martin Robertson.

Burke, Brian (1984) 'Federalism After the Franklin' *Australian Quarterly* 56, 1, pp. 4—9.

Business Council of Australia (1987) *Business Council Bulletin*, 31 and 32.

Butlin, N.G. (1959) 'Colonial Socialism in Australia 1860—1900' in Aitken (1959), pp. 26—78.

———— (1983) 'Trends in Public/Private Relations 1901—75' in Head (1983a), pp. 79—97.

Butlin, N.G., Barnard, A. and Pincus, J.J. (1982) *Government and Capitalism: public and private choice in twentieth century Australia* Sydney: Allen & Unwin.

Cabinet Handbook (1983) Canberra: AGPS.

Caiden, Gerald E. (1967) *The Commonwealth Bureaucracy* Carlton: Melbourne University Press.

Canberra Bulletin of Public Administration (1985) Special Edition: The Ombudsman, 12, 4.

Canberra Development Board (1985) *National Organisations in Canberra*, Revised, 22 March.

Carnoy, Martin (1984) *The State and Political Theory* Princeton: Princeton University Press.

Cass, Bettina (1986) *The Case for Review of Aspects of the Australian Social Security System* Woden, ACT: Department of Social Security.

Cass, Bettina, Keens, Carol and Moller, Jerry (1981) 'Family Policy Halloween: Family Allowances: Trick or Treat?' *Australian Quarterly* 53, 1, pp. 56–73.

Castles, Francis G. (ed.) (1982) *The Impact of Parties: politics and policies in democratic capitalist states* Beverly Hills: Sage.

—— (1985) *The Working Class and Welfare* Sydney: Allen & Unwin.

Catley, R. (1983) 'The Politics of Inflation and Unemployment 1970–1982' in Head (1983a), pp. 272–93.

Catley, Robert and McFarlane, Bruce (1983) *Australian Capitalism: in boom and depression* 2nd edn, Chippendale: Alternative Publishing Co-operative.

Caves, Richard, Ward, Ian, Williams, Philip and Wright, Courtney (1981) *Australian Industry: structure, conduct, performance* Sydney: Prentice-Hall.

Cawson, Alan (1982) *Corporatism and Welfare: social policy and state intervention in Britain* London: Heinemann.

—— (ed.) (1985) *Organised Interests and the State: studies in meso-corporatism* London: Sage.

Chaples, Ernie, Nelson, Helen and Turner, Ken (eds) (1985) *The Wran Model: electoral politics in New South Wales 1981 and 1984* Melbourne: Oxford University Press.

Chapman, R.J.K. (1975) 'Australian Assistance Plan: a study of ineffective planning' *Australian Journal of Social Issues* 10, 4, pp. 283–98.

Clark, Gordon L. and Dear, Michael (1984) *State Apparatus: structures and language of legitimacy* London: Allen & Unwin.

Coaldrake, Peter (1985) 'Parliament and the Executive' in Patience (1985) pp. 219–37.

Cohen, Michael D., March, James G. and Olsen, Johan P. (1972) 'A Garbage Can Model of Organisational Choice' *Administrative Science Quarterly* 17, 1, pp. 1–25.

Committee of Inquiry into Telecommunications in Australia (1982) *Report*, Chairman, J.G. Davidson, Canberra: AGPS.

Connell, R.W. and Irving, T.H. (1980) *Class Structure in Australian History: documents, narrative and argument* Melbourne: Longman Cheshire.

Cooksey, R.J. (1986) *Review of Australia's Defence Exports and Defence Industry* Canberra: AGPS.

Coombs, H.C. (1982) 'Economic Change and Political Strategy' *Social Alternatives* 2, 4, pp. 12–18.

Corbett, David (1965) *Politics and the Airlines* London: Allen & Unwin.
Costar, Brian J. and Woodward, Dennis (eds) (1985) *Country to National: Australian rural politics and beyond* Sydney: Allen & Unwin.
Crawford, Sir John (1973) *A Commission to Advise on Assistance to Industries* Canberra: AGPS.
———— (1979) *Study Group on Structural Adjustment* Report Volume 1, Canberra: AGPS.
Creighton, W.B., Ford, W.J., and Mitchell, R.J. (1983) *Labour Law: Materials and Commentary* Sydney: Law Book Co.
Crisp, L.F. (1972) 'Politics and the Commonwealth Public Service' *Public Administration* 31, 4, pp. 287–309.
———— (1975a) 'Politics and the Commonwealth Public Service', in Spann and Curnow (1975), pp. 176–93.
———— (1975b), 'Specialists and Generalists' in Spann and Curnow (1975), pp. 346–59.
———— (1978) *Australian National Government* 4th edn, Melbourne: Longman Cheshire.
Crossman, R.H.S. (1963 [1867]) *Introduction to Walter Bagehot 'The English Constitution'* London: Fontana.
Crouch, Colin (1979) *State and Economy in Contemporary Capitalism* London: Croom Helm.
———— (1983) 'New Thinking on Pluralism' *Political Quarterly* 54, 4, pp. 363–74.
Crough, G.J. and Wheelwright, E.L. (1982) *Australia: A Client State* Ringwood: Penguin.
Crozier, Brian (1979) *The Minimum State: beyond party politics* London: Hamish Hamilton.
Crozier, Michel, Huntington, Samuel P. and Watanuki, Joji (1975) *The Crisis of Democracy: report on the governability of democracies to the Trilateral Commission* New York: New York University Press.
Curnow, G.R. and Saunders, C.A. (eds) (1983) *Quangos, the Australian Experience* Sydney: Hale and Iremonger.
Curnow, G.R. and Wettenhall, R.L. (eds) (1981) *Understanding Public Administration* Sydney: Allen & Unwin.
Cutt, James (1978) 'Accountability and Efficiency' in Smith and Weller (1978), pp. 219–35.
Dabscheck, Braham (1986) 'Review: John Hyde and John Nurmick (eds) Wages Wasteland: The Australian Wage Fixing System' *Journal of Industrial Relations* 28, 3, pp. 464–65.
Dabscheck, Braham and Niland, John (1981) *Industrial Relations in Australia* Sydney: Allen & Unwin.
Dahl, Robert A. (1961) *Who Governs? Democracy and Power in an American City* New Haven: Yale University Press.
———— (1967) *Pluralist Democracy in the United States: conflict and consent* Chicago: Rand McNally.
———— (1978) 'Pluralism Revisited' *Comparative Politics* 10, 2, pp. 191–203.
Davidson Committee (1982) *Telecommunications Services in Australia: Report*

of the Committee of Inquiry Canberra: AGPS.

Davies, Alan F. (1958) *Australian Democracy: an introduction to the political system* London: Longmans Green.

Deery, Stephen and Plowman, David H. (1985) *Australian Industrial Relations* 2nd edn, Roseville: McGraw-Hill.

Dell, Edmund (1980) 'Collective Responsibility: Fact, Fiction or Facade?' in RIPA (1980), pp. 27−48.

Department of Special Minister of State (1983) *Registration of Lobbyists: guidelines and application forms.*

Deutsch, Karl W. (1986) 'State Functions and the Future of the State' *International Political Science Review* 7, 2, pp. 209−22.

Dillon, M.C. (1985) 'Developments in Public Sector Audit: how effective are efficiency audits?' *Australian Journal of Public Administration* 44, 3, pp. 247−69.

Dobell, Rodney and Zussman, David (1981) 'An Evaluation System for Government: if politics is theatre, then evaluation is (mostly) art' *Canadian Public Administration* 24, 3, pp. 404−27.

Doern, G. Bruce and Aucoin, Peter (eds) (1979) *Public Policy in Canada* Toronto: Gage.

Doern, G. Bruce and Phidd, Richard W. (1983) *Canadian Public Policy* Toronto: Methuen.

Downs, Anthony (1972) 'Up and Down with Ecology: The "issue-attention cycle"' *The Public Interest* 28, pp. 38−50.

Driscoll, R.E. and Behrman, J.N. (eds) (1984) *National Industrial Policies* Cambridge, Mass: Oelgeschlager.

Dror, Yehezkel (1964) 'Muddling Through−"Science" or Inertia?' *Public Administration Review* 24, 3, pp. 154−57.

——— (1968) *Public Policymaking Reexamined* San Francisco: Chandler.

Drysdale, Peter and Kitaoji, Hironobu (eds) (1981) *Japan and Australia: two societies and their interaction* Canberra: ANU Press.

Drysdale, Peter and Shibata, Hirofumi (eds) (1985) *Federalism and Resource Development: the Australian case* Sydney: Allen & Unwin.

Dugteren van, Theo (ed) (1978) *The Political Process: Can It Cope?* Lane Cove: Hodder and Stoughton.

Dunstan, Don (1981) *Felicia: The Political Memoirs of Don Dunstan* Melbourne: Macmillan.

Dye, Thomas R. (1978) *Understanding Public Policy* 3rd edn, Englewood Cliffs: Prentice-Hall.

Economic Planning Advisory Council (1985a) *The Size of Government and Economic Performance—International Comparisons* Council Paper No 4, Canberra: AGPS.

——— (1985b) *Public Sector Expenditure in Australia* Council Paper No 5, Canberra: AGPS.

Eggleston, F.W. (1932) *State Socialism in Victoria* London: P.S. King.

Emy, Hugh V. (1974) *The Politics of Australian Democracy* Melbourne: Macmillan.

——— (1976) *Public Policy: problems and paradoxes* South Melbourne: Macmillan.

—— (1978) *Politics of Australian Democracy* 2nd edn, South Melbourne: Macmillan.

Encel, Sol (1960) 'The Concept of the State in Australian Politics' *Australian Journal of Politics and History* 6, 1, pp. 62–76.

—— (1974) *Cabinet Government in Australia* 2nd edn, Melbourne: Melbourne University Press.

Encel, Sol, Wilenski, Peter and Schaffer, Bernard (1981) *Decisions: case studies in Australian public policy* Melbourne:: Longman Chesshire.

Etzioni, Amitai (1967) 'Mixed Scanning: a "third" approach to decision-making' *Public Administration Review* 27, 5, pp. 385–92.

—— (1986) 'Mixed Scanning Revisited' *Public Administration Review* 46, 1, pp. 8–14.

Evans, Peter B., Rueschemeyer, Dietrich and Skocpol, Theda (eds) (1985) *Bringing the State Back In* Cambridge: Cambridge University Press.

Ewer, Peter and Higgins, Winton (1986) 'Industry Policy Under the Accord: reform vs traditionalism in economic management' *Politics* 21, 1, pp. 29–39.

Fabian Papers (1986) *The Whitlam Phenomenon* Fitzroy: McPhee Gribble, Penguin.

Forsyth, P. (1985) 'Trade and Industry' *Australian Economic Review* 3, pp. 70–81.

Forward, Roy (ed.) (1974) *Public Policy in Australia* Melbourne: Cheshire.

Frankel, Boris (1983) *Beyond the State? Dominant Theories and Socialist Strategies* London: Macmillan.

Frazer, Murray (1986) 'Inadequacies in the Processes of Policy Development in Australia' *Australian Journal of Public Administration* 45, 1, pp. 30–9.

Freedom of Information (1979) *Report by the Senate Standing Committee on Constitutional and Legal Affairs on the Freedom of Information Bill and aspects of the Archives Bill 1978* Canberra: AGPS.

Freudenberg, Graham (1986) 'The Program' in Fabian Papers (1986) pp. 130–44.

Friedman, Milton and Friedman, Rose (1980) *Free to Choose: a personal statement* New York: Harcourt Brace Jovanovich.

Galbraith, John K. (1967) The New Industrial State London: Hamish Hamilton.

—— (1975) *Economics and the Public Purpose* Ringwood: Penguin.

Galligan, Brian J. (1984) 'The State in Australian Political Thought' *Politics* 19, 2, pp. 82–92.

—— (ed.) (1986a) *Australian State Politics* Melbourne: Longman Cheshire.

—— (1986b) *Queensland Railways and Export Coal: the entrepreneurial use of state monopoly power in a select area* Canberra: Department of Political Science, ANU.

—— (1987) *Politics of the High Court: a study of the judicial branch of government in Australia* St Lucia: University of Queensland Press.

Gardner, Margaret and McQueen, Rob (1986) 'Law and Order: The Queensland Power Dispute' in Roman Tomasic and Ric Lucas (eds) (1986) pp. 57–69.

Garland, R.V. (1976) 'Relations Between Ministers and Departments' *ACT RIPA Newsletter* 3, 3, pp. 15–35.

Gerritsen, Rolf (1986) 'The Necessity of "Corporatism": the case of the

Hawke Labor government' *Politics* 21, 1, pp. 45–54.

Glezer, Leon (1982) *Tariff Politics: Australian policymaking 1960–80* Melbourne: Melbourne University Press.

Gold, David A., Lo, Clarence Y.H. and Wright, Erik O. (1975) 'Recent Developments in Marxist Theories of the Capitalist State' *Monthly Review* 27, 5, pp. 29–43 and 6, pp. 36–51.

Goodin, Robert E. (1982) *Political Theory and Public Policy* Chicago: University of Chicago Press.

Goodnow, Jacqueline and Pateman, Carole (eds) (1985) *Women, Social Science and Public Policy* Sydney: Allen & Unwin.

Gough, Ian (1979) *The Political Economy of the Welfare State* London: Macmillan.

Graham, Peter (1986) 'The Australia Card: a burden rather than a relief?' *Australian Quarterly* 58, 1, pp. 4–15.

Grant, Wyn P. (ed.) (1985) *The Political Economy of Corporatism* London: Macmillan.

Grant, Wyn and Nath, Shiv (1984) *The Politics of Economic Policy Making* Oxford: Basil Blackwell.

Graubard, Stephen R. (ed.) (1985) *Australia: The Daedalus Symposium* North Ryde: Angus & Robertson.

Gray, Gwen (1984) 'The Termination of Medibank' *Politics* 19, 2, pp. 1–17.

Graycar, Adam (1974) 'Methodological Issues in Evaluation of Social Development Programmes: the Australian Assistance Plan' *Australian Journal of Social Issues* 9, 4, pp. 251–61.

—— (1979a) *Welfare Politics in Australia: a study in policy analysis* Melbourne: Macmillan.

—— (1979b) 'Political Issues in Research and Evaluation' *Evaluation Quarterly* 3, 3, pp. 460–71.

—— (ed.) (1983) *Retreat from the Welfare State: Australian social policy in the 1980s* Sydney: Allen & Unwin.

Grieve, Norma and Burns, Ailsa (eds) (1986) *Australian Women: new feminist perspectives* Melbourne: Oxford University Press.

Griffen, James (ed) (1967) *Essays in Economic History of Australia 1788–1939* Brisbane: Jacaranda.

Griffiths, John (1985) 'Australian Administrative Law: institutions, reforms and impact' *Public Administration (London)* 63, pp. 445–63.

Groenewegen, Peter (1976) 'Fraser and the New Federalism' *Arena* 42, pp. 10–18.

—— (1982) *Problems and Prospects of Public Sector Growth in Australia* Canberra: ANU Press.

Gruen, F.H. (1985) *The Federal Budget: how much difference do elections make?* Canberra: ANU.

Gunn, Lewis A. (1978) 'Why is Implementation so Difficult?' *Management Services in Government* 33, pp. 169–76.

Hagan, Jim (1981) *The History of the ACTU* Melbourne: Longman Cheshire.

Hall, Peter A. (1984) 'Patterns of Economic Policy: an organisational approach' in Bornstein et al. (1984), pp. 21–53.

Hall, Peter A. (1986) *Governing the Economy* Cambridge: Polity Press.

Ham, Christopher and Hill, Michael (1984) *The Policy Process in the Modern Capitalist State* Sussex: Wheatsheaf.

Hancock, W.K. (1930) *Australia* London: Ernest Benn.

Hancock, Keith (ed.) (1981) *Incomes Policy in Australia* Sydney: Harcourt Brace Jovanovich.

Hardman, D.J. (ed.) (1982) *Government Accounting and Budgeting* Sydney: Prentice-Hall.

Hartle, Douglas G. (1976) 'The Public Servant as Advisor: the choice of policy evaluation criteria' *Canadian Public Policy* 2, 3, pp. 424–38.

Hawker, Geoffrey N. (1981) *Who's Master, Who's Servant? Reforming Bureaucracy* Sydney: Allen & Unwin.

Hawker, Geoffrey, Smith, R.F.I. and Weller, Patrick (1979) *Politics and Policy in Australia* St Lucia: University of Queensland Press.

Head, Brian (ed.) (1983a) *State and Economy in Australia* Melbourne: Oxford University Press.

—— (1983b) 'State and Economy: Theories and Problems' in Head (1983a) pp. 22–54.

—— (1984) 'Recent Theories of the State' *Politics* 19, 1, pp. 36–45.

—— (ed.) (1986) *The Politics of Development in Australia* Sydney: Allen & Unwin.

Heclo, Hugh (1974) *Modern Social Politics in Britain and Sweden* New Haven: Yale University Press.

Heclo, Hugh and Wildavksy, Aaron (1981) *The Private Government of Public Money: community and policy inside British politics* 2nd edn, Berkeley: University of California Press.

Held, David et al. (eds) (1983) *States and Societies* New York: New York University Press.

Henderson, Gerard (1983a) 'The Industrial Relations Club' *Quadrant* 27, 9, pp. 21–29.

—— (1983b) 'Fraserism: myths and realities' *Quadrant* 27, 6, pp. 33–7.

—— (1986) 'Trade Union Chaos: blame the fringe dwellers' *Sydney Morning Herald* 30 September.

Higley, John, Deacon, Desley and Smart, Don (1979) *Elites in Australia* London: Routledge & Kegan Paul.

Hills, Ben (1986) 'The Perils of Polling' *Sydney Morning Herald* 4 November.

Hogwood, Brian W. and Gunn, Lewis A. (1984) *Policy Analysis for the Real World* Oxford: Oxford University Press.

Holloway, John and Picciotto, Sol (eds) (1978) *State and Capital: a Marxist debate* London: Edward Arnold.

Hood, Christopher C. (1976) *The Limits of Administration* London: Wiley.

Hood, Christopher and Wright, Maurice (eds) (1981) *Big Government in Hard Times* Oxford: Martin Robertson.

Hoskyns, Sir John (1983) 'Whitehall and Westminster: an outsider's view' *Parliamentary Affairs* 36, 2, pp. 137–47.

Howard, John (1986) 'Deregulation and Privatisation' *Canberra Bulletin of*

Public Administration 13, 1, pp. 5–27.

——— (1984) 'Perspectives on "Overloaded Government"' *Australian Journal of Public Administration* 43, 4, pp. 332–90.

Hughes, Barry (1980) *Exit Full Employment* Sydney: Angus & Robertson.

Hughes, Colin A. (1984) 'The Proliferation of Portfolios' *Australian Journal of Public Administration* 43, 3, pp. 257–74.

Huntington, Samuel P. (1961) *The Common Defense: strategic programs in national politics* Columbia: Columbia University Press.

——— (1981) *American Politics: the promise of disharmony* Cambridge: Belknap Press.

Hutchinson, Jenny (1982) 'Political Party Conferences' *Current Affairs Bulletin* 59, 6, pp. 4–13.

——— (1985) 'Political Party Conferences 1984' *Current Affairs Bulletin* 61, 9, pp. 3–15.

Hyde, John and Nurick, John (eds) (1985) *Wages Wasteland: a radical examination of the Australian wage fixing system* Sydney: Hale and Iremonger.

INDECS (1986) *State of Play: 4 Indecs economics special report* Sydney: Allen & Unwin.

Industries Assistance Commission (1974) *Annual Report 1973–74*, Canberra: AGPS.

——— (1981) *Annual Report 1980–81* Canberra: AGPS.

——— (1986) *Annual Report 1985–86* Canberra: AGPS.

Isaac, J.E. and Ford, G.W. (eds) (1966) *Australian Labour Relations: readings* Melbourne: Sun.

Jackson, Gordon (1985) 'The Australian Economy' in Graubard (1985) pp. 231–58.

Jackson, Robert J., Jackson, Doreen and Baxter-Moore, Nicolas (1986) *Politics in Canada* Ontario: Prentice-Hall.

Jaensch, Dean (1983) *The Australian Party System* Sydney: Allen & Unwin.

——— (1986) *Getting Our Houses in Order: Australia's Parliament: how it works and the need for reform* Ringwood: Penguin.

Jaensch, Dean and Bierbaum, Nena (compilers) (1985) *The Hawke Government: past, present, future* Adelaide: APSA.

James, Michael (1985) 'Is Small Government Possible?' *Quadrant* 29, 4, pp. 46–9.

——— (1986) 'Cutting Government Down to Size' *Quadrant* 30, 6, pp. 24–30.

Jamrozik, Adam (1983) 'Universality and Selectivity: social welfare in a market economy' in Graycar (1983), pp. 171–88.

Jessop, Bob (1978) 'Capitalism and Democracy: the best possible political shell? in Littlejohn et al. (1978), pp. 10–51.

——— (1982) *The Capitalist State: Marxist theories and methods* Oxford: Martin Robertson.

Jinks, Brian (1982) 'The "New Administrative Law": some assumptions and questions' *Australian Journal of Public Administration* 41, 3, pp. 209–18.

Johns, Richard (1984) 'A Policy Perspective on the Australian Balance of Payments' *Labor Essays, 1984* Melbourne, Drummond, pp. 19–31.

Jones, Barry (1983) 'Industry and Development' in Reeves and Thomson (1983), pp. 26–53.

Jones, Evan (1983) 'Monetarism in Practice' *Australian Quarterly* 55, 4, pp. 433–45.

Jones, G.W. (1985) 'The Prime Minister's Aides' in King (1985), pp. 72–95.

Jordan, A. Grant (1981) 'Iron Triangles, Woolly Corporatism and Elastic Nets: images of the policy process' *Journal of Public Policy* 1, 1, pp. 95–123.

Juddery, Bruce (1974) *At the Centre: the Australian bureaucracy in the 1970s* Melbourne: Cheshire.

Jupp, James (1982) *Party Politics: Australia 1966–81* Sydney: Allen & Unwin.

Kasper, Wolfgang (1982) *Australian Political Economy* Melbourne: Macmillan.

Kay, John (1985) *Who Benefits From Privitisation?* The City-Association Lecture, November 1985, London: Certified Accountants Educational Trust and the City of London Polytechnic.

Kelly, Paul (1984) *The Hawke Ascendancy* North Ryde: Angus and Robertson.

Kemp, D.A. (1983) 'The National Economic Summit: authority, persuasion and exchange' *Economic Record* 59, 3, pp. 209–19.

King, Anthony, (1979) 'The Rise of the Career Politician in Britain and Its Consequences' *British Journal of Political Science* 11, 3, pp. 249–85.

—— (ed.) (1985) *The British Prime Minister* 2nd edn, Basingstoke: Macmillan.

King, Peter (1983) *Australia's Vietnam: Australia in the Second Indo-China War* Sydney: Allen and Unwin.

Kouzmin, Alexander (ed.) (1983) *Public Sector Administration: new perspectives* Melbourne: Longman Cheshire.

Kristianson, G.L. (1966) *The Politics of Patriotism: the pressure group activities of the Returned Servicemen's League* Canberra: ANU Press.

La Nauze, John A. (1972) *The Making of the Australian Constitution* Carlton: Melbourne University Press.

Lane, Jan-Erik (1985) *State and Market: the politics of the public and the private* London: Sage.

Lasswell, H.D. (1963) 'The Decision Process: seven categories of functional analysis' in Polsby, Deutler and Smith (1963).

Lehmbruch, Gerhard and Schmitter, Philippe C. (eds), (1982) *Patterns of Corporatist Policy-making* London: Sage.

Lehner, Franz and Keman, Hans (1984) 'Political-Economic Interdependence and the Management of Economic Crisis' *European Journal of Political Research* 12, pp. 213–20.

Liberal Party of Australia (1982) *Federal Platform as Approved by Federal Council, May 1982* Canberra: The Liberal Party.

Lindblom, Charles E. (1959) 'The Science of "Muddling Through"' *Public Administration Review* 19, 2, pp. 79–88.

—— (1965) *The Intelligence of Democracy* New York: Free Press.

—— (1977) *Politics and Markets* New York: Basic Books.

—— (1979) 'Still Muddling, Not Yet Through' *Public Administration Review* 39, 6, pp. 517–26.

Lipsky, Michael (1980) *Street-Level Bureaucracy: dilemmas of the individual in public services* New York: Sage.

Littlejohn, Gary, Smart, Barry, Wakeford, John and Yuval-Davis, Nira (eds) (1978) *Power and the State* London, Croom Helm.

Lloyd, Clem (1983) 'The Federal ALP: Supreme or Secondary?' in Parkin and Warhust (1983), pp. 230–56.

Lloyd, Clem J. and Troy, Patrick N. (1981) *Innovation and Reaction: the life and death of the Federal Department of Urban and Regional Development* Sydney: Allen & Unwin.

Loveday, Peter (1982) *Promoting Industry: recent Australian experience* St Lucia: University of Queensland.

——— (1984) 'Corporatist Trends in Australia' *Politics* 19, 1, pp. 46–51.

Lucy, Richard (ed.) (1979) *The Pieces of Politics* 2nd edn, South Melbourne: Macmillan.

——— (1985) *The Australian Form of Government* South Melbourne: Macmillan.

Lukes, Steven (1974) *Power: A Radical View* London: Macmillan.

McCallum, Bruce G. (1984) *The Public Service Manager: an introduction to personnel management in the Australian public service* Melbourne: Longman Cheshire.

McEachern, Doug (1980) *A Class Against Itself: power and the nationalisation of the British steel industry* Cambridge: Cambridge University Press.

——— (1986) 'Corporatism and Business Responses to the Hawke Government' *Politics* 21, 1, pp. 19–27.

McFarlane, Bruce J. (1968) *Economic Policy in Australia: the case for reform* Melbourne: Cheshire.

McGhee Roger (1967), 'The Long Boom 1860–1890' in Griffen (1967), pp. 135–185.

McGregor, Craig (1968) *Profile of Australia* Ringwood: Penquin.

McGuinness, P.P. (1985) *The Case Against the Arbitration Commission* St Leonards, New South Wales: Centre for Independent Studies.

Macintyre, Stuart (1985) *Winners and Losers: the pursuit of social justice in Australian history* Sydney: Allen & Unwin.

Mackintosh, John P. (1977) *The British Cabinet* 3rd edn, London: Stevens.

McMillan, J. (1981) 'Freedom of Information: an analysis of arguments about official secrecy and proposals by the federal government to enact a Freedom of Information Bill' *Current Affairs Bulletin* 57, 10, pp. 4–13.

McMillan, John, Evans, Gareth and Storey, Haddon (1983) *Australia's Constitution: time for change?* Sydney: Allen & Unwin.

Macpherson, C.B. (1973) *Democratic Theory: essays in retrieval* Oxford: Clarendon Press.

McQueen, Humphrey (1982) *Gone Tomorrow: Australia in the 80s* Sydney: Angus & Robertson.

Mandel, Ernest (1975) *Late Capitalism* rev. edn, London: New Left Books.

Manley, John F. (1983) 'Neopluralism: a class analysis of Pluralism I and Pluralism II' *American Political Science Review* 77, 2, pp. 368–83.

Marr, David (1984) *The Ivanov Trial* Melbourne: Nelson.

Marsh, Ian (1976) 'Policy Making in the Liberal Party: the opposition experience *Australian Quarterly* 48, 2, pp. 5–17.

——— (1983a) 'Politics, Policymaking and Pressure Groups: some suggestions for reform of the Australian political system' *Australian Journal of Public Administration* 42, 4, pp. 433–58.

———— (1983b) 'The National Economic Summit and the Politics of Reconciliation' *Quadrant* 27, 8, pp. 50–53.

———— (1985) 'The Assets Test: a case study in the politics of expenditure control' *Australian Journal of Public Administration* 44, 3, pp. 197–223.

Mathews, Russell (1983) 'The Commonwealth-State Financial Contract' in Aldred and Wilkes (1983), pp. 37–62.

Matthews, Trevor (1980) 'Australian Pressure Groups' in Mayer and Nelson (1980), pp. 447–73.

———— (1983) 'Business Associations and the State 1850–1979' in Head (1983a), pp. 115–49.

Mayer, Henry and Nelson, Helen (eds) (1980) *Australian Politics: a fifth reader* Melbourne: Longman Cheshire.

Mendelsohn, Ronald (1982) *Fair Go: welfare issues in Australia* Ringwood: Penguin.

Metin, Albert (1977 [1902]) *Socialism Without Doctrine* (tr. R.Ward), Sydney: Alternative Publishing Co-operative.

Miliband, Ralph. (1973) *The State in Capitalist Society* Melbourne: Quartet.

———— (1977) *Marxism and Politics* Oxford: Oxford University Press.

Milio, Nancy (1984) 'The Political Anatomy of Community Health Policy in Australia 1972–82' *Politics* 19, 2, pp. 18–33.

Miller, John A. (1986) 'The Fiscal Crisis of the State Reconsidered' *Review of Radical Political Economics* 18, 1 and 2, pp. 236–60.

Miller, J.D.B. (1954) *Australian Government and Politics: an introductory survey* London: Duckworth.

Mills, Stephen (1986) *The New Machine Men: polls and persuasion in Australian politics* Ringwood: Penguin.

Nethercote, J.R. (ed.) (1982) *Parliament and Bureaucracy* Sydney: Hale and Iremonger.

Nevile, John W. (ed.) (1981) *Policies Against Stagflation* Melbourne: Longman Cheshire.

———— (1983) *Macroeconomic Issues and Policy Options* Canberra: Department of Parliamentary Library.

Nordlinger, Eric (1981) *On the Autonomy of the Democratic State* Cambridge, Mass: Harvard University Press.

Nurick, John (ed.) (1987) *Mandate to Govern: a handbook for the next Australian government* Perth: Australian Institute for Public Policy.

Oakeshott, Michael J. (1962) *Rationalism in Politics and other essays* New York: Basic Books.

O'Brien, Patrick (1985) *The Liberals: factions, feuds and fancies* Ringwood: Penguin.

OECD (1983a) *Industry in Transition* Paris: OECD.

———— (1983b) *Positive Adjustment Policies: managing structural change* Paris: OECD.

———— (1985) *Economic Surveys 1984/5: Australia* Paris: OECD.

———— (1986) *OECD Economic Surveys: United States* Paris: OECD.

Offe, Claus (1984) *Contradictions of the Welfare State* London: Hutchinson.

Olson, Mancur (1982) *The Rise and Decline of Nations: economic growth, stagflation and social rigidities* New Haven: Yale University Press.

Painter, Martin and Carey, Bernard (1979) *Politics Between Departments: the fragmentation of executive control in Australian government* St Lucia: University of Queensland Press.

Palmer, Gill (1986) 'Corporatism in Australia' Paper to APSA Conference, Brisbane, August 1986.

Panitch, Leo (1980) 'Recent Theorizations of Corporatism: reflections on a growth industry' *British Journal of Sociology* 31, 2, pp. 159–87.

Parish, R.M. (1976) 'The Scope of Benefit-Cost Analysis' *Economic Record* 52, pp. 302–14.

Parker, Lee D. (1986) *Value-for-Money Auditing: conceptual development and operational issues* Caulfield: Australian Accounting Research Foundation.

Parker, R.S. (1976) 'The Meaning of Responsible Government' *Politics* 11, 2, pp. 178–84.

—— (1978) 'The Public Service Inquiries and Responsible Government' in Smith and Weller (1978), pp. 334–59.

Parkin, Andrew (1980) 'Power in Australia: an introduction' in Parkin, Summers and Woodward (1980), pp. 263–84.

Parkin, Andrew, Summers, John and Woodward, Dennis (eds) (1980) *Government, Politics and Power in Australia: an introductory reader* 2nd edn, Melbourne: Longman Cheshire.

Parkin, Andrew and Warhurst, John (eds) (1983) *Machine Politics in the Australian Labor Party* Sydney: Allen & Unwin.

Patience, Allan (ed.) (1985) *The Bjelke-Petersen Premiership 1968–83: issues in public policy* Melbourne: Longman Cheshire.

Patience, Allan and Scott, Jeffrey (eds), (1983) *Australian Federalism: future tense* Melbourne: Oxford University Press.

Peacock, A.T. and Wiseman, J. (1961) *The Growth of Public Expenditure in the UK* Princeton: Princeton University Press.

Pemberton, Joanne and Davis, Glyn (1986) 'The Rhetoric of Consensus' *Politics* 21, 1, pp. 55–62.

Pierson, Christopher (1984) 'New Theories of State and Civil Society: recent developments in post-Marxist analysis of the state' *Sociology* 18, 4, pp. 563–71.

Playford, John (1972) 'Who Rules Australia?' in Playford and Kirsner (1972), pp. 108–55.

Playford, John and Kirsner, Douglas (eds) (1972) *Australian Capitalism: towards a socialist critique* Harmondsworth: Penguin.

Plowman, David (1981) *Wage Indexation: a study of Australian wage issues* Sydney: Allen & Unwin.

Polsby, Nelson W. (1979) 'Empirical Investigation of the Mobilisation of Bias in Community Power Research' *Political Studies* 27, 4, pp. 527–41.

Polsby, N.W., Deutler, R.A. and Smith, P.A. (eds) (1963) *Politics and Social Life* Boston: Houghtin Mifflin.

Porter, Michael G. (1978) 'Stablisation, Regulation and Misplaced Entrepreneurship' *Quadrant* 22, pp. 12–16.

Poulantzas, Nicos (1978) *State, Power, Socialism* London: New Left Books.

Pressman, Jeffrey L. and Wildavsky, Aaron (1973) *Implementation: how great expectations in Washington are dashed in Oakland* Berkeley: University of California Press.

Pross, A. Paul (1986) *Group Politics and the Policy Process* Toronto: Oxford University Press.

Public Service Board (1985–6) *Annual Report 1985/6*, Canberra: AGPS.

Rattigan, G.A. (1986) *Industry Assistance: the inside story* Melbourne: Melbourne University Press.

Rawson, D.W. (1986) *Unions and Unionists in Australia* 2nd edn, Sydney: Allen & Unwin.

RCAGA (1975) *Report Task Force on Economic Policy,* Canberra: AGPS.

—— (1976) *Report of the Royal Commission on Australian Government Administration,* Canberra: AGPS.

Reeves, William P. (1969 [1902]) *State Experiments in Australia and New Zealand* Two Volumes, Melbourne: Macmillan.

Reeves, John and Thomson, Kelvin (eds) (1983) *Labor Essays 1983* Melbourne: Drummond.

Reform of the Australian Tax System (1985) Vol 2, draft White Paper, Canberra: AGPS.

Reforming the Australian Public Service (1983) A Statement of the Government's Intention, Canberra: AGPS.

Reid, G.S. (1984) 'The Westminster Model and Ministerial Responsibility' *Current Affairs Bulletin* 61, 1, pp. 4–16.

—— (1978) 'The Changing Political Framework' in van Dugteren (1978), pp. 73–123.

Reinecke, Ian and Schultz, Julianne (1983) *The Phone Book: the future of Australia's communications on the line* Ringwood: Penguin.

Review of Commonwealth Administration (1983) *Report* Canberra: AGPS.

Review of Commonwealth Functions (1981) *Ministerial Statement* Canberra: AGPS.

Richmond, Keith (1980) 'The Major Rural Producer Groups in New South Wales' in Scott (1980), pp. 70–93.

Richardson, J.J. and Jordan, A.G. (1979) *Governing Under Pressure: the policy process in a post-parliamentary democracy* Oxford: Martin Robertson.

RIPA (1980) *Policy and Practice: the experience of government* London: RIPA.

Rittel, H.W.J. and Weber, M.W. (1973) 'Dilemmas in a General Theory of Planning' *Policy Sciences* 4, pp. 155–69.

Robertson, Max (1979) 'Policymaking in the Car Industry' in Lucy (1979), pp. 151–64.

Rose, Richard (1981) 'What if anything is wrong with big government' *Journal of Public Policy* 1, 1, pp. 5–36.

—— (1984) *Understanding Big Government: the programme approach* London: Sage.

Rydon, Joan (1975) 'Frustrations of Federalism' *Australian Quarterly* 47, 4, pp. 94–106.

Sanders, Will (1984) 'Access to Services: ethnicity in Australian Government Administration' *Australian Journal of Public Administration* 43, 3, pp. 275–86.

—— (1985) 'The Politics of Daily Life in Australian Income Security Administration' *Politics* 20, 1, pp. 36–47.

Saunders, Cheryl and Wiltshire, Kenneth (1980) 'Fraser's New Federalism 1975–1980: an evaluation' *Australian Journal of Politics and History* 26, 3, pp. 355–71.

Sawer, Marian (ed.) (1982) *Australia and the New Right* Sydney: Allen and Unwin.

———— (1986) 'The Long March Through the Institutions: Women's Affairs Under Fraser and Hawke' Paper for APSA Conference, Brisbane, August 1986.

Sawer, Marian and Simms, Marian (1984) *A Woman's Place: women and politics in Australia* Sydney: Allen & Unwin.

Schaffer, Bernard B. (1977) 'On the Politics of Policy' *Australian Journal of Politics and History* 23, 1, pp. 146–55.

Schaffer, Bernard and Lamb, Geoffrey (1981) *Can Equity be Organised? Equity, development analysis and planning* Farnborough: Gower.

Schattschneider, Elmer E. (1960) *The Semisovereign People: a realist's view of democracy in America* New York: Holt Rinehart & Winston.

Scott, Roger (ed.) (1980) *Interest Groups and Public Policy* Melbourne: Macmillan.

Scotton, R.B. (1980) 'The Fraser Government and Social Expenditures' in Scotton and Ferber (1980), pp. 1–27.

Scotton, R.B. and Ferber, Helen (eds), (1980) *Public Expenditures and Social Policy in Australia: Volume II: The first Fraser years 1976–78* Melbourne: Longman Cheshire.

Sekuless, Peter (1984) *The Lobbyists: using them in Canberra* Sydney: Allen & Unwin.

Sekuless, Peter and Rees, Jacqueline (1986) *Lest We Forget: the history of the Returned Servicemen's League 1916–86*, Dee Why West: Rigby.

Self, Peter (1975) *Econocrats and the Policy Process: the politics and philosophy of cost-benefit analysis* London: Macmillan.

———— (1985), *Political Theories of Modern Government: its role and reform* London: Allen & Unwin.

Shann, E.O.G. (1948 [1930]) *An Economic History of Australia* Cambridge: Cambridge University Press.

Sharman, Campbell (1980) 'Fraser, the States and Federalism' *Australian Quarterly* 52, 1, pp.9–19.

Sharman, G.C. (1975) 'Federalism and the Study of the Australian Political System' *Australian Journal of Politics and History* 21, 3, pp. 11–24.

Sheridan, Kyoko (ed.) (1986) *The State as Developer: public enterprise in South Australia* Adelaide: Royal Australian Institute of Public Administration.

Shonfield, Andrew (1965) *Modern Capitalism: the changing balance of public and private power*, London: Oxford University Press.

Simeon, Richard (1976) 'Studying Public Policy' *Canadian Journal of Political Science* 9, 4, pp. 548–80.

Simms, Marian (1982) *A Liberal Nation: the Liberal party and Australian politics* Sydney: Hale and Iremonger.

———— (1983) 'The Political Economy of the State in Australia' in Kouzmin (1983), pp. 37–56.

Simon, Herbert A. (1957) *Administrative Behaviour: a study of decision-making processes in administrative organization* 2nd edn, New York: Macmillan.

Singleton, Gwynneth (1985) 'The Economic Planning Advisory Council: the reality of consensus' *Politics* 20, 1, pp. 12–25.

Skocpol, Theda (1980) 'Political Response to Capitalist Crisis: neo-Marxist theories of the state and the case of the New Deal' *Politics and Society* 10, 2, pp. 155–201.

Smart, Don (1978) *Federal Aid to Australian Schools* St Lucia: University of Queensland Press.

Smith, R.F.I. (1977) 'Public Policy and Political Choice: a review article' *Australian Journal of Public Administration* 36, 3, pp. 258–73.

Smith, R.F.I. and Weller, Patrick (eds) (1978) *Public Service Inquiries in Australia* St Lucia: University of Queensland Press.

Smith, R.F.I. and Harman, G.S. (1981) 'Australian Farm Organisations and the Making of Farm Policy' in Drysdale and Kitaoji (1981), pp. 215–35.

Solomon, David (1986) *The People's Palace* Carlton: Melbourne University Press.

Spann, R.N. (1973) *Public Administration in Australia* 3rd edn, Sydney: Government Printer.

—— (1979) *Government Administration in Australia* Sydney: Allen & Unwin.

—— (1981) 'Fashions and Fantasies in Public Administration' *Australian Journal of Public Administration* 40, 1, pp. 12–25.

Spann, R.N. and Curnow, G.R. (eds) (1975) *Public Policy and Administration in Australia: a reader* Sydney: Wiley.

Stanford, J.D. (1978) *The Growth of Public Expenditure in Australia* Leicester: Public Sector Economics Research Centre, University of Leicester.

Starr, Graeme, Richmond, Keith and Maddox, Graham (1978) *Political Parties in Australia* Richmond: Heinemann.

Stewart, Randal G. (1985) 'The Politics of the Accord: Does Corporatism Explain It?' *Politics* 20, 1, pp. 26–35.

Stilwell, Frank (1986) *The Accord ... and Beyond: the political economy of the Hawke Labor government* Sydney: Pluto.

Stretton, Hugh (1977) 'Business and Government' *Australian Journal of Public Administration* 36, 1, pp. 64–78.

—— (1980) 'Social Policy: has the welfare state all been a terrible mistake?' *Labor Essays, 1980* Melbourne: Drummond, pp. 19–39.

—— (1984) 'Review of Martin Rein: "From Policy to Practice"', *Australian Society* 3, 1, pp. 33–34.

—— (1987) *Political Essays* Melbourne: Georgian House.

Strickland, A.J. (1982) 'South Australia's Program – Performance Budgeting Experience' in Nethercote (1982), pp. 113–24.

Summers, Anne (1986) 'Mandarins or Missionaries: Women in the Federal Bureaucracy' in Grieve and Burns (1986), pp. 59–67.

Swan, Peter L. (1979) 'The Libertarian Challenge to Big Government' *Quadrant* 23, pp. 5–11.

Taylor, Charles L. (ed.) (1983) *Why Governments Grow: measuring public sector size* London: Sage.

Theophanous, Andrew C. (1980) *Australian Democracy in Crisis: a radical approach to Australian politics* Melbourne: Oxford University Press.

Therborn, Goran (1978) *What does the Ruling Class do when it rules? state apparatuses and state powers under feudalism, capitalism and socialism* London: New Left Books.

—— (1986) 'Karl Marx Returning: the welfare state and neo-Marxist, cor-
poratist and state theories' *International Political Science Review* 7, 2, pp.
131—64.
Thompson, Elaine (1980) 'The "Washminster" Mutation' in Weller and Jaensch
(1980), pp. 32—40.
—— (1985) 'Ministers, Bureaucrats and Policymaking' in Woodward
et al. (1985), pp. 40—49.
Thynne, Ian and Goldring, John (1981) 'Government "Responsibility" and
Responsible Government' *Politics* 16, 2, pp. 197—207.
Tomasic, Roman (ed.) (1984) *Business Regulation in Australia* North Ryde:
CCH.
Tomasic, Roman and Lucas, Ric (eds) (1986) *Power, Regulation and Resis-
tance* Canberra: CCAE.
Troy, Patrick N. (1978) *A Fair Price: the Lands Commission programme
1972—1977* Sydney: Hale and Iremonger.
Tsokhas, Kosmas (1984) *A Class Apart? Businessmen and Australian Politics
1960—80* Melbourne: Oxford University Press.
Uhr, John (1982) 'Parliament and Public Administration' in Nethercote (1982),
pp. 26—66.
Urry, John (1981) *The Anatomy of Capitalist Societies: the economy, civil
society and the state* London: Macmillan.
Valder, John (1983) *Liberal Party: facing the facts* Report of the Committee
of Review, Canberra: The Liberal Party.
Walter, James (1986) *The Ministers' Minders: personal advisers in national
government* Melbourne: Oxford University Press.
Wanna, John (1981) *Defence Not Defiance* Adelaide: Adelaide CAE.
Warhurst, John (1982a) *Jobs or Dogma?* St Lucia; University of Queensland
Press.
—— (1982b) 'The Industries Assistance Commission and the Making of
Primary Industry Policy' *Australian Journal of Public Administration* 41, 1,
pp. 15—32.
—— (1983) 'Single-issue Politics — The Impact of Conservation and Anti-
abortion Groups' *Current Affairs Bulletin* 60, 2, pp. 19—31.
—— (1985) 'Interest Groups', in Woodward et al. (1985), pp. 308—15.
—— (1986) 'Industry Assistance Issues: state and federal governments' in
Head (1986), pp. 56—71.
Warhurst, John and O'Loghlin, Gillian (1985) 'Federal-State Issues in External
Economic Relations' in Drysdale and Shibata (1985), pp. 190—202.
Weber, Max (1978) *Economy and Society* Guenther Roth and Claus Wittich,
eds, Berkeley: University of California Press.
Weller, Patrick (1983) 'Transition: taking over power in 1983' *Australian
Journal of Public Administration* 42, 3, pp. 303—19.
—— (1985a) *First Among Equals: prime ministers in Westminster systems*
Sydney: Allen & Unwin.
—— (1985b) 'The Hawke Cabinet: collective or responsible?' *Australian
Quarterly* 57, 4, pp. 333—44.
Weller, Patrick and Cutt, James (1976) *Treasury Control in Australia: a study
in bureaucratic politics* Sydney: Novak.

Weller, Patrick and Jaensch, Dean (eds) (1980) *Responsible Government in Australia* Melbourne; Drummond.

Weller, Patrick and Grattan, Michelle (1981) *Can Ministers Cope? Australian federal ministers at work* Melbourne: Hutchinson.

West, Katharine (1984) *The Revolution in Australian Politics* Ringwood: Penguin.

Wettenhall, R.L. (1983a) 'Quangos, Quagos and the Problems of Non-Ministerial Organization' in Curnow and Saunders (1983), pp. 5–52.

———— (1983b) 'Privatisation: a shifting frontier between private and public sectors' *Current Affairs Bulletin* 60, 6, pp. 14–22.

Wheelwright, E.L. and Buckley, Ken (eds) (1975–83) *Essays in the Political Economy of Australian Capitalism* Five Volumes, Sydney: ANZ Books.

Whitfield, Keith (1987) *The Australian Labour Market: perspectives, issues and policies* Sydney: Harper and Row.

Whitlam, E.G. (1983) 'The Cost of Federalism' in Patience and Scott (1983), pp. 28–48.

———— (1985) *The Whitlam Government 1972–75* Ringwood: Penguin.

Whitwell, Greg (1986) *The Treasury Line* Sydney: Allen & Unwin.

Wildavsky, Aaron (1975) *Budgeting: a comparative theory of budgetary processes* Boston: Little, Brown.

———— (1979) *Speaking Truth to Power: the art and craft of policy analysis* Boston: Little, Brown.

———— (1985a) 'The Logic of Public Sector Growth' in Lane (1985), pp. 231–70.

———— (1985b) 'The Once and Future School of Public Policy' *The Public Interest* 79, pp. 25–41.

Wilenski, Peter (1983) 'Small Government and Social Equity' *Politics* 18, 1, pp. 7–25.

———— (1986) *Public Power and Public Administration* Sydney: Hale and Iremonger.

Willetts, Peter (1982) *Pressure Groups in the Global System* London: Frances Pinter

Wilson, Graham K. (1985) *Business and Politics: a comparative introduction* Chatham New Jersey: Chatham House.

Wiltshire, Kenneth W. (1975) *An Introduction to Australian Public Administration* North Melbourne: Cassell.

Withers, Glenn (1978) 'The State of Economics' *Australian Quarterly* 50, 4, pp. 74–79.

———— (ed.) (1983) *Bigger or Smaller Government* Canberra: ANU Press.

Wolfe, Alan (1977) *The Limits of Legitimacy: political contradictions of contemporary capitalism* New York: Free Press.

Women's Electoral Lobby (1977) 'Papers from Seminar Held in Sydney, July 1977' *Australian Quarterly* 47, 3, pp. 3–66.

Woodward, Dennis, Parkin, Andrew and Summers, John (eds) (1985) *Government, Politics and Power in Australia: an introductory reader* 3rd edn, Melbourne: Longman Cheshire.

Index